SOUTH CAROLINA TOKENS

by

TONY CHIBBARO

Edited by
David E. Schenkman

INTERNATIONAL STANDARD BOOK NUMBER: 0-918492-09-2

LIBRARY OF CONGRESS CATALOG CARD NUMBER: 90-071295

THE TOKEN AND MEDAL SOCIETY, INC.
P.O. Box 951988
Lake Mary, FL 32795

CONTENTS

ACKNOWLEDGEMENTS

The author would like to acknowledge the help of all those who assisted in one way or another with this cataloging project. Special thanks are due to two people — Randy Chambers and Austin M. Sheheen, Jr. — without whom the project would have fallen by the wayside. Other collectors that helped in a significant way are Brad Jeffcoat, Norman Eckler, Frank Sanders, Bill Garrett, Joe Studebaker, Thomas McAbee, Bill Graham, Dick Coy, C.R. Clark, Wiley Scruggs, David E. Schenkman, Bill Williams, and Jerry Roughton.

Below appears a list of others who contributed rubbings and/or descriptions. If anyone has been inadvertently omitted from the list, it was not intentional. In the event of such an omission, please contact the author at P.O. Box 420, Prosperity, SC 29127, so the name can be added to a future edition.

Mrs. J.E. Anderson
Wm. C. (Bill) Ballard
James Boswell
Everitt Bowles
Howard Brewington
Calhoun County Museum
Wayne Chapman
Art Coggins
R.W. Colbert
Jim Cooke
Joe Copeland
Louis Crawford
Shane Daniels
Dean H. Davis
J. William Davis
Doug Dill
Lew Egnew
Harry English
Jim Few
Fort Moultrie Museum
Wendell Frick
Georgetown County Library

Mrs. Virginia Geraty
Charlie Grace
Dick Grinolds
Aubrey Haddock
Mrs. Florence Hall
Rich Hartzog
Joe Henderson
George Hosek
Garvin Huggins, Sr.
Paul Jensen
Paul Jeter
Ed Joyce
John Latham
William C. Long
Hal McGirt
Bill Miller
Christopher Lee Moore
Robert Moore, Jr.
Dave Mullins
John G. Nicolosi
Craig Nodine
Jim Partin

Randy Partin
Hank Reidling
Melvin Reiter
The Rice Museum
LoRan Ross
Hink Salley, Jr.
Jerry Schaeper
Jim Shipley
Mrs. Mary G. Silcox
Barry Silverstein
South Carolina State Museum
John Steele
Lou Sutton
Steve Tanenbaum
Harvey Teal
James Twombley
John Umberger
Lloyd E. Wagaman
Randy Woods
Al Zaika
Clem Zambon

The author would also like to thank David E. Schenkman for his editorial expertise, and the Token and Medal Society for undertaking the publication of this work.

INTRODUCTION

In the mid-1970s Randy Chambers compiled the first listing of South Carolina tokens. In 1977 that compilation was published in serial form, in four successive issues of the *TAMS Journal*. Since that time, the number of known South Carolina trade tokens has almost tripled. Therefore this new, updated catalog should be welcomed by today's collectors.

Approximately 1800 tokens from some 250 towns are cataloged in this effort. The majority of these are the "good for" type of trade token popular during the late nineteenth and early twentieth centuries. Modern tokens are omitted for the most part, except those made out of metal and featuring a stated value or the words "good for" in their inscriptions. Modern video arcade tokens are omitted, as are modern plastic tokens, food stamp tokens, wooden nickels, and encased coins. Transportation tokens, although ably cataloged in other works, are included due to their popularity. Parking tokens and car wash tokens, however, are omitted.

Photographs have been printed alongside the catalog entries whenever possible. A rarity rating accompanies each listing, giving the collector some idea of each token's relative availability. As with any catalog, the collector should understand that the rarity ratings herein are only the opinions of the author and are subject to change, sometimes drastically.

This work has been liberally annotated with historical footnotes concerning the token issuers, the tokens themselves, and even the towns in which the tokens were issued. It is the author's opinion that such information provides for a much more enjoyable catalog.

A SHORT HISTORY OF THE USE OF TOKENS IN SOUTH CAROLINA

South Carolina has had a long and varied history, much of which is reflected in the various tokens that have been issued within the state. Although a small state and thereby not having a great many tokens, much can be learned about South Carolina by studying those pieces cataloged herein.

The first token that can arguably be called a South Carolina token was struck even before there was a South Carolina. The Carolina Elephant token, long cataloged in Richard Yeoman's *A Guidebook of United States Coins*, is believed to have been struck in London during the late 1600s. At that time, Carolina was a royal colony (comprised of land that is now North Carolina and South Carolina) under the proprietorship of several of England's prominent citizens. It is thought that the Elephant tokens were struck as a type of advertising piece to promote interest in the new colony. Some specimens in existence today show wear (which suggests circulation as a medium of exchange), but there is no concrete evidence that they circulated in the New World. Most numismatic scholars believe that if any of these tokens did circulate, they did so in England and not in Carolina. For this reason, the Carolina Elephant token will not be cataloged in this work.

Chronologically, the next South Carolina token that the collector would encounter is the R.L. Baker soda water token from Charleston. It bears the date 1837, and thus qualifies for inclusion in the Hard Times Token series. As the only issue from South Carolina in that series, it is quite sought after. It can rightfully be called the "Granddaddy" of South Carolina tokens.

There are a few other South Carolina tokens that fall into the pre-Civil War time period. All of these were issued by merchants in the Charleston area, and they functioned primarily as a means of advertising. Known today as merchant tokens or "storecards," they have previously been cataloged by Miller in *A Catalogue of U.S. Storecards or Merchants Tokens* and more recently by Rulau in *U.S. Merchant Tokens 1845 - 1860*. The issuance of these "storecard" tokens by Charleston area merchants indicates the commercial prominence South Carolina's premier port city enjoyed prior to the Civil War.

The War Between the States brought much change to South Carolina, including a great change in the circulating coinage. Gold and silver coins were immediately hoarded, and even the smaller copper coins became scarce. This shortage was alleviated in part in the Northern states by the use of Civil War tokens, small cent-sized copper tokens issued by various merchants. There are no Civil War tokens presently known from South Carolina. Instead, Confederate currency and other paper scrip seemed to fill the void created by the coin shortage.

Following the Civil War, "Reconstruction" came to South Carolina. The havoc wreaked upon the state during the War and its aftermath necessitated a long period of commercial recovery and this is reflected in the fact that there are very few South Carolina tokens known from the 1860s, 1870s, and 1880s. Those tokens that are known were primarily used during the 1880s and were issued by some of the plantations, merchants, and early industries along the coast. They were of the "trade token" variety; that is, they were redeemable in cash, trade, or merchandise for the value stated.

By the early 1900s, prosperity had begun to return to the state. Two of the industries that were largely responsible for this commercial recovery were the textile industry and the lumber industry. The importance of both of these industries is indicated by the number of trade tokens issued by the various lumber companies and cotton mills. In fact, these two industries account for about half of the trade tokens ever issued in the state.

Both of these industries utilized tokens in much the same way. Many of the early cotton mills (and lumber companies) were located in isolated areas and as a result found it necessary to operate company-owned general stores for the convenience of their employees. Some of these mills then saw it to their advantage to issue their own system of token coinage. This benefitted the company primarily in two ways: by offering to pay the employees in tokens instead of cash, it led them to shop at the company store to the exclusion of other establishments; and, by using this system of private money, the mill company could avoid handling large amounts of cash except on paydays. This second point was very important if the closest bank was over 40 miles away, as was the situation in some of the more isolated mill villages and lumber camps.

For all its good points, this system of private money had its drawbacks. Some cotton mills seemed to "force" it on their employees, not giving them the opportunity to request their pay in cash. To be sure, an employee could wait until payday to receive cash, but one who requested an advance was usually forced to accept tokens. This system tended to keep an employee in debt to the mill company. Other mills charged inflated prices for the goods in their company stores, which had the effect of making a $1.00 token worth only 70 or 80 cents in purchasing power. Also, the system easily lent itself to abuse by enterprising individuals who ran informal black markets in the "loonies," as the tokens were often called in the mill villages. These "entrepreneurs" bought "loonies" from employees for cash at a discount (usually 70 or 80 per cent of face value) and then redeemed them for luxury items such as tobacco or cigarettes.

Of course cotton mills and lumber companies were not the only issuers of trade tokens during the early twentieth century. They are also known from seafood packing companies, vegetable canneries, drug stores, dairies, general stores, military bases, banks, bakeries, school cafeterias, furniture companies, prisons, shoe shops, fraternal organizations, billiard parlors, finance companies, and bottling companies. Grocers, contractors, fruit dealers, confectioners, and jewelers are also known to have issued tokens. Just about all topical interests are represented.

Curiously, there are no true "saloon" tokens cataloged in this work. The author does not know of any token from South Carolina with the word "saloon" in its inscription. There does exist a few tokens that undoubtedly were issued by saloonkeepers, but none of them are blessed with the magic word. This situation seems to exist for several reasons. The word "saloon" evidently was not popular in the state. In fact, this author has never seen a directory listing in which an establishment had the word saloon in its name. To be sure, there were individuals that were listed as saloonkeepers, but names such as "The White Front Saloon" or "The Commercial Saloon" did not seem to be popular. Also, saloons were outlawed in 1893 by the passage of the state dispensary act. This law made it illegal for any establishment to sell liquor by the drink, and the sale of alcohol by the bottle was strictly regulated by the state. This situation lasted in some form until well after Prohibition had ended. Drinking establishments such as bars and saloons were not made legal again until the 1960s.

World War II seemed to bring an end to widespread token usage in this state. Many a token is scarce or unknown today because the bulk of its issue was donated to the scrap metal drives of the war effort. There were a couple of cotton mills (and of course, a few bus companies) that continued to use tokens after the War, but most issuers discontinued the practice in the late 1930s or the early 1940s.

HOW TO USE THIS CATALOG

The tokens cataloged herein are categorized alphabetically by the town in which they were issued. The tokens listed under each town heading are further arranged in alphabetical order by the issuer's last name or the company name. The company name takes precedence over an individual's name when both appear on the token. The following sample listing will illustrate the method by which the tokens are cataloged.

ADAMSBORO   (Marlboro County)   1010

A10   W.B. ADAMS' SON / ADAMSBORO / S.C.
         GOOD FOR / 10¢ / IN MERCHANDISE
            aluminum, 25mm, round, R10

The top line lists the name of the town and the county name (in parentheses) from which the token was issued. The number at the far right of this line is the special catalog number referring to that town. Each town has a different number, ranging from 1000 to 2999.

At the beginning of the second line is the catalog number assigned to that token. The combination of an individual token number with the special town number mentioned previously can be used as a kind of shorthand way of identifying a particular token. The token described above can therefore be identified in "shorthand" as 1010-A10. No other token in the book will have an identical combination of catalog numbers.

The remainder of the second line describes the obverse inscription on the token. A word-for-word representation of the inscription appears in capital letters, with each line being separated by a slash mark (/). Thus, it can be seen that the token described above has three separate lines of text on its obverse.

The third line of the sample listing describes the token's reverse inscription. In most cases this is given in capital letters, with each line of inscription being separated by a slash mark.

Occasionally the reader will encounter an obverse or reverse description (or portion thereof) that is composed of lower case letters in parentheses. This part of the description serves to describe the obverse or reverse, or some other aspect of the token, and is not a word-for-word representation.

The fourth line gives the physical attributes of the token. Normally the composition of the token is followed by its size in millimeters, and then the shape of the planchet. Any type of stencil cut-out (abbreviated as c/o), or manufacturer-made hole (described as holed as made) is identified on this line also. The rarity rating is usually the last thing to appear on this line. Following is a table of these ratings (tokens which were issued after 1960 are designated as "modern," and may not have a rarity rating).

RARITY NUMBER	NUMBER OF SPECIMENS KNOWN
R10	1 to 2
R9	3 to 4
R8	5 to 8
R7	9 to 15
R6	16 to 24
R5	25 to 49
R4	50 to 99
R3	100 to 199
R2	200 to 499
R1	500 or more

SYSTEM SCRIP

Many of the tokens issued in South Carolina were made by one of the companies that specialized in the manufacture of "system" scrip. The reverses of the tokens made by each manufacturer were very similar to the other tokens from that same manufacturer. Therefore, the reverse descriptions of these tokens are abbreviated in the catalog and appear in lower case letters within parentheses. The following listing illustrates how a "system" token will appear.

M500   ANDERSON MILLS STORE / 500 / IN MDSE. / ANDERSON, S.C.
    (Master Metal Scrip - type I)
    copper, 35mm, round, "A" c/o, R10

Notice that the line describing the reverse appears in lower case letters within parentheses. This denotes that it is not a word-for-word rendering of the inscription. Instead, it indicates that the token resembles the type I reverse of the Master Metal Scrip series made by the Ingle - Schierloh Company. Other types of "system" scrip include Ingle System scrip, and scrip made by the Osborne Register Company (abbreviated as Orco). Representative illustrations of each type of reverse from these manufacturers follow.

OSBORNE REGISTER COMPANY (ORCO)

TYPE I (PAT. PEND.)   TYPE II (REG. U.S. PAT. OFF.)

TYPE III (PATENTED)   TYPE IV

MASTER METAL SCRIP
(MADE BY THE INGLE-SCHIERLOH COMPANY)

TYPE I (PAT. PEND.)

TYPE II (DES. PAT. 75656)

INGLE SYSTEM

1909 PATENT DATE

1914 PATENT DATE

A   ABBEVILLE / 145 (serial #) / COTTON / MILLS (all incuse)
     (blank)
       aluminum, 35mm, round, holed as made, R10

       This is probably either a time check or some type of production check which was tendered to the mill workers when a task had been completed. At the end of the day, or possibly on paydays, the checks were turned in to the cashier or foreman and were used to determine the amount of pay a worker was to receive. The Abbeville Cotton Mills was in operation under that name from the early 1900s through most of the 1930s. It specialized in the manufacture of sheetings. The mill continued operation into the 1960s as Abbeville Mills, Inc., a division of Deering Milliken, Inc.

B5   COLUMBIA / CANDY / KITCHEN
     GOOD FOR / 5¢ / IN TRADE
       aluminum, 19mm, round, R10

       Attribution tentative. This confectionery was listed in business directories from 1915 to 1930.

C10   HAGEN BROS. / ABBEVILLE, / S.C.
     GOOD FOR AMUSEMENT ONLY / 10 (numeral incuse)
       aluminum, 23mm, round, R10

       The Hagen Brothers operated a beverage and billiard parlor in Abbeville during the 1930s and 1940s. The token was probably used in some type of amusement game or slot machine located on the premises.

A100   W. B. ADAMS' SON / ADAMSBORO / S.C.
     GOOD FOR / $1<u>00</u> / IN / MERCHANDISE
       aluminum, 35mm, round, R10

A10   (obverse similar to A100)
     GOOD FOR / 10¢ / IN / MERCHANDISE
       aluminum, 25mm, round, R10

       W. B. Adams' son took over his father's general merchandise business sometime between 1904 and 1908, and operated it until the 1930s. There may have been two stores in operation — one in Adamsboro and the other in nearby Newtonville. See listings under Newtonville for other tokens from this business.

AIKEN (Aiken County)

A15 BUSY BEE / 15
(Ingle System - 1909 pat. date)
brass, 18mm, round, R10

    Attribution tentative. The token was attributed, without strong verification, by Wagaman (see Bibliography). It is safe to say that many Busy Bee cafes and restaurants have operated across the country at various times. This is one of the few known Ingle System tokens with a 15 cent denomination.

ALCOLU (Clarendon County)

A100 D. W. ALDERMAN & SONS COMPANY / R.J. ALDERMAN (facsimile signature) / PRESIDENT / ALCOLU, S.C.
GOOD FOR / 1 00 / PAT. JULY 1899 / IN MERCHANDISE ONLY
bimetallic, 39mm, round, R7

A50 (obverse similar to A100)
GOOD FOR / 50 / PAT. JULY 1899 / IN MERCHANDISE ONLY
bimetallic, 32mm, round, R8

A25 (obverse similar to A100)
GOOD FOR / 25 / PAT. JULY 1899 / IN MERCHANDISE ONLY
bimetallic, 28mm, round, R7

A10 (obverse similar to A100)
GOOD FOR / 10 / PAT. / JULY 1899 / IN MERCHANDISE ONLY
bimetallic, 25mm, round, R7

A5 (obverse similar to A100)
GOOD FOR / 5 / PAT. JULY 1899 / IN MERCHANDISE ONLY
bimetallic, 21mm, round, R10

    I have not examined a specimen of A5. The listing is based solely on its inclusion in Randy Chambers' catalog. There is some doubt as to its existence, due to the absence of a corresponding piece in the following set, which was struck with the same obverse dies as the set above.

B100 D. W. ALDERMAN & SONS COMPANY / R.J. ALDERMAN (facsimile signature) / PRESIDENT / ALCOLU, S.C.
GOOD FOR / 1 00 / MERCHANDISE ONLY
brass, 39mm, round, R5

B50 (obverse similar to B100)
GOOD FOR / 50 / MERCHANDISE ONLY
brass, 32mm, round, R5

B25 (obverse similar to B100)
GOOD FOR / 25 / MERCHANDISE ONLY
brass, 28mm, round, R5

B10   (obverse similar to B100)
        GOOD FOR / 10 / MERCHANDISE ONLY
          brass, 25mm, round, R5

        The 1020B series was struck with the same obverse dies as the corresponding tokens of the 1020A series.

C5   D. W. ALDERMAN & SONS COMPANY / P.R. ALDERMAN (facsimile signature) / PRESIDENT / ALCOLU, S.C.
        GOOD FOR / 5¢ / MERCHANDISE ONLY
          brass, 21mm, round, R5

D1   (obverse similar to C5)
        GOOD FOR / 1¢ / IN MERCHANDISE
          brass, 19x26mm, oval, R5

E1   (obverse similar to C5)
        GOOD FOR / 1¢ / IN MERCHANDISE
          nickel, 19x26mm, oval, R10

        David Wells Alderman moved to Clarendon County, S.C. from North Carolina shortly after the Civil War. Over the ensuing years, he purchased large amounts of land and standing timber, and built a fairly large sawmill. He named the town which grew up around his mill Alcolu - "Al" for Alderman, "co" for Mr. Colwell, an early partner in the mill, and "lu" for Lula, his oldest daughter.

        Sometime in the early 1900s R. J. Alderman, one of D. W.'s sons, became president of the business, and it became known as D. W. Alderman & Sons Company. At peak capacity, the mill produced 100,000 feet of cypress and yellow pine lumber per day. The company also built a logging railroad, an electric lighting plant, a large company store with a 200-seat theater upstairs, and close to 200 company-owned houses.

        In 1928, Paul R. Alderman became president of the firm, and the tokens which bear his signature can therefore be dated to after 1928. When P. R. Alderman died in 1946, the company was sold to Williams Furniture Company. In 1957, the mill was sold to Georgia-Pacific, by whom it is still operated. Still standing is the old company store (with theater upstairs), but most of the company-owned houses have been torn down.

F25   M. C. HOWIE / NOT / TRANSFERABLE / ALCOLU, S.C.
        GOOD FOR / 25¢ / IN TRADE
          aluminum, 28mm, round, R10

        An extensive search of business directories has failed to reveal anything about M. C. Howie. However, there was an A. P. Howie listed as a sawmill operator in Alcolu during the early 1920s.

ALLENDALE   (Allendale County)   1025

A50   M. L. HARRIS / ALLENDALE, S.C.
           GOOD FOR / 50 / IN MERCHANDISE
           brass, 31mm, round, R10

           M. L. Harris ran a planing mill near Allendale in the late 1920s and early
           1930s.

B25   H. C. HILL / COMMISSARY / ALLENDALE / S.C.
           GOOD FOR / 25¢ / IN TRADE
           brass, 26mm, round, R10

B1   (obverse similar to B25)
           GOOD FOR / 1¢ / IN TRADE
           brass, 18mm, round, R10

ANDERSON   (Anderson County)   1035

A500   AIKEN STORES, INC. / 5$\underline{00}$ / A S / ANDERSON, S.C.
           (Orco - type IV, dated 1939)
           brass, 32mm, scalloped (12), "C" c/o, R8

A100   (obverse similar to A500 except denomination 1$\underline{00}$)
           (Orco - type IV, dated 1939)
           nickel, 32mm, round, "C" c/o, R2

A50   (obverse similar to A500 except denomination 50)
           (Orco - type IV, dated 1939)
           copper, 29mm, round, "C" c/o, R2

A25   (obverse similar to A500 except denomination 25)
           (Orco - type IV, dated 1939)
           nickel, 26mm, round, "C" c/o, R2

A10   (obverse similar to A500 except denomination 10)
           (Orco - type IV, dated 1939)
           brass, 23mm, round, "C" c/o, R2

A5   (obverse similar to A500 except denomination 5)
           (Orco - type IV, dated 1939)
           nickel, 20mm, round, "C" c/o, R2

           Aiken Stores, Inc. operated company stores for two textile mills in
           Anderson from 1938 to 1941 — Gluck Mills and Orr Mills. The company
           also operated mill stores in Williamston, Calhoun Falls, Langley, Bath, and
           Clearwater. Tokens are known from all of these locations; most are very
           common.

B100   ANDERSON CHEMICAL & MERCANTILE CO. / 1$\underline{00}$ / A C M / CO /
           ANDERSON, S.C.
           (Orco - type IV, dated 1941)
           nickel, 32mm, round, " + " c/o, R7

B50   (obverse similar to B100 except denomination 50)
        (Orco - type IV, dated 1941)
            nickel, 29mm, round, "+" c/o, R7

B25   (obverse similar to B100 except denomination 25)
        (Orco - type IV, dated 1941)
            nickel, 26mm, round, "+" c/o, R7

B10   (obverse similar to B100 except denomination 10)
        (Orco - type IV, dated 1941)
            nickel, 23mm, round, "+" c/o, R5

B5   (obverse similar to B100 except denomination 5)
        (Orco - type IV, dated 1941)
            nickel, 20mm, round, "+" c/o, R6

B1   (obverse similar to B100 except denomination 1)
        (Orco - type IV, dated 1941)
            nickel, 17mm, round, "+" c/o, R8

C1   (obverse similar to B100 except denomination 1)
        (Orco - type IV, dated 1943)
            red fiber, 17mm, round, "+" c/o, R9

D1   (obverse similar to B100 except denomination 1)
        (Orco - type IV, dated 1944)
            red fiber, 17mm, round, "+" c/o, R9

The Anderson Chemical & Mercantile Co. operated the company store for Anderson Cotton Mills during the 1940s and early 1950s. Tokens were discontinued in 1951 when the store was closed down.

E100   ANDERSON COTTON MILL STORE / 1$\underline{00}$
        (Orco - type II) (varieties exist)
            nickel, 32mm, round, "AM" c/o, R6

E50   (obverse similar to E100 except denomination 50)
        (Orco - type II)
            nickel, 27mm, round, "AM" c/o, R7

E25   (obverse similar to E100 except denomination 25)
        (Orco - type II) (varieties exist)
            nickel, 24mm, round, "AM" c/o, R5

E10   (obverse similar to E100 except denomination 10)
        (Orco - type II) (varieties exist)
            nickel, 21mm, round, "AM" c/o, R4

E5   (obverse similar to E100 except denomination 5)
        (Orco - type II) (varieties exist)
            nickel, 19mm, round, "AM" c/o, R4

E1   (obverse similar to E100 except denomination 1)
         (Orco - type II and type III varieties exist)
         nickel, 18mm, round, "AM" c/o, R3
         Varieties of E1 also exist without a cut-out.

F1   ANDERSON COTTON MILL STORE / 1
         (Orco - type III) (varieties exist)
         nickel, 17mm, round, " + " c/o, R4

G1   ANDERSON COTTON MILL STORE / 1
         (Orco - type II)
         brass, 21mm, octagonal, " + " c/o, R7

H100   ANDERSON COTTON MILLS STORE / ANDERSON, / S.C.
         GOOD FOR / 100 / IN MERCHANDISE
         aluminum, 35mm, round, beaded borders on obverse and reverse,
         R9

I100   ANDERSON COTTON MILLS STORE / ANDERSON, / S.C.
         GOOD FOR / 100 / IN MERCHANDISE
         aluminum, 36mm, round, toothed borders on obverse and reverse,
         R9

I50   (obverse similar to I100)
         GOOD FOR / 50 / IN MERCHANDISE
         aluminum, 33mm, round, R9

J5   ANDERSON COTTON MILLS STORE / ANDERSON, / S.C.
         GOOD FOR / 5 / IN / MERCHANDISE
         aluminum, 19mm, round, lined border on obverse, beaded on
         reverse, R9

K5   ANDERSON COTTON MILL STORE / ANDERSON / S.C.
         GOOD FOR / 5 / IN / MERCHANDISE
         aluminum, 19mm, round, beaded borders on obverse and reverse,
         R9

L1   ANDERSON MILLS STORE / 1¢
         GOOD FOR / 1¢ / IN / MERCHANDISE
         brass, 18mm, octagonal, R7

M500   ANDERSON MILLS STORE / 5$\underline{00}$ / IN MDSE. / ANDERSON, S.C.
         (Master Metal Scrip - type I)
         copper, 35mm, round, "A" c/o, R10

M100   (obverse similar to M500 except denomination 1$\underline{00}$)
         (Master Metal Scrip - type I)
         nickel, 35mm, round, "A" c/o, R9

M50   (obverse similar to M500 except denomination 50)
         (Master Metal Scrip - type II)
         nickel, 30mm, round, "A" c/o, R8

M25   (obverse similar to M500 except denomination 25)
          (Master Metal Scrip - type I)
          nickel-plated brass, 24mm, round, "A" c/o, R5

M10   (obverse similar to M500 except denomination 10)
          (Master Metal Scrip - type II)
          nickel, 21mm, round, "A" c/o, R4

M5   (obverse similar to M500 except denomination 5)
          (Master Metal Scrip - type I)
          nickel, 19mm, round, "A" c/o, R5

M1   (obverse similar to M500 except denomination 1)
          (Master Metal Scrip - type II)
          brass, 18mm, round, "A" c/o, R5

N100 ANDERSON MILLS STORE / $1⁰⁰ / ANDERSON / S.C.
          GOOD FOR / 1⁰⁰ / IN / MERCHANDISE / NOT / TRANSFERABLE
          brass, 31mm, round, R6

O100 ANDERSON MILLS STORE / 1⁰⁰ / ANDERSON / S.C.
          GOOD FOR / 1⁰⁰ / IN / MERCHANDISE / NOT / TRANSFERABLE
          brass, 31mm, round, R6

O50   (obverse similar to O100 except denomination 50)
          GOOD FOR / 50¢ / IN / MERCHANDISE / NOT / TRANSFERABLE
          brass, 28mm, round, R6

O25   (obverse similar to O100 except denomination 25)
          GOOD FOR / 25¢ / IN / MERCHANDISE / NOT / TRANSFERABLE
          brass, 26mm, round, R6

O10   (obverse similar to O100 except denomination 10)
          GOOD FOR / 10¢ / IN / MERCHANDISE / NOT / TRANSFERABLE
          brass, 23mm, round, R6

O5   (obverse similar to O100 except denomination 5)
          GOOD FOR / 5¢ / IN / MERCHANDISE / NOT / TRANSFERABLE
          brass, 21mm, round, R6

P1   (obverse similar to O100 except denomination 1)
          GOOD FOR / 1¢ / IN / MERCHANDISE
          aluminum, 21mm, round, R9

Anderson Cotton Mill was one of the most prolific issuers of tokens in South Carolina. There were at least five different sets used at one time or another, if one counts the set used by Anderson Chemical & Mercantile Co. The aluminum tokens seem to be the oldest. It is thought that the company then ordered the 1035-O series, which was made of more wear-resistant brass. However, it was soon discovered that two enterprising employees were surreptitiously purchasing counterfeit tokens from the token manufacturer. An inventory revealed that over $2500 worth of spurious tokens had been accepted at the company store. The company promptly discontinued using this style of token and ordered new "patented" tokens

from the Osborne Register Company and the Ingle Schierloh Company. Interestingly, the two employees were never prosecuted.

Anderson Cotton Mill began operations in the 1880s, being perhaps the first textile plant to operate in a town known for textiles. The company specialized in print cloths.

Q   ANDERSON / STEAM / BAKERY
> GOOD FOR / ONE / LOAF / OF / BREAD
>> brass, 24mm, round, R9

The Anderson Steam Bakery, which was located on Benson Street, operated in the early 1900s. Directory listings disappear around 1915.

R100   APPLETON MILL STORE / 1$\underline{00}$ / IN MDSE. / ANDERSON, S.C.
> (Master Metal Scrip - type II)
>> nickel, 35mm, round, clover-shaped c/o, R8

R50   (obverse similar to R100 except denomination 50)
> (Master Metal Scrip - type II)
>> nickel, 30mm, round, clover-shaped c/o, R8

R25   (obverse similar to R100 except denomination 25)
> (Master Metal Scrip - type I)
>> nickel, 24mm, round, clover-shaped c/o, R7

R10   (obverse similar to R100 except denomination 10)
> (Master Metal Scrip - type II)
>> nickel, 21mm, round, clover-shaped c/o, R6

R5   (obverse similar to R100 except denomination 5)
> (Master Metal Scrip - type II) (varieties exist)
>> nickel, 19mm, round, clover-shaped c/o, R6

R1   (obverse similar to R100 except denomination 1)
> (Master Metal Scrip - type II) (varieties exist)
>> brass, 18mm, round, clover-shaped c/o, R3

S5   (obverse similar to R100 except denomination 5)
> (Master Metal Scrip - type II)
>> zinc, 19mm, round, clover-shaped c/o, R10

Appleton Mill was organized in 1925, when Brogan Mill was purchased by a firm in Boston, Mass. The old Brogan Mill tokens were discontinued and new tokens were ordered from the Ingle Schierloh Company. Over the years the company probably placed several reorders for tokens, as evidenced by the existence of several die varieties of the smaller denominations. The mill made flannels and sheetings.

T5   ATKINSON'S / DRUG STORE / ANDERSON, S.C.
> GOOD FOR ONE / 5 / CENT / GLASS OF SODA
>> aluminum, 24mm, round, R10

W. E. Atkinson operated a drug store circa 1905 to 1915.

ANDERSON (Continued)

1035

U25   BROGAN / MILL STORE
GOOD FOR / 25¢ / IN MERCHANDISE
brass, 28mm, round, R10

U10   (obverse similar to U25)
GOOD FOR / 10¢ / IN MERCHANDISE
brass, size unknown, round, R10

U5   (obverse similar to U25)
GOOD FOR / 5¢ / IN MERCHANDISE
brass, 20mm, round, R10

As previously mentioned, Brogan Mill was purchased by a Boston, Mass. firm in 1925, and Appleton Mill was then organized. Brogan Mill had been in operation since the early 1900s, and specialized in the manufacture of sheetings. Directory listings always showed the spelling as "Brogon," although on all the tokens the spelling is "Brogan."

V   BROGAN / MILLS / 9 (serial #) (all incuse)
(blank)
brass, 21mm, round, holed as made, R8

This is probably some type of production check. Specimens are known with different serial numbers on the obverse.

W   CAROLINA SHOE SHOP / 416 S. / MAIN / ST. / ANDERSON, S.C.
(blank)
aluminum, 26mm, round, R7

X   CAROLINA / SHOE / SHOP / 416 S. MAIN ST. / ANDERSON, S.C.
(blank)
aluminum, 16mm, round, R4

Per Randy Chambers, this shoe shop had a large number of shine boys who would receive a large token (1035W) for shining a pair of boots and a small token (1035X) for a regular pair of shoes. The customers did not pay the shine boys, as was customary, but paid the cashier and he in turn gave the shine boy a token. The store shared in the profits and would exchange the tokens for money at the end of the day. Tokens were used during the 1940s and 1950s.

Y100   COX / MFG. CO. / STORE
GOOD FOR / 100 / IN MERCHANDISE
brass, 36mm, round, R9

Y50   (obverse similar to Y100)
GOOD FOR / 50 / IN MERCHANDISE
brass, 33mm, round, R9

Y25   (obverse similar to Y100)
GOOD FOR / 25 / IN MERCHANDISE
brass, 29mm, round, R9

Y10   (obverse similar to Y100)
         GOOD FOR / 10 / IN MERCHANDISE
              brass, 24mm, round, R9

         The Cox Manufacturing Company was started in the early 1900s. In 1914 the company, which manufactured yarns, was sold and then became Equinox Mill.

Z5   R. R. DERRICK / ANDERSON / S.C.
         GOOD FOR / 5¢ / DRINK
              brass, 25mm, square, R10

         R. R. Derrick operated a restaurant from the late teens to the early thirties.

AA5   EDWARD'S CAFE / & / POOL / ROOM / ANDERSON, S.C.
         GOOD FOR / 5¢ / IN TRADE
              aluminum, 20mm, round, R3

         This establishment was located in the Riverside-Toxaway mill village during the late 1930s and 1940s. Tokens were purchased from the cashier and were used to pay the rack boy for each game of pool played. This prevented the rack boy (who received a commission on each token he turned in) from having to handle cash.

AB100   EQUINOX MILL STORE / 1⁰⁰ / ANDERSON, / S.C.
         (Master Metal Scrip - type II)
              aluminum, 35mm, round, R9

AC50   EQUINOX MILL STORE / 50 / ANDERSON, / S.C.
         GOOD FOR / 50¢ / IN / MERCHANDISE
              aluminum, 31mm, round, R9

         Equinox Mill was formed in 1914 when Cox Manufacturing Company was bought out. The company specialized in the manufacture of cotton duck, a fabric similar to canvas but finer in texture and lighter in weight.

AD100   GLUCK MILL STORE / GOOD FOR / 1⁰⁰ / IN MERCHANDISE / ANDERSON, S.C.
         (same)
              brass, 35mm, round, R9

AD50   (obverse similar to AD100 except denomination 50¢)
         (same)
              brass, 31mm, round, R9

AD25   (obverse similar to AD100 except denomination 25¢)
         (same)
              brass, 29mm, round, R9

AE50   GLUCK MILL STORE / GOOD FOR / 50¢ / IN MERCHANDISE / ANDERSON, S.C.
         (same)
              aluminum, 31mm, round, R9

AE25   (obverse similar to AE50 except denomination 25¢)
    (same)
      aluminum, 28mm, round, R9

AE10   (obverse similar to AE50 except denomination 10¢)
    (same)
      aluminum, 25mm, round, R9

AE5   (obverse similar to AE50 except denomination 5¢)
    (same)
      aluminum, 20mm, round, R8

AF5   GLUCK MILL STORE / 5 / IN MDSE. / ANDERSON, S.C.
    (Master Metal Scrip - type II)
      brass, 19mm, round, "G" c/o, R7

AF1   (obverse similar to AF5 except denomination 1)
    (Master Metal Scrip - type II)
      nickel, 18mm, round, "G" c/o, R6

AG1   (obverse similar to AF5 except denomination 1)
    (Master Metal Scrip - type II)
      brass, 21mm, scalloped (8), no cutout, R7

AH100   GLUCK MILLS STORE / G.M.S. / ANDERSON / S.C.
    GOOD FOR / $1⁰⁰ / IN TRADE
      brass, 31mm, round, R9

AH10   (obverse similar to AH100)
    GOOD FOR / 10¢ / IN TRADE
      brass, 23mm, round, R9

AH5   (obverse similar to AH100)
    GOOD FOR / 5¢ / IN TRADE
      brass, 20mm, round, R9

    Gluck Mills was in operation as early as 1904. The Master Metal Scrip series was first ordered in 1936.

AI   GOSSETT MILLS: tokens were ordered from the Ingle Schierloh Company in 1938, and three hundred were delivered that year. No specimens have been encountered as yet.

AJ50   J. F. HOFFMAN / 50
    (Ingle System - 1909 pat. date)
      copper, 31mm, round, R10

AJ1   (obverse similar to AJ50 except denomination 1)
    (Ingle System - 1909 pat. date)
      copper, 18mm, round, R10

    Lloyd Wagaman attributed this merchant to Louisville, Kentucky. However, the listed 50 cent token was found among a group of cotton mill tokens from the Anderson area. A check of business directories revealed a J. F. Hoffman in the grocery and meat business from 1908 to 1923.

Wagaman has since re-attributed the merchant to Anderson on the strength of this evidence.

AK5   JONES BILLIARD / PARLOR / & CAFE / ANDERSON, S.C.
    GOOD FOR / 5¢ / IN TRADE
      aluminum, 20mm, round, R9

AL25   JONES BILLIARD PARLOR / & / CAFE / 25 / ANDERSON, S.C.
    (Master Metal Scrip - type II)
      brass, 24mm, round, "J" c/o, R5

AL5   (obverse similar to AL25 except denomination 5)
    (Master Metal Scrip - type II)
      brass, 19mm, round, "J" c/o, R4

      According to Randy Chambers, Jones Billiard Parlor started operating in 1933 and closed its doors in 1947. The aluminum tokens (AK5) were used first, but were too easily mistaken for the tokens of Edward's Cafe & Pool Room (AA5), located about half a mile away. To eliminate the problem, Jones ordered Master Metal Scrip tokens (AL25, AL5) and then destroyed all aluminum tokens in his possession. Three specimens were later discovered and escaped destruction.

AM5   MARTIN BROS, / ANDERSON, / S.C.
    GOOD FOR / ONE / 5¢ / CIGAR
      aluminum, 19mm, round, R10

      The Martin Brothers operated a general store in Gluck Mill Village from the early 1900s to the mid-1930s.

AN5   OLYMPIA CANDY CO. / ANDERSON / S.C.
    GOOD FOR / 5¢ / CIGAR OR SODA
      aluminum, 18mm, round, R10

      This business was only listed in the 1914 and 1915 directories.

AO5   ORR COTTON MILLS / ANDERSON / 5 / S.C. / STORE
    (same)
      aluminum, 20mm, round, R10

AP10   ORR COTTON MILLS STORE / GOOD FOR / 10 / IN MERCHANDISE / ANDERSON, S.C.
    (same)
      aluminum, 24mm, round, R10

AP1   (obverse similar to AP10 except denomination 1)
    (same)
      brass, 19mm, round, R10

AQ100   ORR / COTTON MILLS / STORE / GOOD FOR / 1<u>00</u> / IN MDSE. / ANDERSON, S.C.
    (Master Metal Scrip - type II)
      copper, 35mm, round, "O" c/o, R9

AQ50   (obverse similar to AQ100 except denomination 50)
             (Master Metal Scrip - type II)
               copper, 30mm, round, "O" c/o, R8

AQ25   (obverse similar to AQ100 except denomination 25)
             (Master Metal Scrip - type I)
               brass, 24mm, round, "O" c/o, R7

AQ10   (obverse similar to AQ100 except denomination 10)
             (Master Metal Scrip - type II)
               nickel-plated brass, 21mm, round, "O" c/o, R7

AQ5   (obverse similar to AQ100 except denomination 5)
             (Master Metal Scrip - type II)
               copper, 19mm, round, "O" c/o, R7

AR1   (obverse similar to AQ100 except denomination 1)
             (Master Metal Scrip - type II)
               brass, 21mm, scalloped (8), no cutout, R6

AS5   ORR COTTON MILL STORE / 5 / ANDERSON, S.C.
             (Orco - type IV, dated 1944)
               green fiber, 19mm, round, "O" c/o, R10

   Orr Cotton Mill (no relation to Orr, Gray & Co.) was in business as early
as 1904 and remained in operation well into the 1940s. The company made
print cloths and sheetings.

AT5   ORR GRAY. & CO / ANDERSON, / S.C.
             GOOD FOR / ONE / 5¢ / CIGAR
               aluminum, 19mm, round, R4

AU5   (obverse same as AT5)
             GOOD FOR / 5¢ / SODA WATER
               aluminum, 19mm, round, R8

   The Orr, Gray & Co. drug store has long been a fixture in downtown
Anderson. Listed as early as 1904, it is still in business today (under new
management, of course). The two tokens were used in a type of novelty
machine which dispensed a 5¢ token for each nickel placed into the
machine. Every fifth nickel produced three 5¢ tokens and every fifteenth
nickel produced five 5¢ tokens.

AV   SOUTHSIDE / POOL / ROOM / ANDERSON, S.C.
             GOOD FOR / 1 / GAME
               aluminum, 25mm, round, R9

AW   SUBURBAN TRANSIT / (picture of bus) / LINES, INC.
             GOOD FOR / (picture of bus) / ONE FARE
               brass, 16mm, c/o, R4 (Atwood 40A)

             5,000 tokens were struck in 1950.

AX10   TOXAWAY MILL STORE / 10 / ANDERSON / S.C.
             GOOD FOR / 10¢ / IN / MERCHANDISE / NOT / TRANSFERABLE
               brass, 23mm, round, R10

AX5 (obverse similar to AX10 except denomination 5)
GOOD FOR / 5¢ / IN / MERCHANDISE / NOT / TRANSFERABLE
brass, 20mm, round, R8

AX1 (obverse similar to AX10 except denomination 1)
GOOD FOR / 1¢ / IN / MERCHANDISE / NOT / TRANSFERABLE
brass, 18mm, round, R8

AY50 TOXAWAY MILL STORE / 50 / IN TRADE ONLY / ANDERSON, S.C.
(Master Metal Scrip - type II)
brass, 30mm, round, "T" c/o, R8

AY25 (obverse similar to AY50 except denomination 25)
(Master Metal Scrip - type II)
copper, 24mm, round, "T" c/o, R7

AY10 (obverse similar to AY50 except denomination 10)
(Master Metal Scrip - type I)
nickel, 21mm, round, "T" c/o, R7

AY5 (obverse similar to AY50 except denomination 5)
(Master Metal Scrip - type II)
brass, 19mm, round, "T" c/o, R5

AY1 (obverse similar to AY50 except denomination 1)
(Master Metal Scrip - type II)
copper, 18mm, round, "T" c/o, R5

Toxaway Mill was another of the early Anderson mills. In business as early as 1904, the company continued through the mid-1930s. It specialized in yarns and print cloths. The mill was later taken over by Abney Mills of Greenwood, S.C.

AZ100 1960 SILVER JUBILEE YEAR / W A I M / ABC - CBS / ANDERSON, S.C.
ABC - W A I M - CBS / GOOD FOR / $1.00 / ON PURCHASE OF / 1
MINUTE SPOT / DURING 1960 / SILVER JUBILEE YEAR
aluminum, 39mm, round, R9, modern

WAIM is a local radio station that began business in 1935 and still operates.

ANDREWS   (Georgetown County) 1040

A100 ROSEMARY AMUSEMENT CO. / SERVICE / MAKES / MORE / MONEY /
ANDREWS, S.C. (all incuse)
GOOD FOR / $1⁰⁰ / IN TRADE (all incuse)
copper, 38mm, round, reeded edge, R8

This is probably some type of slot machine token. Note that it is the same size as a silver dollar, and also has a reeded edge. It probably dates from the 1950s. The town was originally named Rosemary, but was changed to Andrews by the Seaboard Coast Line Railroad which passed through town.

ARCADIA (Spartanburg County)

A200 ARCADIA MILLS / 2̲0̲0̲
GOOD FOR / 2̲0̲0̲ / IN MDSE. ONLY / AT THE STORE OF
aluminum, 38mm, round, R9

A50 (obverse similar to A200 except denomination 50¢)
GOOD FOR / 50¢ / IN MDSE. ONLY / AT THE STORE OF
aluminum, 32mm, round, R9

A10 (obverse similar to A200 except denomination 10¢)
GOOD FOR / 10¢ / IN MDSE. ONLY / AT THE STORE OF
aluminum, 25mm, round, R7

A5 (obverse similar to A200 except denomination 5¢)
GOOD FOR / 5¢ / IN MDSE. ONLY / AT THE STORE OF
aluminum, 21mm, round, R7

B100 ARCADIA MILLS STORE / ARCADIA, / S.C.
GOOD FOR / 1̲0̲0̲ / IN / MERCHANDISE
brass, 35mm, round, R6

B25 (obverse similar to B100)
GOOD FOR / 25 / IN / MERCHANDISE
brass, 29mm, round, R6

B10 (obverse similar to B100) (varieties exist)
GOOD FOR / 10 / IN / MERCHANDISE
brass, 24mm, round, R6

B5 (obverse similar to B100)
GOOD FOR / 5¢ / IN MERCHANDISE
brass, 19mm, round, R7

C ARCADIA / MILLS
(blank)
brass, 19mm, round, R8

Arcadia Mills began operations in the early 1900s. In the mid-1930s it was sold and renamed Mayfair Mills. 1050C is probably a production token. The 1050A series is the older of the two sets, and may contain additional denominations.

D100 MAYFAIR MILLS STORE / 1̲0̲0̲ / ARCADIA, S.C.
(Orco - type II) (varieties exist)
nickel, 32mm, round, c/o, R3

D50 (obverse similar to D100 except denomination 50)
(Orco - type II)
copper, 27mm, round, c/o, R4

D25 (obverse similar to D100 except denomination 25)
(Orco - type II)
nickel, 24mm, round, c/o, R4

ARCADIA   (Continued)   1050

D10   (obverse similar to D100 except denomination 10)
           (Orco - type II)
               copper, 21mm, round, c/o, R4

D5   (obverse similar to D100 except denomination 5)
           (Orco - type II)
               nickel, 19mm, round, c/o, R4

D1   (obverse similar to D100 except denomination 1)
           (Orco - type III)
               brass, 18mm, round, c/o, R4

           As previously mentioned, Mayfair Mills was organized in the mid-1930s
           when Arcadia Mills changed ownership. The mill continued operation into
           the 1950s and later.

ARKWRIGHT   (Spartanburg County)   1055

A10   ARKWRIGHT MILLS / 10 / ARKWRIGHT / S.C.
               GOOD FOR / 10 / CENTS / IN MERCHANDISE
               aluminum, 21mm, round, R10

A1   (obverse similar to A10 except denomination 1)
               GOOD FOR / 1 / CENT / IN MERCHANDISE
               aluminum, 18mm, round, R10

           The Arkwright mill village was once considered a separate township,
           but is now part of Spartanburg. In business as early as 1904, Arkwright
           Mills is still in operation. The company store was only recently closed down.
           Tokens were last issued in the 1950s, but these show a Spartanburg
           address and are cataloged under that town.

ARLINGTON   (Spartanburg County)   1060

A7   APALACHE / 7¢ / MILLS
           (blank)
               brass, 24mm, round, R10

B6   APALACHE / PLANT
               SPOOLING / 6 / PIECE
               brass, 24mm, round, holed as made, R10

C5½   APALACHE / PLANT
               SPOOLING / 5½ / PIECE
               brass, 25mm, round, holed as made, R10

D2   APALACHE / PLANT
               SPOOLING / 1 (large 2 counterstamped over 1) / PIECE
               brass, 24mm, round, holed as made, R10

E1   APALACHE / PLANT
SPOOLING / 1 / PIECE
brass, 24mm, round, holed as made, R10

These production tokens were re-attributed to Apalache by Randy Chambers. They have been attributed to Arlington, because the town's name was not changed to Apalache until the 1950s. This town has been the site of a textile mill since 1839, when the Cedar Hill cotton factory was established by Thomas Hutchings.

F5   MUTUAL MERCANTILE CO, / ARLINGTON, / S.C.
GOOD FOR / 5¢ / IN TRADE
aluminum, 19mm, round, R10

This company was listed as a general store from 1908 to 1915.

ASHEPOO   (Colleton County)   1065

A100   BRADLEY LB'R. AND MF'G. CO. / ASHEPOO / S.C.
1<u>00</u>
aluminum, 35mm, round, R10

A25   (obverse similar to A100)
25
aluminum, 28mm, round, R10

B100   BRADLEY LUMBER & MFG. CO. / ASHEPOO, / S.C.
GOOD FOR / $1<u>00</u> / IN TRADE
aluminum, 35mm, round, R8

B50   (obverse similar to B100)
GOOD FOR / 50¢ / IN TRADE
aluminum, 31mm, round, R8

B25   (obverse similar to B100)
GOOD FOR / 25¢ / IN TRADE
aluminum, 28mm, round, R7

B10   (obverse similar to B100)
GOOD FOR / 10¢ / IN TRADE
aluminum, 25mm, round, R7

B5   (obverse similar to B100)
GOOD FOR / 5¢ / IN TRADE
aluminum, 21mm, round, R7

B1   (obverse similar to B100)
GOOD FOR / 1¢ / IN TRADE
aluminum, 19mm, round, R6

The Bradley Lumber & Manufacturing Company is listed in Ashepoo from 1919 through the mid-1930s. The company was operated by two

ASHEPOO (Continued) 1065

brothers - Peter B. and Robert S.Bradley, sons of William L. Bradley. (For tokens issued by William L. Bradley, see listings under Stono.) The company was in the lumber business, but it is not known whether it was also involved in the phosphate and fertilizer business at this location.

C100 GRAVES - DENTON / LUMBER / CO. / NOT / TRANSFERABLE / ASHEPOO, S.C.
    GOOD FOR / 1\underline{^{00}}$ / IN TRADE
    aluminum, 31mm, round, R10

C50 (obverse similar to C100)
    GOOD FOR / 50¢ / IN TRADE
    aluminum, 29mm, round, R10

C25 (obverse similar to C100)
    GOOD FOR / 25¢ / IN TRADE
    aluminum, 26mm, round, R10

C10 (obverse similar to C100)
    GOOD FOR / 10¢ / IN TRADE
    aluminum, 23mm, round, R10

C5 (obverse similar to C100)
    GOOD FOR / 5¢ / IN TRADE
    aluminum, 21mm, round, R10

    The Graves - Denton Lumber Company was only listed in 1932.

ASHTON (Colleton County) 1070

A5 F. N. JONES / P.O. / LODGE, S.C. / R.F.D. #1 / ASHTON, S.C.
    GOOD FOR / 5 / IN / MERCHANDISE
    brass, 20mm, round, R10

    Directories show that Frank N. Jones operated a sawmill, cotton gin, and general store from 1912 through 1922. His business was located between Lodge and Ashton.

AWENSDAW (Charleston County) 1080

A110 AWENSDAW / MERCANTILE / CO.
    GOOD FOR / 1$\underline{^{10}}$ / IN / MERCHANDISE
    brass, 33mm, round, R10

B25 AWENSDAW MERCANTILE / COMPANY
    GOOD FOR / 25 / IN MERCHANDISE.
    aluminum, 22mm, round, R10

    During the mid-1930s the Awensdaw Mercantile Company functioned as commissary for the A.C. Tuxbury Lumber Company. National headquarters of this lumber company were in New York City, and local headquarters in Charleston. For additional tokens used by the A.C. Tuxbury Lumber Company, see listings under Bethera and Charleston.

C   SHELMORE / OYSTER / PRODUCTS C<u>o</u>
       (blank)
           brass, 35mm, round, R8

D50 SHELMORE / OYSTER / PRODUCTS CO.
       50 (surrounded by rays)
           brass, 29mm, round, R8

D25 (obverse similar to D50)
       25
           brass, 26mm, round, R8

E10 SHELMORE / O.P. / CO.
       10
           brass, 18mm, round, R8

E5   (obverse similar to E10)
       5
           brass, 18mm, round, R10

F15 SHELMORE
       15
           aluminum, 24mm, round, R9

G10 SHELMORE OYSTER / PRODUCTS CO. / 1939
       10
           aluminum, 33mm, round, R9

The Shelmore Oyster Products Co. was first listed in 1922 as an oyster cannery in Awensdaw. Later this location is listed as a branch, with headquarters in Charleston. The tokens have been attributed to Awensdaw due to the greater likelihood that they were used here.

BADHAM (Dorchester County) 1085

A10 DORCHESTER LUMBER CO. / BADHAM, / S.C.
       GOOD FOR / 10 / IN TRADE
           brass, 24mm, round, R10

B50 DORCHESTER / LUMBER / CO.
       GOOD FOR / 50 / IN / MERCHANDISE
           brass, 29mm, round, R10

B10 (obverse similar to B50)
       GOOD FOR / 10 / IN / MERCHANDISE
           brass, 24mm, round, R10

B5   (obverse similar to B50)
       GOOD FOR / 5 / IN / MERCHANDISE
           brass, 21mm, round, R10

BADHAM (Continued)   1085

This company began operations around the turn of the century and continued through the 1930s. At one time a subsidiary corporation named the Badham Lumber Company operated sawmills in Cosby, Garnett, and Springfield. See listings under Cosby for tokens issued by this subsidiary.

BAMBERG (Bamberg County)   1090

A5   F. W. FREE CO. / BAMBERG, S.C.
GOOD FOR / 5¢ / IN MERCHANDISE
brass, 21mm, round, R10

This company was listed as a general store from 1912 to 1916.

B5   PEOPLES DRUG CO. / 5 / BAMBERG, S.C.
5
brass, 24mm, round, R10

C5   PEOPLES DRUG CO. / BAMBERG / S.C.
GOOD FOR / 5¢ / IN TRADE
aluminum, 19mm, round, R10

The Peoples Drug Company was in business until 1915.

BARNWELL (Barnwell County)   1095

A10 J. A. PORTER / DEALER / IN / GENERAL / MERCHANDISE / BARNWELL, S.C.
GOOD FOR / ¢10¢ / IN TRADE
aluminum, 29mm, round, R10

During the teens and twenties James A. Porter operated a general store and sold livestock.

BATESBURG (Lexington County)   1100

A   BATESBURG DRUG CO. / BATESBURG, / S.C.
GOOD FOR / 1 / GLASS / SODA WATER
aluminum, 25mm, round, R5

The Batesburg Drug Co. operated around 1905.

B5   GUNTER'S / DRUG STORE / BATESBURG, / S.C.
GOOD FOR ONE / 5 / CENT / GLASS OF SODA
brass, 24mm, round, R10

F. B. Gunter operated his drug store between 1908 and 1912.

C   HARDIN & FOX / ONE GLASS / SODA. (all incuse)
     (blank)
       brass, 25mm, round, R7

     A few of these tokens were discovered in Batesburg with those of the Batesburg Drug Company. An 1886 directory reveals that K. Edward Hardin and Thos. S. Fox were both physicians who were practicing medicine at that time in Batesburg. In 1893, K.E. Hardin is listed in the drug store business. It is not known for certain whether these two physicians were in the drug store business themselves, but the above information seems enough to make a positive attribution to Batesburg.

D5   THE PEOPLE'S DRUG STORE / CORNER / MAIN ST. / & / RAILROAD AVE. / BATESBURG, S.C.
     GOOD FOR / 5¢ / SODA
       aluminum, 25mm, round, R10

     It is thought that this store operated around 1908. Local sources believe it was bought out by J. M. Ridgell, who also issued his own tokens.

E5   RAWL'S POOL ROOM / BATESBURG / S.C.
     GOOD FOR / 5¢ / IN TRADE
       aluminum, 19mm, round, R10

This photograph was taken circa 1930 inside J.M. Ridgell's drug store. The man standing is C.B. Spradley, a clerk employed by Ridgell. The elaborately mirrored soda fountain in the background still stands in the building, which housed the Fair Drug Company until 1986.

F5   RIDGELL DRUG CO / BATESBURG / S.C.
GOOD FOR / 5¢ / IN SODA
brass, 24mm, round, R7

J. M. Ridgell operated the Ridgell Drug Company from 1910 into the mid-1940s. The business was then taken over by his son, E.C. Ridgell.

G5   RIKARD & SON / BATESBURG, S.C.
GOOD FOR / 5¢ / AT THE / SODA FOUNTAIN
aluminum, 25mm, round, R10

W. D. Rikard and his son, G. W. Rikard, operated this general store together until about 1914, when G. W. took it over from his father.

H5   WALL'S / DRUG STORE / BATESBURG, S.C.
GOOD FOR ONE / 5 / CENT / GLASS OF SODA
brass, 24mm, round, R10

Wall's Drug Store was in operation from 1914 to 1916.

BATH   (Aiken County)   1105

A500   AIKEN COUNTY STORES INC. / 5$\underline{00}$ / BATH + LANGLEY + / CLEARWATER, / S.C.
(Orco - type I)
brass, 32mm, scalloped (12), "B" c/o, R5

A100   (obverse similar to A500 except denomination 1$\underline{00}$)
(Orco - type II)
nickel, 32mm, round, "B" c/o, R3

A50   (obverse similar to A500 except denomination 50)
(Orco - type II) (varieties exist)
copper, 27mm, round, "B" c/o, R2

A25   (obverse similar to A500 except denomination 25)
(Orco - type II) (varieties exist)
nickel, 24mm, round, "B" c/o, R2

A10   (obverse similar to A500 except denomination 10)
(Orco - type II) (varieties exist)
brass, 21mm, round, "B" c/o, R2

A5   (obverse similar to A500 except denomination 5)
(Orco - type II) (varieties exist)
nickel, 19mm, round, "B" c/o, R2

Varieties of A5 also exist without a cutout.

A1   (obverse similar to A500 except denomination 1)
(Orco - type II)
copper, 18mm, round, "B" c/o, R5

B1   AIKEN COUNTY STORES INC./ 1 / B / BATH + LANGLEY + /
CLEARWATER, / S.C.
    (Orco - type III)
      copper, 17mm, round, R5

    During the 1930s Aiken County Stores Inc. operated a company store
for the Aiken Mills plant in Bath. The company also operated mill stores in
Anderson, Calhoun Falls, Clearwater, Langley, and Williamston. Tokens
from those locations are listed under their respective towns.

C100   AIKEN MANUFACTURING CO'S STORES / BATH, / S.C.
    GOOD FOR / 100 / IN MERCHANDISE
      brass, 36mm, round, R4

C50   (obverse similar to C100)
    GOOD FOR / 50 / IN MERCHANDISE
      brass, 33mm, round, R4

C25   (obverse similar to C100)
    GOOD FOR / 25 / IN MERCHANDISE
      brass, 29mm, round, R4

C10   (obverse similar to C100)
    GOOD FOR / 10 / IN MERCHANDISE
      brass, 24mm, round, R4

C5   (obverse similar to C100)
    GOOD FOR / 5 / IN MERCHANDISE
      brass, 19mm, round, R4

D5   AIKEN / MANUFACTURING / COMPANY / STORE / BATH, S.C.
    GOOD FOR / ONE / 5¢ / DRINK OF COCA-COLA
      brass, 25mm, round, R4

    Until 1915 the Aiken Manufacturing Company was headquartered in
Augusta, Ga. Some type of corporate buy-out occurred in 1916.
Thereafter, the company was called Aiken Mills, Inc. and was controlled
from New York City. In the 1930s, the mill store was operated by Aiken
County Stores Inc. (see listings of this company).

BEAUFORT (Beaufort County)   1115

A   J. R. BELLAMY & SONS / BEAUFORT / S.C.
    (blank)
      aluminum, 32mm, round, R9

    This is probably some type of picker's check. J. R. Bellamy & Sons
were vegetable farmers near Beaufort.

B5   CRESCENT / DRUG CO. / THE / REXALL / STORE / BEAUFORT, S.C.
    GOOD FOR ONE / 5¢ / SODA
      aluminum, 24mm, round, R10

    This store operated in the teens and twenties.

C   HUNT PKG. CO. / SHUCKING / CHECK / BEAUFORT, S.C. (all incuse)
(blank)
 brass, 21mm, round, R7

D   HUNT PKG. CO. / SHUCKING / CHECK / BEAUFORT, N.C. (all incuse)
(blank)
 brass, 21mm, round, R9

 This piece is almost identical to 1115C except for the assumed die-cutting error in the state abbreviation. There is a town named Beaufort in North Carolina, but no mention of a Hunt Packing Company has ever been found in relation to that town.

E5   HUNT PKG. CO. / 5 (all incuse)
(blank)
 brass, 24mm, round, R10

F5   HUNT PACKING CO. / 5 / BEAUFORT, S.C.
(same)
 aluminum, 19mm, round, R10

 The Upson & Hunt Company was in the oyster packing business as early as 1893. In later years Hunt apparently assumed full control of the business, as there is no mention of Upson. Sometime around 1920, L. P. Maggioni & Co. of Savannah, Ga. purchased Hunt Packing Co., but continued to operate under the old name for a period of time. Maggioni later changed the name and operated the cannery into the 1950s.

G5   CHAS. G. LUTHER, PH. G. / AGENT FOR / HUYLER'S / BEAUFORT, S.C.
 GOOD FOR ONE / 5 / CENT (across numeral) / CIGAR OR SODA
 aluminum, 25mm, round, R10

 Charles Gillespie Luther, Ph.G. (Pharmacy Graduate) opened his drug store around the turn of the century and continued to operate it until his death in the 1950s. His son then sold the business, but it is still operated under the name of Luther's Pharmacy.

H   MARINE CORPS / THEATRE / AIR STATION
(blank)
 brass, 26mm, round, R5 (Curto SC 463)

 This token was used for recreational purposes at the Marine Corps Air Station in Beaufort.

I8   ROBERTS CANNING CO. / 8
(blank)
 aluminum, 22mm, round, R9

 The Roberts Canning Co. was operated in 1912 by Mrs. J. K. Roberts. The firm, which canned oysters and vegetables, operated into the 1920s.

BELTON (Anderson County)

A100   BELTON GROCERY / 1<u>00</u> / B G / BELTON, S.C.
       (Orco - type IV, dated 1942)
       nickel, 32mm, round, "B" c/o, R8

A50   (obverse similar to A100 except denomination 50)
       (Orco - type IV, dated 1940)
       nickel, 29mm, round, "B" c/o, R8

A25   (obverse similar to A100 except denomination 25)
       (Orco - type IV)
       nickel, 26mm, round, "B" c/o, R8

A10   (obverse similar to A100 except denomination 10)
       (Orco - type IV)
       nickel, 23mm, round, "B" c/o, R8

A5   (obverse similar to A100 except denomination 5)
       (Orco - type IV, dated 1940)
       nickel, 20mm, round, "B" c/o, R7

A1   (obverse similar to A100 except denomination 1)
       (Orco - type IV, dated 1941)
       nickel, 17mm, round, "B" c/o, R7

B1   (obverse similar to A100 except denomination 1)
       (Orco - type IV, dated 1942)
       red fiber, 17mm, round, "B" c/o, R10

       In the 1940s this business served as the company store for Belton Mills.

C10   BELTON MERCANTILE CO. / 10¢ / BELTON, S.C.
       GOOD FOR / 10¢ / IN TRADE
       brass, 23mm, round, R10

C5   (obverse similar to C10 except denomination 5¢)
       GOOD FOR / 5¢ / IN TRADE
       brass, 20mm, round, R10

       The Belton Mercantile Co. was listed as a general store during the teens and twenties. It may have served as company store for Belton Mills, but directory listings are not clear on this point.

D   BELTON SERVICE COMPANY / B
       GOOD FOR / B / ONE FARE
       nickel, 16mm, round, c/o, R4 (Atwood 110A)

       5,000 tokens were struck in 1946; the company operated only for a short time during that year.

BELVIDERE

       Tokens issued by A.W. Hoshaw's Billiard Hall & Barber Shop, "Belvidere, S.C." are actually from Belvidere, South Dakota. The presence of S.C. in the address is a die-cutting error.

A   APPIN DAIRY / GUERNSEY / MILK / BENNETTSVILLE, / S.C.
GOOD FOR / 1 / QUART / MILK
brass, 26mm, round, R9

B   (obverse similar to A)
GOOD FOR / ONE / PINT OF MILK
brass, 19mm, square, R9

C50 W. H. BRITTON & CO. / NOT / TRANSFERABLE
50 (surrounded by rays)
aluminum, 24mm, round, R7

C25 (obverse similar to C50)
25 (surrounded by rays)
aluminum, 24mm, round, R7

C10 (obverse similar to C50)
10 (surrounded by rays)
aluminum, 24mm, round, R7

C5   (obverse similar to C50)
5 (surrounded by rays)
aluminum, 24mm, round, R7

C2   (obverse similar to C50)
2 (surrounded by rays)
aluminum, 24mm, round, R7

C1   (obverse similar to C50)
1 (surrounded by rays)
aluminum, 24mm, round, R7

In the late 1800s W. H. Britton, in partnership with a man named W. J. Johnson, operated a sawmill, general store, and turpentine still in southern-central North Carolina. Apparently the operation moved around quite a bit; in 1890 it was located in Cameron; in 1891 - Spout Springs; in 1897 - Manchester; in 1900 - Holley Ridge; and again in 1900 - Timberland. Tokens inscribed "Britton & Johnson" were probably used at most, if not all, of the locations. In 1901 the partnership was dissolved, and W. H. Britton then moved his sawmill to Raeford, N.C. It was there that tokens inscribed "W. H. Britton & Co." were first used. In 1906 Britton moved his mill to Bennettsville, S.C. and presumably continued to use the tokens at that location. He later relocated to Lakewood, Florida and Florala, Alabama. It is thought that these tokens were also used there until new tokens with a Florida or Alabama address could be issued.

D5   MARLBORO / DRUG / CO., / BENNETTSVILLE / S.C.
ONE GLASS / 5 / CENT (inside curl of numeral) / SODA
aluminum, 34mm, scalloped (4), R9

The Marlboro Drug Co. opened circa 1900 and operated until 1915.

BESSEMER CITY

Tokens from the American Trading Store, "Bessemer City, S.C.," were actually issued in Bessemer City, North Carolina. This is a die-cutting error.

BETHERA (Berkeley County)   1140

A25   A. C. TUXBURY LBR. CO. / CAMP / 1 / BETHERA, S.C.
GOOD FOR / 25 / IN / MERCHANDISE
aluminum, 26mm, octagonal, R10

The A. C. Tuxbury Lumber Co. is listed in Charleston from 1913 through the late 1930s, as a branch operation of a firm headquartered in New York City. Tokens are known from Camp 1, (listed here) Camp 2 (no location specified), and without a camp specification (see Charleston). The company is also known to have operated in Awensdaw, where tokens with the name Awensdaw Mercantile Co. were issued.

BIG OAK ISLAND   (Charleston County)   1145

A3   J. O. MASSENBURG / SHRIMP
3
aluminum, 18mm, round, R9

James Owen Massenburg moved to Big Oak Island (between James Island and Folly Island) about 1922 and started business operations which included a warehouse, canning factory, and fleet of shrimp boats. The warehouse and cannery were destroyed by fire in the late 1920s. Malicious arson was suspected by Massenburg, and the cannery was not rebuilt due to a lack of insurance. To heap insult upon injury, Massenburg's shrimp boats were destroyed by a hurricane a couple of years later. The token was used to keep track of the number of buckets of shrimp beheaded by the employees. Other denominations were probably issued.

BINGHAM   (Dillon County)   1150

A1   W. C. HATCHELL / 1
(Ingle System - 1909 pat. date)
brass, 18mm, round, R10

W. C. Hatchell operated a general store in Bingham from 1912 to 1921. A W. C. Hatchell (perhaps the same person) was in the grocery business in Darlington in 1914 and 1917. Attribution to Bingham is tentative.

B25   FOR EMPLOYE (sic) ONLY. / C. A. ROACH
GOOD FOR / 25 / IN / MERCHANDISE
brass, 29mm, round, R10

According to the 1910 Bradstreet, C. A. Roach was in the lumber business.

BISHOPVILLE   (Lee County)   1155

A5   ACKERMAN / DRUG CO. / BISHOPVILLE / S.C.
        GOOD FOR / 5¢ / IN SODA
           aluminum, 21mm, round, R9

           The Ackerman Drug Company operated under that name between 1922 and 1926.

B10   CO. 4471, / C C C / DIST. / 1
        GOOD FOR / 10 / CENTS / IN TRADE
           aluminum, 18mm, round, R10

B5   (obverse similar to B10)
        GOOD FOR / 5¢ / IN TRADE
           aluminum, 25mm, round, R10

           During the late 1930s, Company 4471 (Robert E. Lee Company) of the Civilian Conservation Corps was stationed in Lee County, near Bishopville.

C   GOOD FOR LOAF BREAD / H. F. PRATOR
      (blank)
          brass, 19mm, round, R10

          H. F. Prator was a baker in Bishopville circa 1910.

BLACKVILLE   (Barnwell County)   1160

A10   H. D. STILL / & / SONS' / STORE / BLACKVILLE, S.C.
        GOOD FOR / 10¢ / IN TRADE
           aluminum, 22mm, round, R10

          H. D. Still was in business as early as 1886, in partnership with his brother, J. F. Still. Around 1908, one of H. D.'s sons replaced his uncle in the business. By 1912 H. D. had either retired or passed away, as the business was then known as H. D. Still's Sons. Directory listings disappear after 1913.

BLANEY   (Kershaw County)   1165

A50   J. L. GUY, JR. / TRADE / CHECK / BLANEY, S.C.
        50 (surrounded by rays)
           aluminum, 24mm, round, R10

          J. L. Guy, Jr. operated a sawmill and shingle mill in Blaney in 1908. There is no listing for him in Blaney after that time, although he did operate a sawmill in nearby Camden for a period of time thereafter. The town of Blaney later became known as Elgin.

BORDEAUX   (McCormick County)   1175

A50   O. G. CALHOUN / 50 / BORDEAUX, S.C.
GOOD FOR / 50¢ / IN TRADE
aluminum, 28mm, round, R10

O. G. Calhoun operated a farm in McCormick County during the teens and twenties, primarily growing cotton. He also operated a sawmill, cotton gin, and general store. Farming was abandoned during the Depression, the store and gin were closed down, and Calhoun moved to Texas.

BOWMAN   (Orangeburg County)   1180

A5   W. F. P. RISER / BOWMAN, / S.C.
5¢

brass, 19mm, round, R10

William Friendly Perry Riser (1866-1941) moved to Orangeburg County circa 1890. He opened a general store approximately seven miles southeast of Bowman sometime in the 1890s, and operated it into the 1930s.

BRANCHVILLE   (Orangeburg County)   1190

A5   W. P. APPLEBY, / BRANCHVILLE, / S.C.
DRINK / 5¢ / CIGAR
aluminum, 19mm, round, R10

In 1910 W. P. Appleby was listed as a grocer.

B5   F. A. BRUCE JR. & CO. / BRANCHVILLE, / S.C.
GOOD FOR / 5 / IN TRADE
aluminum, 19mm, round, R10

This general store operated in Branchville during the early 1900s.

C5   X. C. JONES / BRANCHVILLE, S.C.
GOOD FOR / 5 / IN TRADE
aluminum, 22mm, octagonal, R10

X. C. Jones was a grocer and fruit dealer from the early teens through the thirties.

BRUNSON   (Hampton County)   1205

A5   W. P. HOGARTH / & / SONS / BRUNSON / S.C.
GOOD FOR / 5¢ / CIGAR OR SODA
aluminum, 19mm, round, R10

W. P. Hogarth & Sons operated a general store in the early 1900s. About 1915, W. P. evidently left the business, as it then became known as the Hogarth Brothers Company.

B10   J. T. RIVERS / BRUNSON, S.C. / NOT TRANSFERABLE
           GOOD FOR / 10¢ / IN MERCHANDISE
             aluminum, 24mm, round, R10

B5   (obverse similar to B10)
           GOOD FOR / 5¢ / IN MERCHANDISE
             aluminum, 20mm, round, R10

        J. T. Rivers ran a general merchandise business in Brunson during the teens and twenties.

BUFFALO   (Union County)   1215

A5   BERRY & KELLER / DRUGGISTS / BUFFALO, S.C.
           GOOD FOR / 5 / CENT (across numeral) / GLASS OF SODA
             aluminum, 20mm, round, R10

B10   BUFFALO COTTON MILLS / BUFFALO / S.C.
           GOOD FOR / 10 / POUNDS / OF ICE
             aluminum, 25mm, round, R9

C5   BUFFALO COTTON MILLS / BUFFALO, / S.C. (similar to B10 except different ornamentation and comma after Buffalo)
           GOOD FOR / 5 / POUNDS / OF ICE
             aluminum, 25mm, octagonal, R8

D5   BUFFALO / 5 / COTTON MILLS
           SPOOLING / 5 / DEPARTMENT
             aluminum, 25mm, round, R10

        The Buffalo Cotton Mill was first listed in 1904. In later years, it became part of Union-Buffalo Mills (see listing of tokens from this company).

E25   MUTUAL DRY GOODS / CO. / BUFFALO, / S.C.
           GOOD FOR / 25¢ / IN MDSE.
             brass, 24mm, round, crescent-shaped c/o, R10

E10   (obverse similar to E25)
           GOOD FOR / 10¢ / IN MDSE.
             brass, 18mm, round, crescent-shaped c/o, R9

E5   (obverse similar to E25)
           GOOD FOR / 5¢ / IN MDSE.
             brass, 21mm, round, crescent-shaped c/o, R9

        This company operated two stores during the early 1900s. The larger was located in nearby Union, while the other was in Buffalo. The Buffalo branch closed down around 1915.

F500   UNION - BUFFALO MILLS STORE / 5⁰⁰ / BUFFALO, S.C.
           (Orco - type I)
             nickel, 32mm, scalloped (12), "B" c/o, R7

This scale model of the Buffalo mill village is presently on display at the South Carolina State Museum.

F100   (obverse similar to F500 except denomination 1<u>00</u>)
        (Orco - type II)
            nickel, 32mm, round, "B" c/o, R6

F50   (obverse similar to F500 except denomination 50)
        (Orco - type II)
            nickel, 27mm, round, "B" c/o, R6

F25   (obverse similar to F500 except denomination 25)
        (Orco - type I)
            nickel, 24mm, round, "B" c/o, R6

F10   (obverse similar to F500 except denomination 10)
        (Orco - type I and type II varieties exist)
            nickel, 21mm, round, "B" c/o, R6

F5   (obverse similar to F500 except denomination 5)
        (Orco - type II)
            nickel, 19mm, round, "B" c/o, R5

F1   (obverse similar to F500 except denomination 1)
        (Orco - type II and type III varieties exist)
            nickel, 18mm, round, "B" c/o, R4

The Union-Buffalo Mills Company was owned by the Duncan and Eaves families. The main mill was in nearby Union, and a branch was located in Fairmont. In 1949 they were sold to United Merchants.

G   B / U.B.M. CO. / 2363 (serial #) / TIME CHECK (all incuse)
        (blank)
            aluminum, 32mm, square, holed as made, R9

This token was used as a time check at the Buffalo Plant of Union-Buffalo Mills Company.

A50   BEAUFORT/JASPER / R.T.A. / 50¢ / BURTON, S.C.
     (same)
       copper, 23mm, round, R5 (Atwood 190B)

A25   (obverse similar to A50 except denomination 25¢)
     (same)
       nickel, 18mm, round, R5 (Atwood 190A)

       These are recent issues of the Beaufort - Jasper Rural Transit Authority.

B2½   HENDERSON PACKING CO. / 2½ / (counterstamped "J")
     (same)
       aluminum, 23mm, scalloped (12), R10

       Although attributed to Beaufort by Randy Chambers, local sources reveal that this packing house was located in Burton.

C   G. W. TRASK & SONS / BURTON, / S.C. (all incuse)
     (same)
       aluminum, 36mm, round, R9

D   (obverse similar to C)
     (blank)
       aluminum, 32mm, round, R9

E   G. W. TRASK & SONS / BURTON, / S.C.
     (blank)
       aluminum, 35mm, round, R9

F   (obverse similar to E)
     (blank)
       aluminum, 32mm, round, R9

G   NEIL W. TRASK / BURTON, S.C.
     (blank)
       brass, 28mm, round, R9

H   (obverse similar to G)
     (blank)
       brass, 22mm, round, R9

       Tokens from Neil W. Trask and G. W. Trask & Sons were used as pickers' checks. The Trasks were large-scale truck farmers, growing produce for Northern markets. They also operated farms near Myrtle Beach, S.C. and Wilmington, N.C.

A500   AIKEN STORES, INC. / 5̲0̲0̲ / A S / CALHOUN FALLS, S.C.
     (Orco - type IV, dated 1939)
       brass, 32mm, round, scalloped (12), "F" c/o, R4

A100   (obverse similar to A500 except denomination 100)
           (Orco - type IV, dated 1939)
              nickel, 32mm, round, "F" c/o, R3

A50   (obverse similar to A500 except denomination 50)
           (Orco - type IV, dated 1939)
              copper, 29mm, round, "F" c/o, R3

A25   (obverse similar to A500 except denomination 25)
           (Orco - type IV, dated 1939)
              nickel, 26mm, round, "F" c/o, R3

A10   (obverse similar to A500 except denomination 10)
           (Orco - type IV, dated 1939)
              brass, 23mm, round, "F" c/o, R2

A5   (obverse similar to A500 except denomination 5)
           (Orco - type IV, dated 1939)
              nickel, 20mm, round, "F" c/o, R2

       Aiken Stores, Inc. operated the company store for Calhoun Mills during the late 1930s and early 1940s. The company also utilized tokens in its stores in Anderson, Bath, Clearwater, Langley, and Williamston.

B100   CALHOUN MILLS STORE / 100 / IN TRADE / NON-TRANSFERABLE
           (Master Metal Scrip - type II)
              nickel, 35mm, round, crescent-shaped c/o, R10

B50   (obverse similar to B100 except denomination 50)
           (Master Metal Scrip - type II)
              brass, 30mm, round, crescent-shaped c/o, R9

B25   (obverse similar to B100 except denomination 25)
           (Master Metal Scrip - type I)
              copper, 24mm, round, crescent-shaped c/o, R8

B10   (obverse similar to B100 except denomination 10)
           (Master Metal Scrip - type unknown)
              nickel, 21mm, round, crescent-shaped c/o, R9

B5   (obverse similar to B100 except denomination 5)
           (Master Metal Scrip - type II)
              brass, 19mm, round, crescent-shaped c/o, R8

B1   (obverse similar to B100 except denomination 1)
           (Master Metal Scrip - type II)
              copper, 18mm, round, crescent-shaped c/o, R9

       Prior to the late 1930s, Calhoun Mills operated its own company store. The 1235B series was probably issued during the 1920s or early 1930s. Calhoun Mills began operations around 1910 and specialized in the manufacture of sheetings.

C50   PEACE'S / SUPER / MARKET / CALHOUN FALLS, S.C. / WITH $10.00
OR MORE PURCHASE
 GOOD FOR / 50¢ / IN MERCHANDISE
  aluminum, size unknown, round, R10

   This description, garnered from a hobby publication, may not be
accurate.

CAMDEN   (Kershaw County)   1240

A25   GOOD FOR / 25 CENTS. / H. BAUM.
 B.H. BAUM / AGT (actual signature)
  purple cardboard, 32mm, round, R7

B25   GOOD FOR / 25 CENTS. / IN TOLL. / H. BAUM.
 NOT GOOD / UNLESS COUNTERSIGNED BY / H. BAUM (actual
signature)
  red cardboard, 38mm, round, R9

B15   (obverse similar to B25 except denomination 15)
 NOT GOOD / UNLESS COUNTERSIGNED BY / H. BAUM (actual
signature)
  blue cardboard, 38mm, round, R9

   Issued circa 1900, these tokens were used by Harry Baum to pay his
farm workers. They could be redeemed for cash or merchandise at the
general store he operated on the farm. At the time, Baum was one of the
largest planters in Kershaw County.

C5   THE CAMDEN DRUG CO. / 5¢ / CAMDEN / S.C.
 5
  aluminum, 24mm, round, R10

   This store operated from about 1910 to 1930.

D   CITY TRANSIT, CAMDEN / (picture of bus) / 1949
 GOOD FOR / (picture of bus) / ONE FARE
  nickel, 16mm, round, c/o, R5 (Atwood 210A)

   3,000 tokens were struck during the late 1940s and early 1950s. In the
early 1950s the bus line was sold to a new owner, who discontinued the
use of tokens.

E5   G. W. CROSBY / CAMDEN, S.C.
 GOOD FOR / 5¢ / IN TRADE
  aluminum, 18mm, round, R10

   G. W. Crosby operated a billiard parlor and cigar store circa 1910 to
1920. The token has not been seen, so description may not be exact.

F10   ERWIN - HERMITAGE CO. INC. / 10 / E H / CO / CAMDEN, S.C.
 (Orco - type IV, dated 1940)
  copper, 23mm, round, R10

CAMDEN   (Continued)   1240

F5   (obverse similar to F10 except denomination 5)
        (Orco - type IV, dated 1940)
            brass, 20mm, round, R10

        The Erwin - Hermitage Co. is thought to have operated the company
    store for Hermitage Mills during the 1940s. Prior to that time, Hermitage
    Mills ran its own store and issued tokens (see listing which follows).

G1   HERMITAGE COTTON MILLS STORE / CAMDEN, / S.C.
        GOOD FOR / 1¢ / IN MERCHANDISE
            aluminum, 18mm, round, R8

H100   S. D. HURST, / GENERAL / MERCHANDISE / CAMDEN, S.C.
        GOOD FOR / 1<u>00</u> / IN / MERCHANDISE
            brass, 35mm, round, R10

H25   (obverse similar to H100)
        GOOD FOR / 25 / IN / MERCHANDISE
            brass, 28mm, round, R10

H10   (obverse similar to H100)
        GOOD FOR / 10 / IN / MERCHANDISE
            brass, 24mm, round, R10

        This general store was in operation between 1914 and 1925.

CAMP JACKSON   (Richland County)   1245

A postcard view of Camp Jackson, circa 1917.

CAMP JACKSON   (Continued)   1245

A10 BASE HOSPITAL / POST / EXCHANGE / CAMP JACKSON, S.C.
GOOD FOR / 10¢ / IN TRADE
   aluminum, 25mm, round, R10

A5 (obverse similar to A10)
GOOD FOR / 5¢ / IN TRADE
   aluminum, 20mm, round, R8 (Curto C36)

   Camp Jackson was organized in June, 1917 as a training base for
troops bound for World War I action in Europe. The 30th and 81st Infantry
Divisions both trained there before being deployed to Europe. After the
war, the 5th Infantry Division trained at Camp Jackson until it was
deactivated in 1921. The camp remained dormant until October 1939. In
August of 1940 it was renamed Fort Jackson. Divisions stationed there
since the outbreak of World War II include the 6th "Sightseeing" Division
(1939); the 30th Division (1940); the 5th Division (1947); the 8th Infantry
Division (1950); the 31st Infantry Division (1951); and the 101st Airborne
Division (1954). Still very active today, the fort has since been designated
as a United States Army Training Center, Infantry.

CAMP SEVIER   (Greenville County)   1250

A50 FIELD / SIGNAL SERVICE / BATTALION / EXCHANGE / 105
GOOD FOR / 50¢ / IN TRADE
   aluminum, 30mm, round, R10

   The 105th Field Signal Service Battalion was stationed at Camp Sevier
from August 1917 until May 1918, when it was deployed to France as part
of the 30th Division.

CAMP WADSWORTH   (Spartanburg County)   1255

A5 CO. "F" 51ST INFANTRY / 5¢
GOOD FOR / 5¢ / IN TRADE
   aluminum, 26mm, round, R10

B5 CO. "G" 51ST INFANTRY / 5¢
GOOD FOR / 5¢ / IN TRADE
   aluminum, 26mm, round, R10

C5 51ST   K (very large) INF.
GOOD FOR / 5¢ / IN TRADE
   aluminum, 26mm, round, R10

D10 COMPANY "C" 52ND INF. / 10 / CTS.
GOOD FOR ONE / 10 / CTS. / PT. MILK
   aluminum, 26mm, round, R10

Camp Wadsworth, as depicted on a postcard.

E10 COMPANY C / 53D. / INFANTRY
GOOD FOR / 10¢ / IN TRADE
aluminum, 18mm, round, R10 (Curto R607-10)

E5 (obverse similar to E10)
GOOD FOR / 5¢ / IN TRADE
aluminum, 20mm, round, R10 (Curto R607-5)

During World War I the 6th Division, which included the 51st, 52nd, 53rd, and 54th Infantry Regiments, was stationed at Camp Wadsworth. The Camp was only in operation for a short period of time during the war.

CARTERSVILLE   (Florence County)   1265

A5 CARTER - EVANS / LUMBER / CO. / CARTERSVILLE, S.C.
GOOD FOR / 5 / IN / MERCHANDISE
aluminum, 20mm, round, R10

This lumber manufacturing concern operated during the teens.

CASHS DEPOT   (Chesterfield County)   1270

A   THE / N. L. H. L. CO. / 52 (serial #) (all incuse)
(blank)
> brass, 35mm, round, holed as made, R10

> Tentatively attributed to the N. L. Hoover Lumber Company, which operated a sawmill from 1908 to 1910. The token was used as a tool or time check.

B10   THE VOSBURG CO. / (ctsp "S") / CASHS DEPOT, S.C.
GOOD FOR / 10 / IN MERCHANDISE
> bimetallic, 24mm, round, R7

> All presently known specimens have been in such poor condition that the aluminum centers are barely readable. Therefore, the description may not be exact. The company, which was headquartered in DuBois, Pa., ran a sawmill in Cashs Depot during the teens.

CASSATT   (Kershaw County)   1275

A   COMPANY / 4470 / C.C.C.
GOOD FOR / 1 / GAME
> brass, 21mm, round, R10

> Company 4470 of the Civilian Conservation Corps was stationed at two different South Carolina locations at one time or another. In 1937 it was based at the Joseph Wheeler Camp in Aiken County, near the town of Montmorenci. Prior to that time, it was stationed at the Kershaw Camp in Kershaw County, near Cassatt. The token was probably utilized at both locations and is therefore listed under both towns. Presumably it was good for a game of pool, since billiards was the standard pastime at most C.C.C. camps in the 1930s.

CATEECHEE   (Pickens County)   1280

A100   NORRIS COTTON MILLS STORE / CATEECHEE / S.C. (ctsp "W")
GOOD FOR / 1$\underline{00}$ / IN / MERCHANDISE ONLY
> brass, 33mm, round, R8

A50   (obverse similar to A100)
GOOD FOR / 50 / IN / MERCHANDISE ONLY
> brass, 30mm, round, R8

A25   (obverse similar to A100)
GOOD FOR / 25 / IN / MERCHANDISE ONLY
> brass, 27mm, round, R8

A10   (obverse similar to A100)
GOOD FOR / 10 / IN / MERCHANDISE ONLY
> brass, 24mm, round, R8

CATEECHEE (Continued) 1280

A5 (obverse similar to A100)
GOOD FOR / 5 / IN / MERCHANDISE ONLY
brass, 20mm, round, R8

Norris Cotton Mill began operation circa 1910. When it was sold to Woodside Mills, the majority of the tokens were counterstamped with a "W" on the obverse.

CAUSEY (Horry County) 1285

A5 MONTGOMERY LUMBER CO. / CAUSEY, / S.C.
GOOD FOR / 5¢ / IN TRADE
aluminum, 20mm, round, R10

This company, headquartered in Suffolk, Va., operated a sawmill in Causey during the teens and twenties. The mill was located in the extreme northern part of the county, near the Lumber River.

CENTRAL (Pickens County) 1295

A25 THE COMMUNITY STORE / CENTRAL / S.C.
GOOD FOR / 25¢ / IN MERCHANDISE
aluminum, 27mm, round, R10

B100 THE COMMUNITY STORE / 1⁰⁰ / IN MDSE. / CENTRAL, S.C.
(Master Metal Scrip - type II)
brass, 35mm, round, "C" c/o, R8

B50 (obverse similar to B100 except denomination 50)
(Master Metal Scrip - type unknown)
brass, 30mm, round, "C" c/o, R9

B25 (obverse similar to B100 except denomination 25)
(Master Metal Scrip - type I)
brass, 24mm, round, "C" c/o, R8

B10 (obverse similar to B100 except denomination 10)
(Master Metal Scrip - type II)
brass, 21mm, round, "C" c/o, R7

B5 (obverse similar to B100 except denomination 5)
(Master Metal Scrip - type I)
brass, 19mm, round, "C" c/o, R7

B1 (obverse similar to B100 except denomination 1)
(Master Metal Scrip - type II)
brass, 18mm, round, "C" c/o, R7

This was the company store for Isaqueena Mills until the mid-1930s, when the mill was sold and became Central Mills. The store probably continued to operate as the company store into the 1940s.

CENTRAL (Continued)   1295

C100   P. M. DURHAM / 1⁰⁰
           (Ingle System - 1909 pat. date)
           brass, 35mm, round, R10

C25   (obverse similar to C100 except denomination 25)
           (Ingle System - 1909 pat. date)
           brass, 24mm, round, R10

           P. M. Durham ran a general store near Central from 1913 to 1917.

CHAPIN (Lexington County)   1300

A5   S. W. BOOZER / CHAPIN, / S.C.
           GOOD FOR / 5¢ / IN TRADE
           aluminum, 18mm, round, R10

           S. W. Boozer was a grocer and soda fountain operator from 1913 to
           the mid-1930s.

CHARLESTON (Charleston County)   1305

A25   A.B.C. / CIGAR STORE / CHAS., S.C.
           GOOD FOR / 25 / IN TRADE
           brass, 24mm, round, R9

A10   (obverse similar to A25)
           GOOD FOR / 10 / IN TRADE
           brass, 18mm, round, R9

B5   (obverse similar to A25 except no ornamentation)
           GOOD FOR / 5¢ / IN TRADE
           brass, 21mm, round, R9

C   R.L. BAKER / GOOD FOR / 1 / GLASS / CHARLESTON, S.C.
           SODA WATER / (picture of urn) / 1837
           German silver, 19mm, round, R6 (Low 108)

           R.L. Baker was listed in the 1835-36 city directory as a druggist,
           operating at the corner of Broad and East Bay Streets. This is the oldest
           token known to have been issued in South Carolina, and, as the only issue
           from the state in the Hard Times Token series, it is quite sought after.

D5   LEON BANOV, / 442 / KING / ST. / CHARLESTON, S.C.
           GOOD FOR / 5¢ / IN TRADE
           aluminum, 19mm, round, R10

           Prior to entering medical school, Leon Banov operated a drug store at
           442½ King Street from 1910 to 1912. Although the store was rather small,
           Banov advertised it as "the largest drug store for its size in the entire state."
           After completing medical school, he was employed as a public health officer
           by the City of Charleston for some fifty years.

A postcard view of King Street, circa 1905.

E   BERNARD S. BARUC / IMPORTER OF FANCY / GOODS & TOYS /
(picture of palmetto tree) / 208 KING STREET / CHARLESTON S.C.
IN UNITATE FORTITUDO / (picture of eagle) /SPIEL MUNZE
brass, 22mm, round, R8 (Miller SC 2)

F   (obverse and reverse same as E)
copper, 22mm, round, R8 (Miller SC 2A)

Previous authors have erroneously identified this issuer as the grandfather of presidential adviser, Wall Street wizard, and native South Carolinian Bernard Baruch (note difference in spelling of last name). Extensive research has failed to prove that Bernard Baruch and Bernard S. Baruc were related. Baruch's own autobiography fails to mention his grandfather even visiting the New World, much less immigrating to Charleston. Neither does the book identify any other relatives with the name Bernard.

Research on the token issuer revealed that he was born in Germany on 4 December 1828 and immigrated to Charleston sometime before 1853. He was married in Charleston to Mathilda R. Oppenheim on 10 October 1855. An 1855 directory listing mentions both his business and residence at 208 King Street. Records in the South Carolina Department of Archives show Baruc to have served two stints in the military, one in 1853 in Co. G, 5th S.C. Cavalry, and again during the Civil War in Co. B, 17th Btn. S.C. Cavalry. He died in New York on 20 October 1904.

G25 "THE SMILE STORE" / BIRLANT'S / 455 KING ST. / CHARLESTON / S.C. / QUARTER DOLLAR
> GOOD FOR / 25¢ / ON / A / $5.00 PURCHASE OR MORE
>> aluminum, 26mm, round, R10

> Mrs. Dora Birlant was the proprietor of this retail dry goods store.

H100 E. E. BISHOP / 1<u>00</u>
> (Ingle System - 1909 pat. date)
>> copper, 35mm, round, R9

H5 (obverse similar to H100 except denomination 5)
> (Ingle System - 1909 pat. date)
>> copper, 20mm, round, R10

> Eunice E. Bishop operated a grocery store at 34 Amherst Street circa 1914.

I100 BLUESTEIN BROTHERS / J.S. / BLUESTEIN / PROP. / TAILORING / GUARANTEED / 494 KING ST. / CHARLESTON / S.C.
> GOOD FOR / $1.00 / ON / SUIT OR OVERCOAT
>> aluminum, 39mm, round, R10

> This firm, which specialized in men's clothing and furnishings, operated under the proprietorship of Joseph S. Bluestein during the late teens and twenties.

J10 W. J. H. BRANDT / 10
> (Ingle System - 1909 pat. date)
>> nickel-plated brass, 21mm, round, R10

> W. J. H. Brandt operated a grocery store at 62 Drake Street from 1904 to 1921.

K25 E. P. BURTON LUMBER CO. / 25 / IN / MERCHANDISE / CHARLESTON, S.C.
> GOOD FOR / 25 / IN / MERCHANDISE
>> brass, 26mm, round, R10

K5 (obverse similar to K25 except denomination 5)
> GOOD FOR / 5 / IN / MERCHANDISE
>> aluminum, 19mm, round, R10

L5 E. P. BURTON / LUMBER CO. / 1910 / CHARLESTON / S.C.
> GOOD FOR / 5 / AT / OUR STORE
>> aluminum, 20mm, round, R10

M E. P. B. LBR. CO. / 776 (serial #) (all incuse)
> (blank)
>> brass, 38mm, round, holed as made, R10

> The E. P. Burton Lumber Company, headquartered in Philadelphia, Pa., operated a sawmill and wholesale lumber yard in the Charleston area from the early 1900s to the early 1920s.

N100   C. H. CASTENS, JR. / 1 00
       (Ingle System - 1909 pat. date)
         composition unknown, 35mm, round, R10

       Carsten H. Castens, Jr. took over his father's grocery business at 524 Meeting Street sometime between 1904 and 1908, and continued to operate it into the 1920s. In the latter years, the business evolved into more of a bakery and confectionery. The token's description may not be exact.

O100   N C O / 1.00 / C A F B
       (blank)
         aluminum, 38mm, round, R3 (Curto A37-100)

O50   (obverse similar to O100 except denomination 50)
       (blank)
         aluminum, 28mm, round, R3 (Curto A37-50)

O25   (obverse similar to O100 except denomination 25) (varieties exist)
       (blank)
         aluminum, 26mm, round, R3 (Curto A37-25)

O5   (obverse similar to O100 except denomination 5)
       (blank)
         aluminum, 22mm, round, R3 (Curto A37-5)

P100   N C O / 1.00 / C A F B
       (blank)
         gold-colored aluminum, 38mm, round, R3 (Curto A38-100)

P50   (obverse similar to P100 except denomination 50)
       (blank)
         gold-colored aluminum, 28mm, round, R3 (Curto A38-50)

P25   (obverse similar to P100 except denomination 25)
       (blank)
         gold-colored aluminum, 26mm, round, R3 (Curto A38-25)

P5   (obverse similar to P100 except denomination 5)
       (blank)
         gold-colored aluminum, 22mm, round, R3 (Curto A38-5)

Q100   N.C.O. OPEN MESS / CHAS. A.F.B. / B-325 / CHARLESTON, S.C.
       GOOD FOR / $1 00 / IN TRADE
         aluminum, 31mm, hexagonal, R8 (Curto A488-100v)

Q5   (obverse similar to Q100)
       GOOD FOR / 5¢ / IN TRADE
         aluminum, 23mm, round, R8 (Curto A488-5)

R100   (obverse same as Q100)
       GOOD FOR / $1 00 / IN TRADE
         brass, 31mm, hexagonal, R8

S100   NCO OPEN MESS / CHAS. A.F.B. / B-325 / CHARLESTON, S.C.
(obverse similar to R100 and S100 except no periods after NCO and no propeller-like ornament)
    GOOD FOR / $1<u>00</u> / IN TRADE
      brass, 31mm, hexagonal, R8

S25   (obverse similar to S100)
    GOOD FOR / 25¢ / IN TRADE
      brass, 23mm, square, R8

S5   (obverse similar to S100)
    GOOD FOR / 5¢ / IN TRADE
      brass, 22mm, round, R8

T100   (obverse same as S100)
    GOOD FOR / $1<u>00</u> / IN TRADE
      aluminum, 31mm, hexagonal, R8

      The Charleston Air Base was first commissioned in 1941, three days after the Japanese bombed Pearl Harbor. The Army Air Corps utilized the runways of the Charleston Municipal Airport at that time. The base was deactivated shortly after the conclusion of World War II. In 1953 it was reopened by the 456th Troop Carrier Group of the Tactical Air Command. In 1955, the 1608th Military Air Command took control of the base. The name of this unit was changed to the 437th Military Air Lift Wing in 1965. The 437th still mans the base.

      The NCO Club was built circa 1953 and still occupies Building 325, hence the designation "B-325" on some of the tokens.

U   CHARLESTON / C (stencil cut-out) / C. RY. & LT. CO.
    GOOD FOR / ONE FARE
      nickel, 16mm, round, c/o, R4 (Atwood 240A)

      The Charleston Consolidated Railway and Lighting Co. was organized about 1910, replacing the Charleston Consolidated Railway, Gas, & Electric Company. The tokens were issued in 1919 and were in use until July 1938, even though the company was taken over by the South Carolina Power Company in 1926.

V   CHARLESTON / CANNING / CO.
    (picture of three tomatoes on vine)
      brass, 26mm, octagonal, R7

      The Charleston Canning Co. first appears in the directories in 1893, being operated by B.F. McCabe and a partner named Hunt. The company continued to operate until 1915, canning oysters and vegetables.

W   CHARLESTON / HUNTING / & FISHING / CLUB.
    (same)
      brass, 21mm, round, R6

X   CHARLESTON / HUNTING / & FISHING / CLUB (different dies)
    (same)
      brass, 21mm, round, R8

Y   CHARLESTON / HUNTING / & FISHING / CLUB. (different dies)
       (same)
         aluminum, 21mm, round, R8

       During the early 1900s the Charleston Hunting & Fishing Club was located at 92-94 Society Street. The tokens were used in some type of slot machine or amusement game.

Z5   CHARLESTON NEWS / 5 / AGENCY (all incuse)
       (blank)
         brass, 23mm, octagonal, R10

       The Charleston News Agency was operated by A.L. Stroud at 336 King Street in the 1920s.

AA   THE CITIZENS & SOUTHERN BANK OF SOUTH CAROLINA / (picture of building) / JUNE 29, 1929
       (picture of the S.C. state seal)
         brass, 32mm, round, reeded edge, R6

This advertisement for the Cleremont Cafe appeared in a 1904 city directory.

AB5   CLEREMONT / CAFE / 228 KING ST.
       GOOD FOR / 5¢ / IN TRADE
         brass, 21mm, round, R8

       Stephen R. Mooney was the proprietor of the Cleremont Restaurant and Cafe (and later the Hotel Cleremont) which was located at 228 King Street in the early 1900s.

AC   COBURG DAIRY / GOLDEN GUERNSEY (across picture of milk jug) / CHARLESTON, S.C.
       GOOD FOR / 1 / QT. / GOLDEN GUERNSEY MILK
         brass, 27mm, scalloped (9), R9

AD   COBURG DAIRY / CHARLESTON, S.C.
       GOOD FOR / ONE / QUART / PASTEURIZED MILK
         aluminum, 24mm, round, center hole, R9

AE   (obverse and reverse similar to AD)
         zinc, 24mm, round, center hole, R10

AF COBURG DAIRY / G / CHARLESTON, S.C.
GOOD FOR / ½ GAL. / GOLDEN GUERNSEY MILK
brass, 23mm, octagonal, R10

AG COBURG / DAIRY / CHARLESTON, / S.C.
GOOD FOR / ½ GAL. / PASTEURIZED / MILK
aluminum, 25mm, square, R10

In 1920 The Coburg Dairy opened on the west side of the Ashley River with about 100 Jersey Cows, but the herd was phased out in the 1940s. The company utilized tokens for about 20 years, discontinuing them in the 1950s. The dairy is still in operation, but recently moved to the North Charleston area.

AH5 COSMOPOLITAN / 186 / MEETING / STREET / CLUB
5
brass, 21mm, round, R8

COSMOPOLITAN CLUB
186 MEETING ST.
Restaurant, & Billiard & Parlor,
CIGARS.
PERMANENT AND TRANSIENT BOARDING.
PETER J. CONWAY, Manager.

A 1906 city directory advertisement for the Cosmopolitan Club.

AI5 COSMOPOLITAN / 186 / MEETING / STREET / CLUB (different obverse and reverse dies, with dotted borders)
5
brass, 21mm, round, R8

The Cosmopolitan Club operated in the early 1900s under the management of Peter J. Conway. The business offered cigars, billiards, food, and permanent and transient boarding to its patrons.

AJ5 DAVIS CAFE. / CHARLESTON / S.C.
GOOD FOR / 5¢ / IN TRADE
brass, 21mm, round, R10

This cafe was in operation at 37 Columbus Street in 1914.

AK5 DELORME DRUG CO. INC. / ON THE / SQUARE / COR. KING & / CALHOUN / CHARLESTON, / S.C.
GOOD FOR / 5 / CENTS (inside curl of numeral) / AT / THE FOUNTAIN
composition unknown, 25mm, round, R10

The Delorme Drug Co. was in business during the late teens and early twenties.

AL5 DEWEY / 1 (additional varieties exist with numbers 2 through 9)
GOOD FOR 5¢ IN TRADE / DEWEY
brass, 21mm, round, R3

This stock amusement or slot-machine token was heavily used in the Charleston area. The control number on the obverse may vary from specimen to specimen.

AM100 WORTH $1.00 / DUVAL BROKERAGE CO. / 286 KING ST. / CHARLESTON, S.C. / ON / FIRST / MONEY / TRANSACTION
KEEP ME FOR GOOD LUCK / (picture of horseshoe, etc.)
aluminum, 32mm, round, R9

AN100 THE HOUSE OF SERVICE / GOOD FOR A / CHARGE ACCOUNT / ON YOUR TERMS / AT THE / FEDERAL CLOTHING STORES / 244 KING STREET / CHARLESTON / S.C. / A SQUARE DEAL TO ALL
GOOD AS / 1\frac{00}{}$ / CASH / ON YOUR NEXT PURCHASE OF / $10 OR MORE / COMPLIMENTS / OF / J. NATHAN (signature) / PRESIDENT / GOOD ONLY DURING / 1922
brass, 32mm, round, R9

During the early 1920s A. S. Rosenstein managed the Federal Clothing Store at 224 King Street.

AO5 FRANK FIELDS, / 424 / KING / STREET, / CHARLESTON, S.C.
GOOD FOR / 5 / IN / MERCHANDISE
brass, 21mm, round, R10

Frank Fields ran a billiard hall and lunch room at 424 King Street during the mid-teens. The business was known as the Maceo Pool Room in 1914.

This photograph, taken circa 1900, appeared in *Charleston, S.C. and Vicinity Illustrated*, a book printed specially for distribution at the 1901 Charleston Exposition.

AP5 FOLLIN BROS. COMPANY / CIGARS / 260 / KING / STREET
GOOD FOR ONE / 5 / CENT (across numeral) / GLASS OF SODA
aluminum, 24mm, round, R9

In the early 1880s Gustavus A. and John E. Follin followed their father's footsteps into the wholesale tobacco and cigar manufacturing business. During its early years the business was located at 175 East Bay Street, later moving to the 260 King Street location mentioned on the token. The company manufactured the following brands of cigars - King Clay, Key West Cuban, La Fernandina, and Garcia.

AQ THE GEER DRUG CO. / DON'T / GAMBLE WITH / SERVICE / BUY FROM GEER / SERVING WITH SERVICE
ROUND AND ROUND SHE GOES / WHERE SHE STOPS NOBODY KNOWS
aluminum, 32mm, round, R9

This wholesale drug and pharmaceutical sales firm has operated since the early 1900s.

AR GRAY / LINE / CHARLESTON, S.C.
GOOD FOR / CHARLESTON / SULLIVANS / IS. / ONE FARE
nickel, 24mm, round, center hole, R5 (Atwood 240C)

5000 tokens were struck in 1941. This suburban bus line ran from downtown Charleston across the Cooper River Bridge to Sullivans Island. The company ceased operations in 1951.

AS HAVILAND STEVENSON & CO. / WHOLESALE / DRUGGIST'S / ESTABLISHED / 1825 / CHARLESTON, S.C.
(eagle with banner which reads ESTABLISHED A.D. 1825)
copper, 28mm, round, R7 (Miller SC 3)

AT (obverse and reverse same as AS)
brass, 28mm, round, R7

AU DEALERS IN STOVES / (padlock depicted) / WHOLESALE & RETAIL / IRON & HARDWARE
(reverse same as AS)
brass, 28mm, round, R10

AV THE RAIL SPLITTER OF THE WEST / (man depicted splitting a log)
(reverse same as AS)
copper, 28mm, round, R10 (Miller SC 3A)

AW (obverse and reverse same as AV)
brass, 28mm, round, R10 (Miller SC 4)

AX (obverse and reverse same as AV)
silvered brass, 28mm, round, R10 (Miller SC 4A)

The Haviland, Stevenson Co. was listed in the wholesale drug business in the 1860 Charleston city directory. Prior to that time, the firm went through a succession of name changes, primarily due to changes in the business partnership. Stevenson did not join the firm until sometime after

1852, and was not mentioned by name after 1860. Therefore the tokens can probably be dated to sometime in the late 1850s or early 1860s. The wholesale business of the firm was conducted at 25 Hayne Street, while a retail store was located for a time at 260 King Street.

AU, AV, AW, and AX are considered "mules" — fabrications made indiscriminately for collectors sometime during the nineteenth century. They were struck from original dies not intended for use together.

The High School of Charleston, circa 1902.

AY5 LUNCH ROOM / HIGH SCHOOL / OF / CHARLESTON / CHARLESTON, S.C.
      GOOD FOR / 5¢ / IN TRADE
        brass, 20mm, round, R9

      The High School of Charleston was located at 24 George Street in the early 1900s.

AZ5 JNO. J. LANDERS / 118 / EAST BAY
      GOOD FOR / 5¢ / IN TRADE
        brass, 21mm, round, R9

      From 1904 to 1918 John J. Landers operated a restaurant and sold cigars at 118 East Bay Street.

BA M. A. LORENZI / 559 / KING ST. / FREE POOL
      NATIONAL BILLIARD MAN'F'G. CO. / N B M Co (between crossed cues) / CIN,O.
        brass, 24mm, round, R10

      Maurice (sometimes listed as Morris) A. Lorenzi operated a saloon at 559 King Street in the late 1880s and early 1890s.

BB   LOS GRINGOS (in script across picture of horseman) / 80 N. MARKET ST.
GOOD / FOR ONE / FREE DRINK / LIMIT ONE PER / CUSTOMER
aluminum, 35mm, round, R8, modern

BC5   J. MANNOS / 50 / ARCHDALE / ST. / CHARLESTON, S.C.
GOOD FOR / 5 / IN TRADE
brass, 19mm, round, R9

James Mannos operated a restaurant at 50 Archdale Street circa 1905.

BD5   T. W. MAPPUS / GROCER / 4½ / MILE HOUSE / CHARLESTON, S.C.
GOOD FOR / 5 / IN MERCHANDISE
aluminum, 25mm, round, R10

Theodore W. Mappus advertised himself as a dealer in choice family groceries, glassware, tinware, tobacco, and cigars. His business was located in the 4½ Mile House, which was 4½ miles north of Charleston on the State Road between Charleston and Columbia (now known as the Old Meeting Street Road).

BE5   D. MARCHETTI / 4 BROAD ST.
GOOD FOR ONE / 5 / CENT CIGAR
aluminum, 19mm, round, R10

Dominico Marchetti was listed as a fruit dealer in the early 1900s.

BF50   MARSHALL / BATH / HOUSE
GOOD FOR / 50¢ / IN TRADE
brass, 29mm, round, R10

BF5   (obverse similar to BF50)
GOOD FOR / 5¢ / IN TRADE
brass, 20mm, round, R10

Attribution tentative. Both of the tokens were originally purchased in Charleston (one being unearthed in the area).

BG5   METROPOLITAN CIGAR CO. / COR. / MEETING / AND / QUEEN / STS.
GOOD FOR / 5 / IN TRADE
aluminum, 24mm, round, R9

In 1914 H. M. Burn (Pres. and Treas.) and N. D. Sassard (Vice Pres.) were listed as officers of the Metropolitan Cigar Company.

BH5   A. J. H. NOLTE / 5
(Ingle System - 1909 pat. date)
brass, 20mm, round, R10

BH1   (obverse similar to BH5 except denomination 1)
(Ingle System - 1909 pat. date)
brass, 18mm, round, R10

From 1913 to 1915 A. J. H. Nolte operated a grocery store at 78 Anson Street.

BI5   H. NOLTE / CHARLESTON, S.C.
        TURNER HALL 5¢ CIGAR
          brass, size unknown, round, R10

        Henry Nolte operated a grocery and saloon around the turn of the century. The token's line description may not be exact, since it was garnered from a hobby publication.

BJ5   J. F. PIEPER / CHARLESTON, / S.C.
        GOOD FOR ONE / 5¢ / CIGAR
          brass, 21mm, round, R9

BK5   J. F. PIEPER, / CHARLESTON / S.C. (different dies)
        GOOD FOR ONE / 5¢ / CIGAR
          brass, 21mm, round, R8

        J. Frederick Pieper operated a grocery store from the early 1890s to the mid-teens. In the late 1890s his store was located at 590 King Street.

BL   GOOD FOR 1 CHIEF JURIST CIGAR / J. S. PINKUSSOHN CO.
        (same)
          aluminum, 34mm, round, R10

        J. S. Pinkussohn went into the cigar manufacturing business with his two brothers (Jacob and Samuel) in the 1880s. The business continued into the 1920s. Branches were located in Columbia and Savannah, Ga. at one time or another. Description of the token may not be exact.

BM50   PLANTERS HOTEL / CHARLESTON / S.C.
        PAY TO / 50 (denomination incuse and painted white) / CASHIER.
          black hard rubber, 36mm, round, R10

        The Planter's Hotel was a familiar landmark to 19th century Charlestonians. First opening in 1809, Alexander Calder and his wife operated it for many years. Later proprietors included Orran Byrd, J. W. Gamble, and Gorman & McCord. It may have operated during the Civil War, because it is known to have undergone repairs in 1866. The hotel disappears from the directories about 1880. In 1935, the rapidly deteriorating building was purchased by the City of Charleston and was restored with federal funds. It is now part of the Dock Street Theatre complex, still in use.

BN5   HENRY PLENGE / PHARMACIST / CHARLESTON, / S.C.
        GOOD FOR ONE / 5¢ / GLASS OF SODA
          aluminum, 24mm, round, R10

        Henry Plenge clerked at the drug stores of Herman Baer, C. J. Luhn, and C. F. Panknin during the 1870s and 1880s. In 1892 he opened his own pharmacy at 8 Broad Street. The business continued in his name into the 1940s.

BO10   POST EXCHANGE / FOUNTAIN / CHARLESTON, S.C.
        GOOD FOR / 10¢ / IN TRADE
          aluminum, 25mm, round, R10

PLANTERS' HOTEL,

Late Calder House,

CORNER OF CHURCH AND QUEEN STREETS.

THE ABOVE HOUSE HAS BEEN LEASED BY

GORMAN & McCORD,

Who have had seven or eight years' experience, as employees in the CHARLESTON HOTEL, and feel confident that they can give entire satisfaction to those who may favor them with a call.

Rates of Board, per Day, $2.00.

COACHES ATTACHED TO THE HOTEL

ALWAYS IN ATTENDANCE AT RAILROADS AND STEAMBOATS.

PASSENGERS ARRIVING AT THE HOUSE, AND LEAVING THE SAME DAY

TAKEN FOR ONE FARE.

An 1860 directory advertisement for the Planters' Hotel.

BO5 (obverse similar to BO10)
GOOD FOR / 5¢ / IN TRADE
aluminum, 20mm, round, R9

These tokens were probably used at the Charleston Naval Shipyard.

BP10 W. R. PRITCHARD / CHARLESTON, / SOUTH CAROLINA
GOOD FOR / 10¢ / IN TRADE
aluminum, 25mm, round, R10

In 1916 William R. Pritchard operated a merchandise brokerage at 181 East Bay Street.

BQ5 C. J. F. RABENS. / COR. / KING / & / SHEPARD STS.
5
brass, 21mm, round, R8

Christian John Frederick Rabens operated a grocery store at the corner of King and Shepard Streets from the early 1900s to the late 1920s.

BR5 H. R. RABINS / N.E. COR. / LINE & KING / STS.
GOOD FOR / 5¢ / CIGAR
brass, 22mm, round, R9

Henry R. Rabens (note misspelling of his last name on the token) owned a grocery store and bottled soft drinks from 1910 to 1921 at the corner of Line and King Streets. The building later housed the locally famous Rabens' Tavern.

BS REPHAN'S SANITARY DAIRY / CHARLESTON, S.C.
GOOD FOR / 1 / QUART MILK
aluminum, 24mm, round, clover-shaped center hole, R7

Harry Rephan operated his dairy at 529 King Street from the teens through the fifties. The token was issued after World War II.

BT ROSE / BANK / FARM / COMPANY
10
aluminum, 24mm, round, R10

The Rose Bank Farm Company operated in the Charleston area around 1915.

BU S.C. POWER CO. / SCPC / CHARLESTON
GOOD FOR / SCPC / ONE FARE
brass, 16mm, round, c/o, R3 (Atwood 240B)

BV (obverse and reverse same as BU)
nickel, 16mm, round, c/o, R10 (Atwood 998A)

300,000 tokens were struck in 1949; they were used until 1955. The South Carolina Power Co. took over operations from the Charleston Consolidated Railway and Lighting Company in 1926. Streetcars were in operation until 1938, and thereafter only buses were utilized by the company.

BW5 S. E. F.
GOOD FOR / 5¢ / IN TRADE
brass, 21mm, round, R10

Tentatively attributed to S. Edwin Follin, who started out as a clerk at the Follin Bros. Company (see 1305-AP5). He later opened his own retail cigar and tobacco business, known as the Follin Cigar Store.

BX5 J. H. SCHMONSEES / 79 / COLUMBUS / ST. / CHARLESTON, / S.C.
GOOD FOR / 5¢ / CIGAR
brass, 21mm, round, R10

In the mid-teens John H. Schmonsees sold groceries, fruit, and cigars in his establishment at 79 Columbus Street.

BY5 C. H. SCHULTZ / 95 / CALHOUN ST.
GOOD FOR / 5¢ / IN TRADE
brass, 21mm, round, R10

C. Henry Schultz ran a grocery store during the early 1900s.

BZ1 SEASIDE CANNERY, CHARLESTON, S.C. / 1
1
brass, 19mm, round, R8

This cannery was in operation in the 1920s and 1930s.

CA5 GEO. W. SEIGNIOUS, / DRUGGIST / CHARLESTON, S.C.
GOOD FOR / 5¢ / CIGAR.
brass, 21mm, round, R10

George W. Seignious owned a drug store at 130 Spring Street from the early 1900s to the early 1930s.

CB10 SHIPYARD RIVER / CHARLESTON, / S.C. / MERCANTILE CO.
GOOD FOR / 10 / IN TRADE
aluminum, 18mm, round, R10

CC5 SHIPYARD RIVER / CHARLESTON, / S.C. / MERCANTILE CO. (similar wording to CB 10 but different arrangement and style)
GOOD FOR / 5 / IN TRADE
aluminum, 21mm, round, R9

CD In an early TAMS listing of embossed shell cards, Rulau & Mitchell cataloged a shell card of STENHOUSE & CO., Charleston, S.C. It was part of the Tilton collection, which was cataloged and sold in the late 1800s. The token has failed to surface since, and thus an exact description is not available.

CE6 H. A. STRAMM, / BAKERY / 212 / ST. PHILIP ST. / CHARLESTON, / S.C.
GOOD FOR / 6 CENT / LOAF OF BREAD
brass, 31mm, round, R9

Herman A. Stramm operated a bakery at 212 St. Phillip Street in the early 1900s. The business later evolved into a cigar store-restaurant, and then a grocery.

CF5   GOOD FOR / 5¢ / F. C. W. SUHRSTEDT
(blank)
> brass, 21mm, round, R10

> Frederick C. W. Suhrstedt ran a dairy in the late 1890s and early 1900s. He resided at 252 Ashley Avenue.

CG110 A. C. TUXBURY / LUMBER / CO.
GOOD FOR / 1 <u>10</u> / IN / MERCHANDISE (counterstamped "S")
> brass, 33mm, round, R10

CH1   A. C. TUXBURY LUMBER CO. / CAMP / 2
GOOD FOR / 1 / IN MERCHANDISE
> brass, 19mm, round, R10

> The A. C. Tuxbury Lumber Company, headquartered in New York City, operated a sawmill in Charleston from 1913 through 1937. The company also had operations in Awensdaw and Bethera. See listings under those towns for additional tokens. The exact location of Camp 2 is not presently known, so the token is tentatively cataloged here.

CI25   U.S.S. DENEBOLA / SHIP / SERVICE / STORE
GOOD FOR / 25 / IN TRADE
> aluminum, 24mm, round, R10

CI10   (obverse similar to CI25)
GOOD FOR / 10 / IN TRADE
> aluminum, 22mm, round, R9 (Curto N8-10)

CI5   (obverse similar to CI25)
GOOD FOR / 5 / IN TRADE
> aluminum, 19mm, round, R9 (Curto N8-5)

> According to the *Dictionary of American Naval Fighting Ships, Volume II* this ship was originally built as the *Edgewood* in Seattle, Washington by Skinner and Eddy in 1919. In 1921, she was refitted for naval use as a destroyer tender at the Philadelphia Navy Yard, and was renamed *Denebola* (after the name of a first magnitude star in the northern constellation Leo). She left Philadelphia in January of 1922 and sailed to Charleston for further outfitting, staying until September of that year. The ship continued as part of the Atlantic Fleet during the 1920s, travelling in maneuvers to the Mediterranean and the Caribbean. She probably revisited Charleston several times during this period. The general style of the token dates to the 1920s, so it can be safely assumed that it was in use while the ship was stationed in Charleston.

> In the early 1930s, the *Denebola* served as a barracks ship at Norfolk, Virginia for the crews of battleships undergoing modernization. It is likely that the tokens were also used during this period. The ship also served during World War II, seeing action as a destroyer tender in the Atlantic and the Mediterranean. It was decommissioned at San Francisco in 1946 and never served in the Navy again. She received one battle star for service in World War II.

A postcard view of the *U.S.S. Denebola*, tied up at Charleston.

CJ   JOHN WALLACH, Charleston, S.C. Listed with incomplete description in the Rulau-Mitchell catalog of embossed shell cards. It is made of silvered brass, with an 1867-dated Liberty seated reverse.

CK   WEST END / DAIRY / CHARLESTON, S.C.
         GOOD FOR / 1 / QT. / MILK
           zinc, 24mm, round, R7

CL   (obverse similar to CK)
         GOLDEN GUERNSEY / GOOD FOR / 1 / QT. / MILK
           zinc, 21mm, round, R8

CM WEST END DAIRY / CHARLESTON / S.C.
GOOD FOR / ½ GAL. / GRADE A MILK
aluminum, 26mm, octagonal, R9

This dairy was located for many years at the west end of Bee Street
(hence its name). It operated into the late 1970s.

CN5 A. W. WIETERS / GROCER / CORNER / CALHOUN AND / ELIZABETH /
STS. / CHARLESTON, / S.C.
GOOD FOR / 5 / CENTS (within curl of numeral) / IN MERCHANDISE
brass, 32mm, round, R10

August W. Wieters operated a grocery and saloon at 82 Calhoun Street
in the late 1890s and early 1900s.

CO5 O. H. WIETERS, / GROCER / 186 / KING ST. / CHARLESTON, S.C.
GOOD FOR / 5¢ / IN / MERCHANDISE
brass, 24mm, round, R9

CP5 O. H. WIETERS / 184 - 186 / KING ST. / CHARLESTON, S.C.
GOOD FOR / 5¢ / IN TRADE
brass, 21mm, round, R9

Otto H. Wieters ran a grocery store at 186 King Street from 1904 to
1927. He also operated a bowling alley at 184 King Street for a period of
time; this was reportedly the first bowling alley in Charleston.

CQ W. W. WILBUR. AUCTION & COMMISSION MERCHANT /
CHARLESTON. SO.CA / (picture of auctioneer holding a gavel) / 1846
MERCHANTS & MANUFACTURERS AGENT / COLLECTION BROKER
NOTARY PUBLIC &c / (picture of palmetto tree)
brass, 28mm, round, R7 (Miller SC 5)

CR (obverse and reverse same as CQ)
copper, 28mm, round, R7 (Miller SC 5A)

CS (obverse similar to CQ but slightly different die with period after SO.CA)
(reverse same as CQ)
German silver, 28mm, round, R10 (Miller SC 6)

CT (obverse and reverse same as CS)
copper, 28mm, round, R6 (Miller SC 7)

CU (obverse and reverse same as CS)
brass, 28mm, round, R3 (Miller SC 8)

CV (obverse and reverse same as CS)
silvered brass, 28mm, round, R9

CW (obverse same as CS)
(reverse similar to CQ but period between BROKER and NOTARY, and
a bushier-looking palmetto tree)
German silver, 28mm, round, R10

CX (obverse and reverse same as CW)
copper, 28mm, round, R4 (Miller SC 7A)

CY   (obverse and reverse same as CW)
           brass, 28mm, round, R4 (Miller SC 8A)

CZ   (new obverse die with words GOING AT ONLY A PENNY added around
           auctioneer)
           (reverse same as CW)
           brass, 28mm, round, R2 (Miller SC 9)

DA   (obverse and reverse same as CZ)
           copper, 28mm, round, R4 (Miller SC 10)

DB   (obverse and reverse same as CZ)
           cupronickel, 28mm, round, R10 (Miller SC 10A)

DC   (obverse and reverse same as CZ)
           German silver, 28mm, round, R10 (Miller SC 11)

DD   (obverse and reverse same as CZ)
           silvered brass, 28mm, round, R9

   During the 1840s and 1850s W. W. Wilbur was in the auction and
commission merchant business. As far as is presently known, and contrary
to popular belief, he was not involved in the slave trade.

EASY IDENTIFICATION CHART

CATALOG NUMBER	OBVERSE	REVERSE	COMPOSITION	MILLER NUMBER
CQ	No period after CA	Thin tree	Brass	SC 5
CR	No period after CA	Thin tree	Copper	SC 5A
CS	Period after CA	Thin tree	German silver	SC 6
CT	Period after CA	Thin tree	Copper	SC 7
CU	Period after CA	Thin tree	Brass	SC 8
CV	Period after CA	Thin tree	Silvered brass	
CW	Period after CA	Bushy tree	German silver	
CX	Period after CA	Bushy tree	Copper	SC 7A
CY	Period after CA	Bushy tree	Brass	SC 8A
CZ	GOING....A PENNY	Bushy tree	Brass	SC 9
DA	GOING....A PENNY	Bushy tree	Copper	SC 10
DB	GOING....A PENNY	Bushy tree	Cupronickel	SC 10A
DC	GOING....A PENNY	Bushy tree	German silver	SC 11
DD	GOING....A PENNY	Bushy tree	Silvered brass	

   The author has examined over 200 specimens of the W. W. Wilbur
tokens and has come to the conclusion that the tokens numbered SC12 and
SC13 by Miller and Rulau are actually weakly struck or badly worn examples
of SC9 and SC10. Therefore they are not listed as separate varieties.

CHARLESTON (Continued)

DE WONDERLAND / CHARLESTON / S.C.
(blank)
brass, 19mm, round, R8

Wonderland was a penny arcade located on King Street in the early 1900s.

Tokens issued for use by R. RICHTER with advertising on the reverse for the WULBERN FERTILIZER CO. of Charleston were used in the town of Mappus, located on the outskirts of Charleston. See listings under Mappus.

CHERAW (Chesterfield County)

A5 BULL'S GROCERY / CHERAW, / S.C.
GOOD FOR / 5¢ / IN TRADE
brass, 21mm, round, R10

W. A. Bull was listed as a grocer during the teens.

B CHERAW / GOOD ONLY / DATE SOLD / AMUSEMENT CO.
CHILD / ADMISSION / OR / ADULT PASS
brass, 25mm, round, center hole, R8

C5 CHIQUOLA CLUB / GAMES / CHERAW, S.C.
5
aluminum, 26mm, octagonal, R10

This postcard view shows the Chiquola Club and the Hotel Covington.

D50   MAYNARD LUMBER CORP. / GOOD / ONLY AT / COMPANY STORE
GOOD FOR / 50¢ / IN TRADE
aluminum, 31mm, round, R10

This corporation was based in Cheraw in the late 1930s and the 1940s.

E   G. W. TREADWAY / SECOND ST. / CHERAW, S.C.
(same)
aluminum, 21mm, round, R10

G. W. Treadway operated a restaurant and billiard parlor in 1910.

CHESNEE   (Spartanburg County)   1315

A100   CHESNEE MILLS STORE / 1$\frac{00}{}$ / MDSE. ONLY / CHESNEE, S.C.
(Orco - type I)
nickel, 32mm, round, barbell-shaped c/o, R9

A25   (obverse similar to A100 except denomination 25)
(Orco - type I)
copper, 24mm, round, barbell-shaped c/o, R8

A10   (obverse similar to A100 except denomination 10)
(Orco - type I)
brass, 21mm, round, barbell-shaped c/o, R8

A5   (obverse similar to A100 except denomination 5)
(Orco - type I) (varieties exist)
nickel, 19mm, round, barbell-shaped c/o, R7

Organized around 1912, Chesnee Mills was a manufacturer of cotton goods. The company operated through the 1940s as a branch of Saxon Mills of Spartanburg.

CHESTER   (Chester County)   1320

A1   G. W. BYARS & CO. / 1
(Ingle System - 1909 pat. date)
composition unknown, 18mm, round, R10

G. W. Byars & Co. ran a general store during the teens and twenties. Obverse description may not be exact.

B5   THE CHESTER DRUG CO, / REXALL / STORE, / CHESTER, / S.C.
GOOD FOR / 5¢ / SODA
aluminum, 25mm, square with clipped corners, R10

Owned and operated by Henry DeVega and H. R. Woods, this company was in business from 1908 through the 1940s.

C100   ONE WITH EACH $20.00 PURCHASE / CLARK / FURNITURE / CO. / CHESTER, S.C.
GOOD FOR / $1.00 / ON A / $20.00. / CASH / PURCHASE
aluminum, 38mm, round, R10

This company was involved in retail furniture sales from the teens through the thirties.

D100   J. F. CLOUD / WYLIE MILL, / CHESTER, / S.C.
GOOD FOR / 100 / IN MERCHANDISE
aluminum, 35mm, round, R10

John F. Cloud ran a general store in the Wylie Mill village during 1912 and 1913.

E5   McCULLOUGH / & / FERGERSON / CHESTER / S.C.
GOOD FOR / 5¢ / CIGAR OR DRINK
aluminum, 19mm, round, R10

This grocery store operated from 1908 to 1912.

F100   PETTY & CO. / CHESTER, S.C.
GOOD FOR / 1<u>00</u> / IN MERCHANDISE
aluminum, 38mm, round, R10

F50   (obverse similar to F100)
GOOD FOR / 50 / IN MERCHANDISE
aluminum, 33mm, round, R10

F10   (obverse similar to F100)
GOOD FOR / 10 / IN MERCHANDISE
aluminum, 22mm, round, R10

G10   J. W. WHITE / R.F.D. / NO. 3 / CHESTER, S.C.
GOOD FOR / 10 / IN / MERCHANDISE
aluminum, 24mm, round, R10

During the teens J. W. White operated a general store one mile west of Chester on rural route #3.

CHESTERFIELD   (Chesterfield County)   1325

A5   CHESTERFIELD BRICK CO. / CHESTERFIELD / S.C.
GOOD FOR / 5 / IN / MERCHANDISE
aluminum, 21mm, round, R10

During the early 1900s this company was intermittently listed as a manufacturer of brick and clay pipe.

CHICK SPRINGS   (Greenville County)   1330

A5   CHICK SPRINGS / CO. / GOOD / FOR 1 BOTTLE / CHICK SODA / 5¢
THE MOST / SANITARY / PLANT IN / THE / U.S.A.
aluminum, 19mm, round, R10

The Chick Springs Co. operated a resort hotel and bottling company during the early 1900s. Chick Springs was the site of a health resort as early as the 1870s.

CHOPPEE   (Georgetown County)   1335

A   CHOPPEE SCHOOL
GOOD FOR / 1 / MEAL / ELEMENTARY
aluminum, 23mm, round, R10

CITY VIEW   (Greenville County)   1337

A50   FRANKLIN FINANCE / 1318 WOODSIDE AVE. / CITY VIEW
50¢
aluminum, 26mm, round, R10

City View is a separate municipality overlooking the city of Greenville, hence its name. For other tokens issued by this company, see listings under Greenville.

CLEARWATER   (Aiken County)   1345

A500   AIKEN COUNTY STORES INC. / 5$\underline{00}$ / BATH + LANGLEY + / CLEARWATER, / S.C.
(Orco - type I)
brass, 32mm, scalloped (12), "C" c/o, R5

A100   (obverse similar to A500 except denomination 1$\underline{00}$)
(Orco - type II)
nickel, 32mm, round, "C" c/o, R3

A50   (obverse similar to A500 except denomination 50)
(Orco - type II)
copper, 27mm, round, "C" c/o, R2

A25   (obverse similar to A500 except denomination 25)
(Orco - type II) (varieties exist)
nickel, 24mm, round, "C" c/o, R2

A10   (obverse similar to A500 except denomination 10)
(Orco - type II) (varieties exist)
brass, 21mm, round, "C" c/o, R2

A5   (obverse similar to A500 except denomination 5)
        (Orco - type II) (varieties exist)
            nickel, 19mm, round, "C" c/o, R2

A1   (obverse similar to A500 except denomination 1)
        (Orco - type II)
            copper, 18mm, round, "C" c/o, R7

B1   AIKEN COUNTY STORES INC. / 1 / C / BATH + LANGLEY + /
        CLEARWATER, / S.C.
        (Orco - type III)
            copper, 17mm, round, R7

    Aiken County Stores Inc. operated the company store for Seminole
Mills during the 1930s. The company also operated mill stores in other S.C.
towns. (See Bath, Langley, Anderson, Calhoun Falls, and Williamston.)

C5   SEMINOLE / MANUFACTURING / COMPANY / STORE, / CLEARWATER,
        S.C.
            GOOD FOR / ONE / 5¢ / DRINK OF COCA - COLA
            brass, 25mm, round, R10

    The Seminole Mfg. Co. operated a large cotton mill in Clearwater from
1913 into the 1940s.

CLEMSON COLLEGE   (Pickens County)   **1350**

A100   THE CLEMSON / AGRICULTURAL / COLLEGE / CLEMSON COLLEGE /
        S.C.
            GOOD FOR / 1⁰⁰ / IN / MERCHANDISE
            aluminum, 33mm, round, R10

A50   (obverse similar to A100)
            GOOD FOR / 50 / IN / MERCHANDISE
            aluminum, 29mm, round, R10

A25   (obverse similar to A100)
            GOOD FOR / 25 / IN / MERCHANDISE
            aluminum, 26mm, round, R10

A10   (obverse similar to A100)
            GOOD FOR / 10 / IN / MERCHANDISE
            aluminum, 23mm, round, R10

A5   (obverse similar to A100)
            GOOD FOR / 5 / IN / MERCHANDISE
            aluminum, 20mm, round, R10

    The Clemson Agricultural College is now known as Clemson University,
the second largest university in the state. It is not known how the above
tokens were used.

B5   GOOD FOR / 5¢ / WINSLOW / SLOAN / AT / FOUNTAIN
(blank)
aluminum, 25mm, round, R10
Around 1910 Winslow Sloan operated a general store.

CLINTON   (Laurens County)   1355

A100   CLINTON COTTON MILL / STORE
GOOD FOR / 1⁰⁰ / IN / MERCHANDISE
brass, 35mm, round, R8

A25   (obverse similar to A100)
GOOD FOR / 25 / IN / MERCHANDISE   (varieties exist)
brass, 29mm, round, R7

A10   (obverse similar to A100)
GOOD FOR / 10 / IN / MERCHANDISE   (varieties exist)
brass, 24mm, round, R7

A5   (obverse similar to A100)
GOOD FOR / 5 / IN / MERCHANDISE   (varieties exist)
brass, 21mm, round, R6

This large cotton mill started operations around the turn of the century and continued through the 1960s. The company made print cloths and sheetings.

B5   AT JEANS / CLINTON S.C.
GOOD FOR / 5¢ / CIGAR OR SODA
aluminum, 19mm, round, R10

P. S. Jeans ran a grocery store, soda fountain, and small soda water bottling company from 1908 to the late 1930s.

C5   NABORS / & / ADAIR.
GOOD FOR / 5¢ / IN TRADE
brass, 19mm, round, R10

Nabors and Adair were partners in a confectionery and ice cream parlor in the teens.

D5   YOUNGS PHARMACY, / CLINTON, / S.C.
GOOD FOR / 5¢ / IN TRADE
aluminum, 19mm, round, R10

Young's Pharmacy operated from 1904 through the late 1940s. The token was probably issued around 1910.

CLIO   (Marlboro County)   1360

A5   CLIO DRUG CO., / CLIO, / S.C.
        GOOD FOR / 5¢ / IN TRADE
           aluminum, 19mm, round, R10

B   CLIO DRUG CO. / CLIO, S.C.
        FIVE OF THESE GOOD FOR / 1 / GLASS / OF / SODA
           aluminum, 25mm, round, R10

        The Clio Drug Co. was in business from 1910 to 1933.

C5   COVINGTON COMPANY, / INC. / CLIO, / S.C. / NOT / TRANSFERABLE
        GOOD FOR / 5¢ / IN MERCHANDISE
           brass, 20mm, round, R10

        This company operated a general store during the teens and the twenties.

CLOVER   (York County)   1365

A   CLOVER COTTON / MANFG. / CO. / CLOVER S.C.
        TWO PLY / SPOOLING
           brass, 24mm, round, R10

        Undoubtedly this was a production token. The Clover Cotton Mfg. Co. was in business as early as 1893, specializing in the manufacture of cotton yarns. The mill was sold to Clover Mills Co. in 1920, and again in 1937 to Clover Spinning Mills, Inc.

COLUMBIA   (Richland County)   1380

A5   W. W. ABBOTT / 1300 / MAIN ST. / COLUMBIA, S.C.
        GOOD FOR / 5¢ / IN TRADE
           aluminum, 27mm, scalloped (8), R10

        This merchant ran a cigar and tobacco shop on Main Street from 1904 to 1916.

B10   ARCADE PLACE / COLUMBIA, / S.C.
        GOOD FOR / 10 / IN TRADE
           aluminum, 22mm, round, R10

        Harry and E. B. Cantey operated this cigar store and soda fountain circa 1916.

C5   B. P. K. / P.O. FRUIT STORE / COLUMBIA, S.C.
        GOOD FOR / 5 / IN TRADE
           brass, 21mm, round, R10

        Tentatively attributed to Wm. Karas, who operated a fruit stand on the premises of the Post Office Restaurant at 1728 Main Street from 1917 to 1922.

D10   J. Q. BALLENTINE / 10
(Ingle System - 1909 pat. date)
brass, 21mm, round, R10

John Quincy Ballentine sold groceries and meats at 1908 Blanding Street during the teens and early twenties.

E100   V. Z. BURKE / 1⁰⁰
(Ingle System - 1909 pat. date)
brass, 35mm, round, R10

E5   (obverse similar to E100 except denomination 5)
(Ingle System - 1909 pat. date)
brass, 20mm, round, R10

E1   (obverse similar to E100 except denomination 1)
(Ingle System - 1909 pat. date)
brass, 18mm, round, R10

During the early teens Virgil Z. Burke operated a grocery store at 2110 Hampton Street.

F   CAPITAL / CABANA / MOTOR INN / COLUMBIA / S.C.
GOOD FOR 1 FREE DRINK / IN THE PIRATES COVE
brass, 33mm, round, R8, modern

G   CAROLINA TRANSIT CO. COLUMBIA, S.C. / C T CO
GOOD FOR / C T CO / ONE FARE
nickel, 23mm, round, c/♂, R5 (Atwood 310B)

A total of 20,000 tokens were struck in 1926 and 1927. Organized in 1925, the Carolina Transit Company operated buses along the routes of discontinued streetcar lines in the Columbia area.

H5   COLUMBIA / BOWLING / CENTER / COLUMBIA, S.C.
GOOD FOR / 5¢ / IN TRADE
aluminum, 20mm, round, R10

I10   GOOD FOR / 10¢ / WITH / BOTTLE / COLUMBIA DAIRIES
(same)
aluminum, 23mm, round, R10

J   COLUMBIA / DAIRIES
GOOD FOR / 1 / QT. / MILK
aluminum, 21mm, scalloped (8), R10

The Columbia Dairies Co. began operations around 1927 and stayed in business into the 1940s.

K   COLUMBIA ELECTRIC STREET RAILWAY / COLUMBIA, S.C.
GOOD FOR / ONE FARE
bimetallic - aluminum with copper "C" in center of planchet, 19mm, round, R9 (Atwood 310A)

Consolidated in January, 1892, the Columbia Electric Street Railway operated several streetcar lines in downtown Columbia. Although the company was taken over by the Columbia Railway, Gas, & Electric Co. in

1911, streetcar service continued until 1936. The majority of the tokens were destroyed many years ago when a member of the company threw them into the Atlantic Ocean from a dock in Kennebunkport, Maine.

L   COLUMBIA OFFICE SUPPLY / 1112 / LADY STREET / COLUMBIA, SC
GOOD FOR / 1 SKELLY 1 / ONE CUP OF COFFEE
brass, 29mm, round, R8, modern

M5   W. L. CORLEY & CO. / LUMBER / COLUMBIA, S.C.
GOOD FOR / 5 / IN / MERCHANDISE
aluminum, 22mm, round, R10

N25   J. R. CORNWELL / 25 c. / BARBER SHOP, 1636 MAIN STREET
(blank)
white cardboard, 28mm x 53mm, rectangular, R9

N15   (obverse similar to N25 except denomination 15)
(blank)
white cardboard, 28mm x 53mm, rectangular, R9

N10   (obverse similar to N25 except denomination 10)
(blank)
white cardboard, 28mm x 53mm, rectangular, R9

O15   J. R. CORNWELL / 15 c. / BARBER SHOP, 1636 MAIN STREET
(blank)
orange cardboard, 32mm x 60mm, rectangular, R10

J. R. Cornwell was a black barber who ran a shop on Main Street in Columbia for many years. He was listed at 1629 Main from 1914 to 1945, so these tokens must predate 1914.

P   HENRY V. DICK & CO. / CHARLOTTE, N.C. / RALEIGH, N.C. / COLUMBIA, S.C. / GREENVILLE, S.C.
YOU PAY (in script divided by large arrow)
aluminum, 32mm, round, R8

This refrigeration, heating, and radio supply dealer was in business during the 1940s.

Q25   DRAUGHON'S / 25 / COLLEGE
(same)
aluminum, 29mm, round, R10

Q5   (obverse similar to Q25 except denomination 5)
(same)
aluminum, 25mm, round, R10

This small business college also operated a branch in Knoxville, Tennessee.

R5   EAGLE / CONFECTIONERY
GOOD FOR / 5¢ / IN TRADE
brass, 21mm, round, center hole, R10

The Eagle Confectionery was listed only in 1914 and 1915.

S   EDISTO / FARMS / DAIRY / COLUMBIA, S.C.
        GOOD FOR / 1 / QT. / MILK
        aluminum, 26mm, round, center hole, R10

T   EDISTO / FARMS / DAIRY / COLUMBIA, S.C.
        GOOD FOR / 1 / QT. / MILK
        zinc, 26mm, round, center hole, R10

        The Edisto Farms Dairy was listed in the 1940s. A branch was located in Orangeburg, and additional tokens of the company are listed under that town.

U   FAIRWOLD FARMS DAIRY / PURE MILK / AND / CREAM / COLUMBIA, S.C.
        GOOD FOR / 1 / PINT / OF / MILK
        aluminum, 20mm, round, R10

        The Fairwold Dairy Depot was located at 1228 Main St. in 1911.

V100   THE HOUSE OF SERVICE / GOOD FOR A / CHARGE ACCOUNT / ON YOUR TERMS / AT THE / FEDERAL CLOTHING STORES / 1538 MAIN STREET / COLUMBIA / S.C. / A SQUARE DEAL TO ALL
        GOOD AS / 1\frac{00}{}$ / CASH / ON YOUR FIRST PURCHASE OF / $10 OR MORE / COMPLIMENTS / OF / J. NATHAN (signature) / PRESIDENT / GOOD ONLY DURING / 1922
        brass, 33mm, round, R10

        S. G. Cohen was the manager of this branch of the Federal Department Stores. Other stores in the chain, which operated throughout the Southeast, were located in Charleston and Greenville.

W50   B. A. FULMER / 50
        (Ingle System - 1909 pat. date)
        copper, 31mm, round, R10

W5   (obverse similar to W50 except denomination 5)
        (Ingle System - 1909 pat. date)
        copper, 20mm, round, R10

W1   (obverse similar to W50 except denomination 1)
        (Ingle System - 1909 pat. date)
        copper, 18mm, round, R10

        From 1908 to 1917 Bachman A. Fulmer operated a grocery store at 1531 Richland.

X5   R. P. FUNDERBURK / 5
        (Ingle System - 1909 pat. date)
        composition unknown, 20mm, round, R10

X1   (obverse similar to X5 except denomination 1)
        (Ingle System - 1909 pat. date)
        composition unknown, 18mm, round, R10

        Robert P. Funderburk ran a grocery at 700 Taylor St. from 1908 to 1936.

AM5 McMILLANS DRUG STORE
GOOD FOR / 5¢ / CIGAR OR SODA
aluminum, 19mm, round, R10

   W. C. McMillan operated a drug store at 1214 Main Street from 1904 to 1915.

AN50 MOD / STORE / J. G. RICHARDS
GOOD FOR / 50¢ / IN TRADE
aluminum, 32mm, round, R10, modern

AN25 (obverse similar to AN50)
GOOD FOR / 25¢ / IN TRADE
aluminum, 29mm, round, R10, modern

AN10 (obverse similar to AN50)
GOOD FOR / 10¢ / IN TRADE
aluminum, 16mm, round, R10, modern

AN5 (obverse similar to AN50)
GOOD FOR / 5¢ / IN TRADE
aluminum, 26mm, round, R10, modern

   The John G. Richards Center is a present-day juvenile detention center outside of Columbia. The tokens were used during the early 1970s in conjunction with a behavior modification program designed to develop work skills and life skills in the young detainees. The juveniles were paid with tokens for doing various jobs, and they could later be spent at the "MOD Store" for soft drinks, candy, toiletries, etc.

AO10 NEW CABANA / CLUB / COLUMBIA, / S.C.
GOOD FOR / 10¢ / IN TRADE
brass, 22mm, round, R10

AP100 ONE ON EACH SUIT ORDER / OWEN / & / PAUL / MERCHANT
TAILORS / 1119 WASHINGTON / COLUMBIA / CLEANING & PRESSING
GOOD FOR / $ 1.00 $ / ON A SUIT
aluminum, 38mm, round, R10

   The tailoring firm of Owen & Paul first opened in 1917. The firm is still in business, although no members of the original families are presently involved.

AQ5 P. B.,G. / 1329 MAIN ST. / COLUMBIA, S.C.
GOOD FOR / 5 / IN TRADE
brass, 21mm, round, R10

   Peter B. Gretes was listed as a fruit dealer and restaurant operator at 1329 Main Street from 1903 to the early 1920s.

AR5 PALACE / CONFECTIONERY / COLUMBIA, / S.C.
GOOD FOR / 5¢ / SODA OR ICE CREAM
aluminum, 24mm, round, R10

   In 1908 this establishment was located at 1204 Main Street.

AS5   PALMETTO COMMISSARY CO. / COLUMBIA / S.C. / STORE
GOOD FOR / 5 / IN MERCHANDISE
brass, 19mm, round, R10

AT   PALMETTO COTTON / SPOOLER / ROOM / MILLS
(blank)
brass, 24mm, round, R10

Palmetto Cotton Mills specialized in the manufacture of yarns and
fabrics. The mill operated from the early 1900s to the early 1920s. 1380-AT
was probably some type of production token, while 1380-AS5 was used by
the company store.

AU5   PALMETTO PHARMACY / CORNER / GATES / & / GERVAIS / STS. /
COLUMBIA, S.C.
GOOD FOR / 5¢ / IN TRADE
aluminum, 21mm, round, R10

This pharmacy was in business from 1915 to 1940.

AV25   J. S. PINKUSSOHN / CIGAR CO. / COLUMBIA, / S.C.
GOOD FOR / 25¢ / IN TRADE
brass, 24mm, square, R10

As stated under the Charleston listing, a branch of this company was
located in Columbia. Operating from the early 1900s to the late 1920s, this
branch dealt in wholesale and retail cigars and tobacco.

AW100 The PLAZA NEWS STAND of the PLAZA HOTEL is purported to have
issued tokens. A $1.00 denomination maverick token was attributed to
Columbia by the seller in a 1970s mail bid sale. This author has not
examined the specimen nor confirmed the attribution.

AX5   P. R. REESE
GOOD FOR / 5¢ / SODA
aluminum, 25mm, round, R10

Paul R. Reese ran a drug store at 1105 Washington St. in the teens.
After his death, the store was operated by his wife, Pauline, until the late
1930s.

AY5   J.B. RIEDLINGER / BAKERY / AND / CONFECTIONERY / COLUMBIA,
S.C.
GOOD FOR ONE / 5¢ / LOAF OF BREAD
aluminum, 24mm, round, R10

John B. Riedlinger operated a bakery and confectionery at 1907 Main
Street during the late 1800s and early 1900s. Around 1910, the business
was purchased by W. J. Heidt, who continued it under the name Riedlinger
Bakery Company.

AZ   S.C. ELECTRIC / BUS / & GAS CO.
GOOD FOR / BUS / ONE FARE
nickel, 16mm, round, c/o, R1 (Atwood 310C)

BA   (obverse and reverse same as AZ)
             zinc, 16mm, round, c/o, R2 (Atwood 310D)

BB   (obverse and reverse same as AZ)
             steel, 16mm, round, c/o, R2 (Atwood 310E)

BC   (obverse and reverse same as AZ)
             brass, 16mm, round, c/o, R2 (Atwood 310F)

BD   (obverse and reverse same as AZ)
             bronze, 16mm, round, c/o, R2 (Atwood 310G)

   South Carolina Electric and Gas began operating buses in Columbia in 1936. Although the company still runs Columbia's transit system, tokens were discontinued in 1968. Over one million of the various varieties were struck, and they are quite common today.

BE5   S.C. / PENITENTIARY / CANTEEN
             GOOD FOR / 5¢ / IN MERCHANDISE
             aluminum, 20mm, round, R10

BE1   (obverse similar to BE5)
             GOOD FOR / 1¢ / IN MERCHANDISE
             brass, 17mm, round, R9

BF5   GEO. SABBAGHA
             GOOD FOR / 5¢ / IN TRADE
             brass, 21mm, round, center hole, R10

BG5   GEO. SABBAGHA / 1424 ASSEMBLY
             GOOD FOR / 5 / IN TRADE
             brass, 20mm, round, R10

   George Sabbagha operated a hot dog stand in the late teens on Assembly Street. Later, he ran a grocery store and meat counter. Description may not be accurate.

BH5   S. A. SABBAGHA / 1810 / MAIN ST.
             GOOD FOR / 5 / IN TRADE
             brass, 21mm, round, R10

   During the teens, S. A. Sabbagha operated a confectionery and billiard parlor. From the late teens through the mid-forties he ran a grocery store and meat counter.

BI5   THE SAVOY. / S. T. / WESBERRY, / PROP.
             GOOD FOR / 5¢ / IN TRADE
             aluminum, 26mm, round, R10

   In 1912 Samuel T. Wesberry was listed as the proprietor of The Savoy, a billiard hall located at 1345 Main Street.

BJ   SCOFIELD AUTO-MUSIC CO. / COLUMBIA / S.C.
    (blank)
      brass, 18mm, round, R9

      The Scofield Auto-music Co. was listed in the late teens. The token was probably used in some type of coin-operated musical piano.

BK25   J. C. SEEGERS & CO. / (picture of barrel) / S.C. / COLUMBIA
    25 (within wreath)
      German silver, 27mm, round, R10   (Miller SC 14)

BK10   (obverse similar to BK25)
    10 (within wreath)
      brass, 20mm, round, R9

      The 1875 city directory listed J. C. Seegers as operating a brewery, ice house, and wholesale liquor dealership on North Richardson Street. In later years Seegers operated the brewery at his farm on Barhamville Road. In the early 1900s, his son may have taken over the bottling works, as a F. W. Seegers is listed in the bottling business in 1904.

BL5   SMALL'S / GROCERY / FOREST DRIVE / COLUMBIA, / S.C.
    GOOD FOR / 5¢ / WHEN / RETURNED WITH BOTTLE
      brass, 20mm, round, R10

BM   THE SMITHDEAL MUSIC CO. / EVERYTHING / IN / MUSIC / COLUMBIA, / S.C.
    SEND US PIANO PROSPECT / IF WE SELL / YOU GET / $5<u>00</u>
      brass, 31mm, round, R10

BN   SMITHDEAL / 1802 / MAIN ST. / COLUMBIA, S.C. / EVERYTHING / IN MUSIC
    GOOD FOR / 25 / MINUTES / AT / SMITHDEAL'S / WRIGHT CIN'TI, O.
      aluminum, 26mm, round, R9

BO   GOOD FOR / 25 / MINUTES / AT / SMITHDEAL'S
    (same)
      aluminum, 28mm, round, R10

      From 1904 to 1933 the Smithdeal Music Co. sold musical instruments and sheet music at 1802 Main Street.

BP   SOUTH CAROLINA BAPTIST / HOSPITAL / COLUMBIA, / S.C.
    RADIO TOKEN / DAHLBERG (in script)
      zinc, 17mm, round, center hole, R9

BQ100   SOUTH CAROLINA / $1<u>00</u> / STATE PRISON
    $1<u>00</u>
      green plastic, 36mm, round, R1, modern

BQ50   (obverse similar to BQ100 except denomination 50¢)
    50¢
      yellow plastic, 29mm, round, R1, modern

COLUMBIA (Continued)   1380

BQ25 (obverse similar to BQ100 except denomination 25¢)
25¢
green plastic, 26mm, round, R1, modern

BQ10 (obverse similar to BQ100 except denomination 10¢)
10¢
yellow plastic, 23mm, round, R1, modern

BQ5 (obverse similar to BQ100 except denomination 5¢)
5¢
green plastic, 20mm, round, R1, modern

BQ1 (obverse similar to BQ100 except denomination 1¢)
1¢
yellow plastic, 16mm, round, R1, modern

BR10 SOUTH CAROLINA / 10¢ (upside down) / STATE PRISON
10¢
yellow plastic, 23mm, round, R6, modern

See listings under S.C. Penitentiary Canteen (1380-BE series) for other tokens used at this prison.

BS SUBURBAN TRANSIT CO.
GOOD FOR / ONE FARE (varieties exist)
nickel, 23mm, round, "S" c/o, R3 (Atwood 310H)

BT (obverse and reverse same as BS)
zinc, 23mm, round, "S" c/o, R3 (Atwood 310I)

BU (obverse and reverse same as BS)
steel, 23mm, round, "S" c/o, R3 (Atwood 310J)

The Suburban Transit Co. offered bus service in West Columbia from 1938 to 1969, when the line was taken over by South Carolina Electric & Gas. A total of 195,000 tokens were struck between 1938 and 1961.

BV SUNSHINE LAUNDRY / AND / CLEANERS / ONE DAY SERVICE / GOOD LUCK
(1951 University of South Carolina football schedule)
aluminum, 38mm, round, R10

Still in business today, Sunshine Laundry and Cleaners has operated at various locations in Columbia since 1937.

BW5 T. C. / 1207 MAIN ST. / COLUMBIA, S.C.
GOOD FOR / 5¢ / IN TRADE
aluminum, 19mm, round, R10

BX5 THOMAS' / DRUG / STORE / COLUMBIA / S.C.
GOOD FOR / 5¢ / IN TRADE
aluminum, 19mm, round, R10

The Thomas Drug Store was located at 1611 Main Street from 1908 to 1915.

BY TIME FINANCE / CO., INC. / AL 3-9419 / COLA, S.C. / LOANS
GOOD LUCK / (picture of cloverleaf)
aluminum, 36mm, round, R10

BZ TWIN / LAKES
GOOD FOR / 1 / RIDE
aluminum, 19mm, round, R9

Twin Lakes amusement park was located on the outskirts of Columbia, on property which is now part of the Fort Jackson Army Training Center.

Twin Lakes in 1937, as depicted on a postcard.

CA5 UNION STATION DRUG CO. / SODA / AND / CIGARS / COLUMBIA, S.C.
GOOD FOR / 5¢ / IN CIGARS
aluminum, 20mm, round, R10

This company was in operation as early as 1904 and as late as 1940.

CB50 GOOD FOR 50¢ / ON A / PURCHASE / OF $5.00 OR MORE / AT / VAN METRE'S / COLUMBIA / S.C.
GOOD FOR / ¢50¢ / IN TRADE
aluminum, 32mm, round, R9

J. M. Van Metre operated a furniture store in Columbia from 1904 until his death. The store continued to operate in his name through the late 1940s. Van Metre also ran an undertaking business.

COLUMBIA (Continued)   1380

CC5 G. K. XEPAPAS / 1506 MAIN ST. / COLUMBIA, S.C.
GOOD FOR / 5 / IN TRADE
brass, 21mm, round, R8

George K. Xepapas ran a fruit store for over 30 years, from the early 1900s to the mid 1930s.

CD Y.M.C.A. / COLUMBIA, / S.C.
GOOD FOR / 1 TOWEL / OR / 1 CAKE SOAP
aluminum, 23mm, octagonal, R10

During the early 1900s the Columbia Y.M.C.A. was located at 1246 Main Street.

CONESTEE (Greenville County)   1390

A100 CONESTEE MILLS STORE / 1<u>00</u>
GOOD FOR / $1<u>00</u> / IN MERCHANDISE
aluminum, 35mm, octagonal, R10

A5 (obverse similar to A100 except denomination 5)
GOOD FOR / 5¢ / IN MERCHANDISE
aluminum, 21mm, octagonal, R9

B10 CONESTEE MILLS STORE / 10
GOOD FOR / 10 / IN / MERCHANDISE
aluminum, 22mm, octagonal, R10

B5 (obverse similar to B10 except denomination 5)
GOOD FOR / 5 / IN / MERCHANDISE
aluminum, 19mm, octagonal, R10

Conestee Mills operated from the mid-teens to the late 1930s. The company specialized in making sheetings and drills (coarse, twilled cloths often used in the manufacture of uniforms).

CONWAY (Horry County)   1395

A10 ADAMS PHARMACY INC. / 10 / CONWAY, S.C.
(Orco - type II)
brass, 21mm, round, R10

A5 (obverse similar to A10 except denomination 5)
(Orco - type II)
nickel, 19mm, round, R10

A1 (obverse similar to A10 except denomination 1)
(Orco - type II)
brass, 18mm, round, R9

This pharmacy is listed in the late 1930s and early 1940s.

B5   W. B. CHESTNUT & CO. / 30 AVE. / CONWAY, / S.C.
GOOD FOR / 5¢ / DRINK
aluminum, 24mm, round, R9

W. B. Chestnut opened his general store sometime around 1912. In later years, he only stocked groceries. The store closed around 1940.

C   CONWAY DRUG CO. / CONWAY, / S.C.
GOOD FOR / 1 / GLASS / SODA WATER
aluminum, 24mm, round, R9

The Conway Drug Co. was in business as early as 1904 and as late as 1927.

D   CONWAY LUMBER CO. / CAMP #1 / CONWAY, S.C.
A set of five obverse dies with this inscription is known to exist. To date none of the tokens have been seen or reported.

E100   CONWAY TRADING COMPANY / CONWAY / S.C.
GOOD FOR / NOT / 1$\underline{00}$ / TRANSFERABLE / IN MERCHANDISE ONLY
brass, 35mm, round, R10

E50   (obverse similar to E100)
GOOD FOR / NOT / 50 / TRANSFERABLE / IN MERCHANDISE ONLY
brass, 32mm, round, R10

F5   (obverse similar to E 100)
GOOD FOR / 5¢ / IN / MERCHANDISE / NOT / TRANSFERABLE
aluminum, 20mm, round, R10

The Conway Trading Company operated as commissary for the Conway Lumber Co. in the late 1920s and early 1930s.

G100   THE JERRY COX CO. / 1$\underline{00}$ / CONWAY, S.C.
(Orco - type I and type II varieties exist)
brass, 32mm, round, R6

G50   (obverse similar to G100 except denomination 50)
(Orco - type II) (varieties exist)
nickel, 27mm, round, R6

G25   (obverse similar to G100 except denomination 25)
(Orco - type I and type II varieties exist)
brass, 24mm, round, R6

G10   (obverse similar to G100 except denomination 10)
(Orco - type II) (varieties exist)
nickel, 21mm, round, R6

G5   (obverse similar to G 100 except denomination 5)
(Orco - type II) (varieties exist)
brass, 19mm, round, R6

G1   (obverse similar to G100 except denomination 1)
(Orco - type III)
copper, 18mm, round, R8

The mercantile business which evolved into The Jerry Cox Co. was started by the firm of Burroughs & Collins, a very prominent company in the early history of Horry County. Burroughs & Collins had interests in the lumber & turpentine industry, a steamship company, a local railroad, real estate, and a retail mercantile business. Wanting to divest themselves of the mercantile portion of their business interests, they sold it to Mr. Jerry Cox and a Mr. Lundy. The new company was called the Cox - Lundy Company. Later, Lundy sold his interest to Cox and the name was changed to The Jerry Cox Company. Cox had an agreement with Burroughs & Collins to supply credit to their lumber company workers. The Jerry Cox Company later evolved into a department store which is still open today.

One of the Burroughs & Collins turpentine stills, circa 1895.

H   HORRY TRANSIT COMPANY / (picture of bus)
         GOOD FOR / (picture of bus) / ONE FARE
         bronze, 16mm, round, R5 (Atwood 320A)

         5,000 tokens were struck in 1947.

CONWAY (Continued)   1395

I5   NORTON DRUG CO. / PHARMACIST / CONWAY, S.C.
     GOOD FOR / 5¢ / AT SODA FOUNTAIN
       aluminum, 24mm, round, R10

       This establishment operated from the late 1890s to the early 1920s.

J100 THE VENEER MFG. CO. / EUREKA / STORE / CONWAY, S.C.
     GOOD FOR / 100 / IN TRADE
       aluminum, 35mm, round, R10

       The Eureka Store and the Veneer Manufacturing Co. are listed in the 1920s, 30s, and 40s.

CORDESVILLE (Berkeley County)   1405

A100 SOUTH ATLANTIC / LUMBER CO. / CORDESVILLE / S.C.
     GOOD FOR / $1⁰⁰ / IN TRADE
       brass, 35mm, round, R10

A50   (obverse similar to A100)
     GOOD FOR / 50¢ / IN TRADE
       brass, 31mm, round, R10

A25   (obverse similar to A100)
     GOOD FOR / 25¢ / IN TRADE
       brass, 28mm, round, R10

COSBY (Hampton County)   1410

A10   BADHAM LUMBER CO.
     GOOD FOR / 10 / IN MERCHANDISE
       aluminum, 24mm, round, R10

       This company was a subsidiary of the Dorchester Lumber Company of Badham, S.C. which operated in the late 1920s and early 1930s. The office was in Garnett, with mills in nearby Cosby and Springfield. Tokens were used in Cosby, Springfield, and possibly in Garnett.

COWARD (Florence County)   1415

A50   COXE LUMBER / COMPANY / COWARD STORE
     GOOD FOR / 50¢ / IN TRADE
       brass, 28mm, round, R10

       This firm is listed in the late 1930s as a branch operation of a company headquartered in Wadesboro, N.C.

COWPENS   (Spartanburg County)   1420

A5   COWPENS DRUG STORE / 5 / COWPENS / S.C.
          GOOD FOR / 5¢ / DRINK / OR / CIGAR
          brass, 21mm, round, R8
          This store operated in the teens, twenties, and thirties.

B5   THE COWPENS MFG. CO. / WILL PAY / 5¢ / IN MDSE. / ONLY / SO.
          RUB. STP. WKS. / RICHMOND, VA.
          FOR THE CONVENIENCE OF EMPLOYEES
          brass, 22mm, square, R10

C10   COWPENS MILLS STORE / 1932 / NOT TRANSFERABLE
          GOOD FOR / 10¢ / IN / MERCHANDISE ONLY
          brass, 26mm, round, R10

D1   (obverse similar to C10)
          GOOD FOR / 1¢ / IN MDSE. ONLY
          brass, 18mm, round, R10

E1   COWPENS MILLS STORE / 1933 / NOT TRANSFERABLE
          GOOD FOR / 1¢ / IN MDSE. ONLY
          brass, 18mm, round, R10

          The Cowpens Manufacturing Company, in business as early as 1893,
          underwent a name change in 1920 to Cowpens Mills, Inc. The company
          manufactured cotton goods and sheetings.

F5   SIMPSON - MOORE DRUG CO.
          GOOD FOR ONE / 5 / CENT / GLASS OF SODA
          brass, 24mm, round, R10
          This retail drug store operated in Cowpens between 1917 and 1919.

CROCKETVILLE   (Hampton County)   1430

A100 HENRY W. LIGHTSEY / CROCKETVILLE, / S.C.
          GOOD FOR / 1⁰⁰ / IN / MERCHANDISE.
          aluminum, 36mm, round, R7

A50   (obverse similar to A100)
          GOOD FOR / 50 / IN / MERCHANDISE.
          aluminum, 33mm, round, R7

A25   (obverse similar to A100)
          GOOD FOR / 25 / IN / MERCHANDISE
          aluminum, 29mm, round, R7

A10   (obverse similar to A100)
          GOOD FOR / 10¢ / IN MERCHANDISE
          aluminum, 24mm, round, R9

A5   (obverse similar to A100)
          GOOD FOR / 5 / IN / MERCHANDISE
          aluminum, 20mm, round, R7

CROCKETVILLE (Continued)   1430

B100   W. FRED LIGHTSEY, / CROCKETVILLE, / S.C. / NOT / TRANSFERABLE
GOOD FOR / 1⁰⁰ / IN / MERCHANDISE.
aluminum, 36mm, round, R6

B50   (obverse similar to B100)
GOOD FOR / 50 / IN / MERCHANDISE.
aluminum, 33mm, round, R6

B25   (obverse similar to B100)
GOOD FOR / 25 / IN / MERCHANDISE
aluminum, 29mm, round, R6

B10   (obverse similar to B100)
GOOD FOR / 10 / IN / MERCHANDISE
aluminum, 24mm, round, R7

B5   (obverse similar to B100)
GOOD FOR / 5 / IN / MERCHANDISE.
aluminum, 21mm, round, R7

The Lightsey brothers, W. Fred and Henry W., started in business around 1905. Originally, Fred ran a general store and Henry operated a general store and a sawmill. About 1910 they combined their businesses around 1910 into one large operation named the Lightsey Brothers, and moved it to the town of Miley shortly thereafter. (See Miley for more Lightsey Brothers tokens.)

DARLINGTON (Darlington County)   1450

A5   W. D. COGGESHALL / FLOYD / FARM / DARLINGTON, S.C.
GOOD FOR / 5¢ / IN MERCHANDISE
aluminum, 21mm, round, R10

W. D. Coggeshall was first listed in 1904, as a seller of general merchandise and fertilizer. In 1936 the W. D. Coggeshall Co. evolved into a department store.

B100   DARLINGTON MFG. CO. / 1⁰⁰ / D M / CO. / DARLINGTON, S.C.
(Orco - type IV, dated 1940)
brass, 32mm, round, cup-shaped c/o, R10

B50   (obverse similar to B100 except denomination 50)
(Orco - type IV, dated 1940)
nickel, 29mm, round, cup-shaped c/o, R10

B5   (obverse similar to B100 except denomination 5)
(Orco - type IV, dated 1940)
nickel, 20mm, round, cup-shaped c/o, R9

C1   (obverse similar to B100 except denomination 1)
(Orco - type IV, dated 1943)
red fiber, 17mm, round, cup-shaped c/o, R10

DARLINGTON   (Continued) 1450

D   DARLINGTON / MFG. CO. / SPOOLING
(blank)
     brass, 29mm, round, R10

E   DARLINGTON / MFG. CO. / 152 (serial #) / SPOOLING (all incuse)
(blank)
     brass, 29mm, round, R10

     One of the few cotton mills in the Pee Dee area of South Carolina, the Darlington Mfg. Co. was in business as early as 1893. The company, which specialized in cotton goods and print cloth, continued production into the 1940s.

F5   GOOD ONLY / AT / DARLINGTON / VENEER / COMPANY / INC.
GOOD FOR / 5¢ / IN MERCHANDISE
     aluminum, 20mm, round, R10

     The Darlington Veneer Company became incorporated around 1927 and is still operating. The token was probably used in the 1930s.

G   HARRIS MUSIC C⁰ / PIANOS, / ORGANS, / SHEET MUSIC / ETC. / DARLINGTON, S.C.
HARRIS MUSIC C⁰ / ALL KINDS / OF / SEWING / MACHINES / ETC. / DARLINGTON, S.C.
     aluminum, 30mm, round, R10

     The Harris Music Co. was listed under piano sales in 1904.

H5   IDEAL / STEAM / BAKERY, / DARLINGTON. S.C.
GOOD FOR / 5¢ / LOAF OF BREAD
     aluminum, 24mm, round, R9

DENMARK   (Bamberg County) 1465

A5   MATTHEWS DRUG STORE / 5 / DENMARK, / S.C.
5
     brass, 24mm, round, R10

     J. S. Matthews was listed in the retail drug business in 1908 and 1910.

B5   THE MAYFIELD CO. / DENMARK, / S.C.
GOOD FOR / 5¢ / IN MERCHANDISE
     brass, 21mm, round, R9

     This general store operated from 1913 to 1923. See listing under the town of Lees for another token of the company.

C   W. M. MOTTE / BAKERY / DENMARK / S.C.
GOOD FOR / ONE / CREAM LOAF
     brass, 29mm, scalloped (4), R9

     William M. Motte ran a bakery from 1908 to 1923.

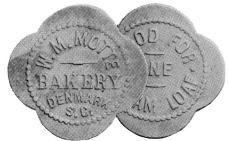

DILLON   (Dillon County)   1470

A25   DILLON / HIGH / SCHOOL / CAFETERIA
25 c / IN TRADE (across numerals)
aluminum, 29mm, round, R3

B25   J. V. MARTIN JR. HIGH SCHOOL
GOOD FOR / 25¢ / IN TRADE
brass, 29mm, round, R7

C100   W. C. TOLAR / MERCHANDISE / DILLON, S.C.
GOOD FOR / $1<u>00</u> / IN / MERCHANDISE / NOT TRANSFERABLE
brass, 31mm, round, R9

    W. C. Tolar ran a sawmill near Dillon for many years. Originally in partnership with a man named Wellington in 1908, he became the sole owner in 1912. He operated the sawmill himself until 1940, when the firm became known as W.C. Tolar & Son. In 1947 it was listed as the W. C. Tolar Lumber Company.

DONALDS   (Abbeville County)   1475

A5   DODSON & AGNEW
GOOD FOR / 5¢ / IN TRADE
aluminum, 19mm, round, R10

    Dodson & Agnew ran a general store from 1908 to around 1910.

DORLEN   (Georgetown County)   1485

A1   E. L. KELLY / DORLEN, / S.C.
GOOD FOR / 1¢ / IN TRADE   (varieties exist)
brass, 18mm, round, R9

DOVESVILLE   (Darlington County)   1490

A10   EDWARDS / LUMBER / CO. / DOVESVILLE / S.C.
GOOD FOR / 10¢ / IN MDSE.
aluminum, 18mm, round, R10

B5   EDWARDS LUMBER CO. / DOVESVILLE, / S.C.
GOOD FOR / 5 / IN MERCHANDISE
aluminum, 19mm, round, R10

C50   MASSIE LUMBER CO. / DOVESVILLE, / S.C.
GOOD FOR / 50 / IN / MERCHANDISE
brass, 31mm, round, R10

    The Massie Lumber Co. operated from 1904 to 1912.

DRAKE   (Marlboro County)   1495

A5   W. B. DRAKE / DRAKE, / S.C.
       GOOD FOR / 5 / IN MERCHANDISE
         brass, 19mm, round, R9

         W. B. Drake operated a general store from the 1890s to the 1920s.

DRAYTON   (Spartanburg County)   1500

A25   GOOD FOR / 25 / IN MERCHANDISE / DRAYTON MILL STORE
       FOR CONVENIENCE OF / EMPLOYEES / ONLY / NOT REDEEMABLE
       IN CASH
         aluminum, 27mm, round, R10

A5   (obverse similar to A25 except denomination 5)
       (reverse similar to A25)
         aluminum, 21mm, round, R9

B   DRAYTON MILL / STORE / DRAYTON, S.C.
       GOOD FOR MDSE. / WHEN / ACCOMPANIED / BY BOTTLE
         aluminum, 25mm, octagonal, R10

C100   DRAYTON MILLS STORE / 1$\underline{00}$ / DRAYTON, S.C.
       (Orco - type II)
         nickel, 32mm, round, square-shaped c/o, R10

C50   (obverse similar to C100 except denomination 50)
       (Orco - type II)
         brass, 27mm, round, square-shaped c/o, R10

C25   (obverse similar to C100 except denomination 25)
       (Orco - type II)
         nickel, 24mm, round, square-shaped c/o, R9

C10   (obverse similar to C100 except denomination 10)
       (Orco - type II)
         brass, 21mm, round, square-shaped c/o, R9

C5   (obverse similar to C100 except denomination 5)
       (Orco - type II)
         nickel, 19mm, round, square-shaped c/o, R9

C1   (obverse similar to C100 except denomination 1)
       (Orco - type II)
         copper, 18mm, round, square-shaped c/o, R7)

         Drayton Mills began operating before 1905 and continued into the 1950s. The company made cotton goods.

DUNBARTON (Barnwell County) 1510

A25 SOUTHERN STATES / LUMBER / CO. / DUNBARTON / S.C.
GOOD FOR / 25 / IN MERCHANDISE
aluminum, 29mm, round, R10

This company, which was headquartered in Pittsburgh, Pa., operated a sawmill in Dunbarton during 1912 and 1913.

EASLEY (Pickens County) 1525

A50 W. G. FRICKS / EASLEY, / S.C.
GOOD FOR / 50¢ / IN TRADE
aluminum, 29mm, round, R10

A25 (obverse similar to A50)
GOOD FOR / 25¢ / IN TRADE
aluminum, 26mm, round, R10

A10 (obverse similar to A50)
GOOD FOR / 10¢ / IN TRADE
aluminum, 23mm, round, R10

A5 (obverse similar to A50)
GOOD FOR / 5¢ / IN TRADE
aluminum, 20mm, round, R10

W. G. Fricks was first listed in the general merchandise business in 1912. Later he was listed as a grocer, and remained business until the early 1930s.

B15 GLENWOOD COTTON MILLS / 50 LBS. / EASLEY, S.C.
ICE CHECK / 15¢
aluminum, 29mm, round, R10

B7½ (obverse similar to B15 except denomination 25 LBS.)
ICE CHECK / 7½¢
aluminum, 25mm, round, R10

Glenwood Cotton Mills began operation before 1904 and continued through the 1940s. The company specialized in making sheeting and print cloth.

C5 T. E. HUNNICUTT / EASLEY, / S.C.
GOOD FOR / 5 / IN TRADE
brass, 19mm, round, R9

T. E. Hunnicutt sold groceries and meat during the teens. Some of his tokens are counterstamped with an "M".

D100 J. C. MUNDY & CO. / EASLEY / MILL / No. 1
GOOD FOR / 1⁰⁰ / IN / MERCHANDISE ONLY
brass, 31mm, round, R5

EASLEY   (Continued)   1525

D50   (obverse similar to D100)
GOOD FOR / 50 / IN / MERCHANDISE ONLY
brass, 28mm, round, R5

D25   (obverse similar to D100)
GOOD FOR / 25 / IN / MERCHANDISE ONLY
brass, 26mm, round, R5

D10   (obverse similar to D100)
GOOD FOR / 10 / IN / MERCHANDISE / ONLY
brass, 23mm, round, R5

D5   (obverse similar to D100)
GOOD FOR / 5 / IN / MERCHANDISE / ONLY
brass, 20mm, round, R10

J. C. Mundy & Co. was listed in 1923. Although there is no mention in that directory, it is presumed that this business operated the company store for Easley Mills.

EASTOVER   (Richland County)   1530

A100   J. M. GATES. / EASTOVER, / S.C.
GOOD FOR / 1⁰⁰ / IN / MERCHANDISE
aluminum, 35mm, round, R10

J. M. Gates ran a general store from 1904 to 1933.

EDDY LAKE   (Horry County)   1540

A100   THIS CHECK IS GOOD FOR / IN GOODS / AT THE STORE OF / EDDY LAKE CYPRESS CO. / G. OFFICER (actual signature) / SUBJECT TO DISCOUNT OF / 25% IF PAYABLE / IN CASH. / ONE DOLLAR
ONE DOLLAR / $1 / NOT TRANSFERABLE
gray cardboard, 37mm, round, R10

A25   (obverse similar to A100 except denomination TWENTY-FIVE CENTS)
TWENTY-FIVE CENTS / 25 / NOT TRANSFERABLE
lilac cardboard, 37mm, round, R10

This company operated a sawmill during the first decade of this century. The dock and shipping terminal were located in Port Harrelson.

EDGEFIELD   (Edgefield County)   1545

A   ADDISON MILLS / 529 (serial number) / TIME CHECK (all incuse)
(blank)
> brass, 36mm, square, holed as made, R10

> Addison Mills began operations in 1917. The company, which made cotton gauze and other hospital supplies, was bought out by Kendall Mills of Boston, Mass. in 1926.

B5   B. TIMMONS / EDGEFIELD / S.C.
GOOD FOR / 5¢ / IN TRADE
> aluminum, 19mm, round, R10

> B. Timmons ran a drug store from 1908 to 1912.

EFFINGHAM   (Florence County)   1555

A100   DARGAN LUMBER CO. / EFFINGHAM, / S.C.
GOOD FOR / 100 / IN / MERCHANDISE
> aluminum, 33mm, round, R9

B5   DARGAN / 5 / LUMBER CO.
GOOD FOR / 5 / IN MERCHANDISE
> aluminum, 24mm, round, R10

> This business was founded in Lynchburg, S.C. in 1900. It moved to Effingham about 1902 and operated there until 1915 when it moved again, this time to Pamplico. The company was sold in 1920.

EHRHARDT   (Bamberg County)   1558

A10   J. M. KIRKLAND & CO. / MERCHANTS / EHRHARDT, S.C.
GOOD FOR / 10¢ / IN MERCHANDISE
> aluminum, 25mm, round, R10

A5   (obverse similar to A10)
GOOD FOR / 5¢ / IN MERCHANDISE
> aluminum, 20mm, round, R10

> J. M. Kirkland operated a general store during the teens and twenties.

ELLENTON   (Aiken County)   1565

A100   ASHLEY CO. / ELLENTON, S.C.
GOOD FOR / $100 / IN MERCHANDISE
> brass, 28mm, round, R9

A50   (obverse similar to A100)
GOOD FOR / 50¢ / IN MERCHANDISE
> brass, 28mm, round, R8

A25 (obverse similar to A100)
GOOD FOR / 25¢ / IN MERCHANDISE
brass, 28mm, round, R9

A10 (obverse similar to A100)
GOOD FOR / 10¢ / IN MERCHANDISE
brass, 28mm, round, R9

This company was involved in several business endeavors — a sawmill, logging railroad, farm, and the commissary at which the tokens were used. It operated during the twenties and thirties.

B5 M. F. BUSH
GOOD FOR / 5¢ / IN MERCHANDISE
aluminum, 20mm, round, R10

During the 1920s and 1930s M. F. Bush operated a general store.

C100 H. M. CASSELS / ELLENTON, S.C.
GOOD FOR / $1⁰⁰ / IN MERCHANDISE
aluminum, 36mm, octagonal, R10

At one time or another H. M. Cassels operated a sawmill (1890s to 1914), telephone exchange (1913 to 1918), general store (1890s to 1930s), cotton gin (1908 to 1927), and fertilizer company (1921 to 1927). After 1932, the listing appears as Cassels Co., Inc. and is mentioned only as a general store. Local sources recall that it was called the "Long Store" because it ran the length of an entire block. The store's slogan was "We sell everything from a sword to a toothpick."

The entire town of Ellenton was moved about ten miles north and was renamed New Ellenton when the Savannah River Nuclear Weapons Plant was built.

ELLIOTT (Lee County)   1570

A50 J. S. BROWN / ELLIOTT, / S.C.
50
aluminum, 33mm, round, R10

A5 (obverse similar to A50)
5
aluminum, 19mm, round, R10

J. S. Brown ran a general store during the late 1890s and early 1900s.

ELLOREE (Orangeburg County) 1575

A100 THE FARMER'S BANK / 4% / PAID / ON SAVINGS / PARLER, S.C. /
ELLOREE, S.C.
GOOD FOR / $1.00 / WHEN / ACCOMPANIED BY / $100.00 /
SAVINGS DEPOSIT
aluminum, 38mm, round, R10

EMBREE (Bamberg County) 1580

A10 EDISTO RIVER / LUMBER / CO. / EMBREE, / S.C.
GOOD FOR / 10¢ / IN / MERCHANDISE
aluminum, 23mm, round, R10

B5 EDISTO RIVER LUMBER CO. / EMBREE, / S.C.
GOOD FOR / 5 / IN TRADE / & / NOT TRANSFERABLE
aluminum, 27mm, octagonal, R10

This company, which operated during the late teens and early twenties,
was headquartered at Chicago, Illinois. The town of Embree was not much
more than a railroad watering stop where the Southern Railroad passed
over the Edisto River.

ENOREE (Spartanburg County) 1585

A100 ENOREE MFG. COMPANY / 1 / ENOREE, / S.C.
GOOD FOR / ONE / 1 / DOLLAR / IN MERCHANDISE
aluminum, 29mm, round, R8

A50 (obverse similar to A100 except denomination 50)
GOOD FOR / 50 / CENTS / IN MERCHANDISE
aluminum, 27mm, round, R10

A25 (obverse similar to A100 except denomination 25)
GOOD FOR / 25 / CENTS / IN MERCHANDISE
aluminum, 24mm, round, R10

A5 (obverse similar to A100 except denomination 5)
GOOD FOR / 5 / CENTS / IN MERCHANDISE
aluminum, 19mm, round, R9

B100 ENOREE MILL STORE / ENOREE, / S.C.
GOOD FOR / 1\frac{00}{}$ / IN MDSE. ONLY
aluminum, 35mm, round, R10

B50 (obverse similar to B100)
GOOD FOR / 50¢ / IN MDSE. ONLY
aluminum, 31mm, round, R8

The Enoree Mfg. Co. was in operation as early as 1893. In the late
1920s it was purchased by Riverdale Mills of Spartanburg.

Post Office Block, Fairfax, S. C.

This postcard view of Fairfax, S.C. was taken circa 1910.

A100   F. G. CRADDOCK / 1$\underline{00}$
      (Ingle System - 1909 pat. date)
      copper, 35mm, round, R10

A5   (obverse similar to A100 except denomination 5)
      (Ingle System - 1909 pat. date)
      copper, 20mm, round, R10

      Francis Gordon Craddock ran a general store from the early teens to
the late twenties.

B5   FAIRFAX COOL SPOT / FAIRFAX / S.C.
      GOOD FOR / 5¢ / IN TRADE
      aluminum, 19mm, round, R10

C25   H. R. HARTER / 25
      (Ingle System - 1909 pat. date)
      unknown composition, 24mm, round, R10

      During the teens and the early twenties H. R. Harter operated a general
store. Obverse inscription may not be exact.

D100   T. T. SPEAKS / 1$\underline{00}$
      (Ingle System - 1909 pat. date)
      brass, 35mm, round, R10

      T. T. Speaks operated a grocery store during the early teens.

E   THOMAS' / DAIRY / FAIRFAX / S.C.
      GOOD FOR / 1 / QT. / PASTEURIZED MILK
      aluminum, 21mm, round, R10

FAIRMONT   (Spartanburg County)   1615

A5   UNION - BUFFALO / FAIRMONT / S.C. / MILLS STORE
GOOD FOR / 5¢ (within wreath) / IN MERCHANDISE
nickel, 20mm, round, R10

B500 UNION BUFFALO MILLS STORE / 5$\underline{00}$ / FAIRMONT, S.C.
(Orco - type I)
nickel, 32mm, scalloped (12), "F" c/o, R10

B10   (obverse similar to B500 except denomination 10)
(Orco - type II)
nickel, 21mm, round, "F" c/o, R8

B5   (obverse similar to B500 except denomination 5)
(Orco - type II)
nickel, 19mm, round, "F" c/o, R8

B1   (obverse similar to B500 except denomination 1)
(Orco - type II and type III varieties exist)
nickel, 18mm, round, "F" c/o, R5

Union - Buffalo Mills, headquartered in Union, operated the cotton mill in Fairmont from the late 1920s through the 1940s.

FERGUSON   (Berkeley County)   1630

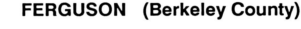

A100 SANTEE MERCANTILE CO. / NOT / TRANSFERABLE / FERGUSON, S.C.
GOOD FOR / 1$\underline{00}$ / PATD. / JULY 1899. / IN MERCHANDISE
bimetallic, 39mm, round, R4

A50   (obverse similar to A100)
GOOD FOR / 50 / PAT / APPLD FOR / IN MERCHANDISE
bimetallic, 32mm, round, R4

A25   (obverse similar to A100)
GOOD FOR / 25 / PAT / APPLD FOR / IN MERCHANDISE
bimetallic, 28mm, round, R4

A10   (obverse similar to A100)
GOOD FOR / 10 / PAT / APPLD FOR / IN MERCHANDISE
bimetallic, 25mm, round, R4

A5   (obverse similar to A100)
GOOD FOR / 5 / PATD. / JULY 1899. / IN MERCHANDISE
bimetallic, 20mm, round, R4

The Santee Mercantile Co. operated as the company store for the Santee River Cypress Lumber Co. (see listings which follow).

B100 SANTEE RIVER CYPRESS LUMBER CO. / FERGUSON, / BERKELEY CO. / S.C.
GOOD FOR / 1 / DOLLAR / IN / MERCHANDISE
aluminum, 35mm, round, R10

FRANCIS BEIDLER, Pres't. & Treas.
CHICAGO, ILL.

M. BAUGHMAN CROSS, Secy
FERGUSON, S.C.

F. R. SEELEY, Gen'l. Mgr.
MANF'G. AND SALES
FERGUSON, S. C.

SANTEE RIVER CYPRESS LUMBER CO.

SALES
DEPARTMENT

MANUFACTURERS OF
AND DEALERS IN

SHINGLES AND LATH.
HARDWOODS.

CYPRESS LUMBER.

SAP GUM
RED GUM, CYPRESS,
BAY POPLAR, OAK,
COTTONWOOD, PINE,
ASH, HICKORY,
ELM, SYCAMORE,
MAPLE

PLANING MILL
MOULDINGS,
BALUSTERS,
PICKETS,
BOX SHOOKS.

AMERICAN LUMBERMAN TELECODE
AND SOUTHARDS CODE.

IN REPLY PLEASE MENTION INITIALS.

FERGUSON, ORANGEBURG. Co. S.C.

A letterhead of the Santee River Cypress Lumber Co.

B10   (obverse similar to B100)
         GOOD FOR / 10 / CENTS / IN / MERCHANDISE
         aluminum, 25mm, round, R10

B5   (obverse similar to B100)
         GOOD FOR / 5 / CENTS / IN / MERCHANDISE
         aluminum, 21mm, round, R10

C100   SANTEE RIVER CYPRESS LUMBER CO. / FERGUSON, / S.C.
         GOOD FOR / 100 / IN MERCHANDISE
         aluminum, 36mm, round, R4

C10   (obverse similar to C100)
         GOOD FOR / 10 / IN MERCHANDISE
         aluminum, 24mm, round, R10

C5   (obverse similar to C100)
         GOOD FOR / 5 / IN MERCHANDISE
         aluminum, 19mm, round, R10

D100   (obverse and reverse similar to C100 but slightly smaller and struck with
         different dies)
         aluminum, 35mm, round, R4

E50   SANTEE RIVER CYPRESS LBR. CO.
         GOOD FOR / 50¢ / IN MERCHANDISE
         aluminum, 29mm, octagonal, R4

E25   (obverse similar to E50)
         GOOD FOR / 25¢ / IN MERCHANDISE
         aluminum, 28mm, round, R4

E10   (obverse similar to E50)
GOOD FOR / 10¢ / IN MERCHANDISE
aluminum, 22mm, octagonal, R4

E5   (obverse similar to E50)
GOOD FOR / 5¢ / IN MERCHANDISE
aluminum, 20mm, round, R4

This company, which was headquartered in Chicago, was in business as early as 1893. It operated a sawmill until the early 1920s. The town no longer exists, as the entire area was covered with water when Lake Marion was constructed.

FINGERVILLE (Spartanburg County)   1635

A10   COHANNET / 1922 / MILLS
GOOD FOR / 10 / IN / MERCHANDISE
aluminum, 24mm, round, R10

B5   COHANNET / MILLS / FINGERVILLE / S.C.
GOOD FOR / 5 / IN MERCHANDISE
aluminum, 22mm, round, R10

Cohannet Mills was in operation from 1912 to the mid-1920s, when it was taken over by Franklin Process Spinning Mills (see listings which follow). The mill specialized in the manufacture of cotton yarns.

C100   FRANKLIN PROCESS SPINNING MILLS INC. / 1930
GOOD FOR / $1.00 / IN / MERCHANDISE / ONLY
brass, 35mm, round, R8

C50   (obverse similar to C100)
GOOD FOR / 50¢ / IN / MERCHANDISE / ONLY
brass, 31mm, round, R8

C25   (obverse similar to C100)
GOOD FOR / 25¢ / IN / MERCHANDISE / ONLY
brass, 28mm, round, R8

C10   (obverse similar to C100)
GOOD FOR / 10¢ / IN / MERCHANDISE ONLY
brass, 26mm, round, R8

D5   (obverse similar to C100)
GOOD FOR / 5¢ / IN MDSE. ONLY
brass, 20mm, round, R8

In the mid-1920s Franklin Process Spinning Mills took over the mill in Fingerville, and operated it through the 1960s. The company's headquarters was located in Providence, Rhode Island.

The town was named for its founder, John Finger, who was the owner-operator of one of the earliest cotton mills in the state.

A5 　ELLERBE'S / PHONE / 48
　　　GOOD FOR / 5 / IN / MERCHANDISE.
　　　　aluminum, 22mm, round, R10

　　　　A. Clyde Ellerbe operated a drug store at 201 E. Evans Street from the
early teens to the late twenties.

B 　FLORENCE COACH COMPANY / (picture of bus)
　　　GOOD FOR / (picture of bus) / ONE FARE
　　　　zinc, 16mm, round, c/o, R4   (Atwood 430A)

C 　(obverse and reverse same as B)
　　　　steel, 16mm, round, c/o, R4   (Atwood 430B)

D 　(obverse and reverse same as B)
　　　　brass, 16mm, round, c/o, R4   (Atwood 430C)

E 　(obverse and reverse same as B)
　　　　nickel, 16mm, round, c/o, R4   (Atwood 430D)

　　　　In 1942 the Florence Coach Company began operating buses in
Florence. The company was in business through the late 1940s and
possibly into the 1950s. A total of 21,000 tokens were struck of the above
four varieties.

F100 　THE FLORENCE DAILY TIMES / GOOD FOR / ONE DOLLAR IN TRADE /
　　　AT ANY / STORE IN FLORENCE / IN PAYMENT FOR / DOLLAR DAY
　　　BARGAINS / ADVERTISED IN THE / FLORENCE / DAILY TIMES /
　　　DOLLAR DAY DOLLAR
　　　　GOOD FOR ONE DOLLAR IN TRADE / (picture of female shopper) /
　　　　1\underline{00}$
　　　　　brass, 38mm, round, R10

G100 　FLORENCE V.F.W. POST #3181 / ALL / AMERICA / CITY / FLORENCE,
　　　S.C. (all incuse)
　　　　GOOD FOR / 1\underline{00}$ / IN TRADE (all incuse)
　　　　copper, 38mm, round, R9, modern

　　　　Probably this was a slot machine token used in the 1960s.

H10 　HERRING BROTHERS / 10
　　　　(Ingle System - 1909 pat. date)
　　　　brass, 21mm, round, R10

H5 　(obverse similar to H10 except denomination 5)
　　　　(Ingle System - 1909 pat. date)
　　　　brass, 20mm, round, R10

H1 　(obverse similar to H10 except denomination 1)
　　　　(Ingle System - 1909 pat. date)
　　　　brass, 18mm, round, R10

　　　　The Herring Brothers operated a general store in Florence from the
early 1900s into the early 1920s.

I10   HOLMES SCHOOL / FLORENCE / S.C.
       GOOD FOR / 10¢ / IN MERCHANDISE
       brass, 26mm, round, R9

I1   (obverse similar to I10)
       GOOD FOR / 1¢ / IN / MERCHANDISE
       brass, 16mm, round, R10

J5   HOLMES / SCHOOL / FLORENCE / S.C.
       GOOD FOR / 5¢ / IN TRADE
       brass, 23mm, round, R9

The Charles Ingram Lumber Company's letterhead.

K100   CHARLES INGRAM STORE, INC. / FLORENCE, / S.C.
       GOOD FOR / $1⁰⁰ / IN MERCHANDISE
       aluminum, 31mm, round, R6

K50   (obverse similar to K100)
       GOOD FOR / 50¢ / IN MERCHANDISE
       aluminum, 28mm, round, R7

K25   (obverse similar to K100)
       GOOD FOR / 25¢ / IN MERCHANDISE
       aluminum, 26mm, round, R6

K10   (obverse similar to K100)
       GOOD FOR / 10¢ / IN MERCHANDISE
       aluminum, 25mm, round, R10

    The Charles Ingram Store operated as company store for the Dargan - Ingram Lumber Co. in the 1930s. Later, it was the commissary for the Charles Ingram Lumber Co.

L   KAFER'S / BAKERY
       GOOD FOR / ONE LOAF / BREAD
       brass, 26mm, round, R10

    Arthur O. Kafer operated a bakery and confectionery as early as 1904 and as late as 1947.

FLORENCE (Continued) 1645

M SELECTED DAIRIES / INC. / FLORENCE, S.C.
GOOD FOR / 1 / QT. / HOMOGENIZED MILK
aluminum, 23mm, round, R8

N (obverse similar to M)
GOOD FOR / 1 / QT. / PASTEURIZED MILK
aluminum, 19mm, square, R9

O (obverse similar to M)
GOOD FOR / ½ / PT. / CREAM
aluminum, 26mm, scalloped (4), R10

P (obverse similar to M)
GOOD FOR / 1 / QT. / CHOCOLATE MILK
aluminum, 23mm, octagonal, R10

FORT JACKSON (Richland County) 1660

A FORT JACKSON / S.C.
(insignia of the 8th Army)
nickel, 21mm, round, R5 (Curto F80)

B (obverse and reverse same as A)
brass, 21mm, round, R5

These were probably some sort of slot machine tokens. See Camp Jackson for a detailed history of the fort.

FORT MOTTE (Calhoun County) 1670

A100 W. C. HANE (all incuse)
1⁰⁰ / IN TRADE (all incuse)
brass, 20mm, round, R9 (varieties exist)

A50 (obverse same as A100)
50¢ / IN TRADE (all incuse)
brass, 20mm, round, R9

A25 (obverse same as A100)
25¢ / IN TRADE (all incuse)
brass, 20mm, round, R9

A10 (obverse same as A100)
10¢ / IN TRADE (all incuse)
brass, 20mm, round, R9

FORT MOTTE   (Continued)   1670

A5   (obverse same as A100)
              5¢ / IN TRADE (all incuse)
              brass, 20mm, round, R9

              Around the turn of the century W. C. Hane operated a small general
              store near the site of the old Hickory Grove Plantation, approximately two
              miles from Fort Motte.

FORT MOULTRIE   (Charleston County)   1675

A10   POST EXCHANGE / 10¢ / FORT MOULTRIE, S.C. (all incuse)
              (incuse picture of a key)
              brass, 35mm, round, R9 (Curto F137-10)

A5   (obverse similar to A10 except denomination 5¢)
              (blank)
              brass, 29mm, round, R9 (Curto F137-5)

B50   POST EXCHANGE / FORT / MOULTRIE. (counterstamped "PX")
              GOOD FOR / 50¢ / IN TRADE
              brass, 29mm, round, R9

B25   (obverse similar to B50) (varieties exist)
              GOOD FOR / 25 / CENTS / IN TRADE
              brass, 25mm, round, R8

Fort Moultrie, as depicted on a postcard.

FORT MOULTRIE   (Continued)   1675

B10 (obverse similar to B50)
GOOD FOR / 10¢ / IN TRADE
brass, 21mm, round, R10 (Curto F138)

C10 POST EXCHANGE / 10 / FORT MOULTRIE, S.C.
P 10 E
aluminum, 26mm, octagonal, R9 (Curto F327)

Fort Moultrie, originally built for the defense of Charleston Harbor against British warships during the Revolutionary War, is one of South Carolina's most historic landmarks. In 1862, it participated in the opening salvo of the Civil War when Confederate gunners fired upon Union-held Fort Sumter. The fort was also garrisoned during the Spanish-American War, and World Wars I & II. The site is now a National Historic Monument and is operated by the National Park Service.

FOUNTAIN INN   (Greenville County)   1685

A FOUNTAIN INN M'F'G. CO.
80 (incuse serial #)
brass, 23mm, round, R10

This was probably some type of production token. The Fountain Inn Mfg. Co. made cotton yarns and damasks circa 1900 to 1917.

B5 REDICK'S / PHARMACY / FOUNTAIN / INN, / S.C.
GOOD FOR / 5¢ / IN TRADE
aluminum, 19mm, round, R10

M. E. Redick ran a drug store from 1912 to 1936.

C5 J. E. RODGERS / FOUNTAIN INN, / S.C.
GOOD FOR / A 5¢ / DRINK
aluminum, 20mm, round, R10

J. E. Rodgers operated a grocery store during the early 1920s.

FROGMORE   (Beaufort County)   1695

A8 GOOD FOR / 8¢ / GEO. W. LOWDEN / AT FROGMORE / FACTORY
NOT TRANSFERABLE / PAYABLE / TO / 8¢ / EMPLOYEES ONLY
aluminum, 25mm, round, R10

George W. Lowden operated a large oyster packing company during the early 1900s. The main cannery was located in Savannah, Ga. with branches in Frogmore and Bluffton, S.C.

GABLE (Clarendon County)   1705

A100   CHRISTAL STORE / GABLE, S.C.
       GOOD FOR / 1$\underline{00}$ / (aluminum center partially illegible) / IN
       MERCHANDISE
       bimetallic, 38mm, round, R10

A10   (obverse similar to A100)
       GOOD FOR / 10 / PAT. / APPLD FOR / IN MERCHANDISE
       bimetallic, 24mm, round, R10

A7½   (obverse similar to A100)
       GOOD FOR / 7½ / PAT. / JULY 1899 / IN MERCHANDISE
       bimetallic, 22mm, octagonal, R10

A5   (obverse similar to A100)
       GOOD FOR / 5 / (aluminum center partially illegible) / IN
       MERCHANDISE
       bimetal, 20mm, round, R10

       This establishment was listed as a general store from 1917 to 1930.

GAFFNEY (Cherokee County)   1710

A5   CHEROKEE DRUG CO. / GAFFNEY, / S.C.
       GOOD FOR / 5 / CENT / DRINK
       aluminum, 24mm, round, R9

       The Cherokee Drug Company operated from 1904 to 1940.

B50   ERWIN & CO. INC. / 50 / GAFFNEY, S.C.
       (Orco - type II)
       copper, 27mm, round, "E" c/o, R10

B10   (obverse similar to B50 except denomination 10)
       (Orco - type II)
       brass, 21mm, round, "E" c/o, R8

B5   (obverse similar to B50 except denomination 5)
       (Orco - type II) (varieties exist)
       copper, 19mm, round, "E" c/o, R8

       Operating in the late 30s and early 40s, this general store may have
       served as company store for one of the cotton mills in the area.

C5   C. C. HUMPHRIES (incuse) / GOOD FOR / 5¢ / GAFFNEY (incuse)
       (blank)
       brass, 23mm, round, R10

D100   LIMESTONE MILLS STORE / 1$\underline{00}$ / GAFFNEY, S.C.
       (Orco - type I)
       nickel, 32mm, round, R9

D50   (obverse similar to D100 except denomination 50)
       (Orco - type I)
       nickel, 27mm, round, R9)

D25 (obverse similar to D100 except denomination 25)
(Orco - type I)
nickel, 24mm, round, R8

D10 (obverse similar to D100 except denomination 10)
(Orco - type I)
nickel, 21mm, round, R8

D5 (obverse similar to D100 except denomination 5)
(Orco - type I and type II varieties exist)
nickel, 19mm, round, R7

E50 (obverse similar to D100 except denomination 50)
(Orco - type I)
brass, 27mm, round, R9

E10 (obverse similar to D100 except denomination 10)
(Orco - type I)
brass, 21mm, round, R9

E1 (obverse similar to D100 except denomination 1)
(Orco - type I, type II, and type III varieties exist)
brass, 18mm, round, R4

F100 LIMESTONE MILLS STORE / 1⁰⁰ / GAFFNEY, N.C. (die-cutting error)
(Orco - type I)
nickel, 32mm, round, R9

G100 LIMESTONE / MILLS STORE / GAFFNEY, S.C.
GOOD FOR / $1⁰⁰ / IN / MERCHANDISE
aluminum, 35mm, round, R9

G25 (obverse similar to G100)
GOOD FOR / 25¢ / IN MERCHANDISE
aluminum, 27mm, round, R8

G10 (obverse similar to G100)
GOOD FOR / 10¢ / IN MERCHANDISE
aluminum, 25mm, round, R8

G1 (obverse similar to G100)
GOOD FOR / 1¢ / IN MDSE.
aluminum, 19mm, round, R8

H1 (obverse similar to G100)
GOOD FOR / 1¢ / IN MDSE.
aluminum, 18mm, octagonal, R8

I100 LIMESTONE MILLS STORE / GAFFNEY, / S.C.
GOOD FOR / 100 / IN MERCHANDISE
aluminum, 35mm, round, R8

I50 (obverse similar to I100)
GOOD FOR / 50 / IN MERCHANDISE
aluminum, 33mm, round, R8

I25 (obverse similar to I100)
GOOD FOR / 25 / IN MERCHANDISE
aluminum, 29mm, round, R8

I10 (obverse similar to I100)
GOOD FOR / 10 / IN MERCHANDISE
aluminum, 24mm, round, R8

I5 (obverse similar to I100)
GOOD FOR / 5 / IN MERCHANDISE
aluminum, 19mm, round, R8

Specializing in the manufacture of print cloth, Limestone Mills was in business as early as 1904; it continued to operate through the 1940s.

J5 LIPSCOMB & RICHARDSON / GAFFNEY, / S.C.
GOOD FOR / 5 / IN MERCHANDISE
aluminum, 20mm, round, R9

K5 J. L. MOREHEAD / GAFFNEY, S.C.
GOOD FOR / 5¢ / IN MERCHANDISE
aluminum, 19mm, round, R10

J. L. Morehead operated a grocery store and confectionery during the teens.

L5 PEELER & LEMMOND / GROCERS / GAFFNEY, S.C.
GOOD FOR ONE / 5¢ / GLASS OF SODA.
aluminum, 25mm, round, R10

M RAPID TRANSIT CO. / ZONE / 1
(blank)
white fiber, 20mm, round, R6 (Atwood 450A)

N RAPID TRANSIT CO. / ZONE / 2
(blank)
gray fiber, 23mm, round, R6 (Atwood 450B)

O RAPID TRANSIT CO. / ZONE / 3
(blank)
red fiber, 27mm, round, R6 (Atwood 450C)

P RAPID TRANSIT COMPANY / (picture of bus) / GAFFNEY, S.C.
ZONE ONE / (picture of bus)
brass, 16mm, round, c/o, R6 (Atwood 450D)

Q (obverse similar to P)
ZONE TWO / (picture of bus)
nickel, 23mm, round, c/o, R6 (Atwood 450E)

Bus service in Gaffney began prior to World War II, but tokens were not used until then. The fiber tokens (M, N, and O) were used during the War, while the metal varieties (P and Q) were struck in 1948. 7000 specimens of P were struck, and 2000 of Q.

GAFFNEY (Continued)   1710

R100   L. C. RODGERS / 1⁰⁰ / GAFFNEY, S.C.
(Ingle System - 1909 pat. date)
brass, 35mm, round, R10

R25   (obverse similar to R100 except denomination 25)
(Ingle System - 1909 pat. date)
brass, 24mm, round, R10

R5   L. C. RODGERS / 5
(Ingle System - 1909 pat. date)
brass, 20mm, round, R9

R1   (obverse similar to R5 except denomination 1)
(Ingle System - 1909 pat. date)
brass, 18mm, round, R9

During the teens and twenties Rodgers ran a grocery store and meat counter.

GALIVANTS FERRY (Horry County)   1715

A200   THIS CHECK IS GOOD FOR / IN GOODS / AT THE STORE OF / GEO. J.
HOLLIDAY (actual signature) / TWO DOLLARS
TWO DOLLARS / $2 / NOT TRANSFERABLE
gray cardboard, 37mm, round, R9

A100   (obverse similar to A200 except denomination ONE DOLLAR)
ONE DOLLAR / $1 / NOT TRANSFERABLE
orange cardboard, 37mm, round, R9

A50   (obverse similar to A200 except denomination FIFTY CENTS)
FIFTY CENTS / 50 / NOT TRANSFERABLE
white cardboard, 37mm, round, R9

A25   (obverse similar to A200 except denomination TWENTY-FIVE CENTS)
TWENTY-FIVE CENTS / 25 / NOT TRANSFERABLE
yellow cardboard, 37mm, round, R9

A10   (obverse similar to A200 except denomination TEN CENTS)
TEN CENTS / 10 / NOT TRANSFERABLE
red cardboard, 37mm, round, R9

A5   (obverse similar to A200 except denomination FIVE CENTS)
FIVE CENTS / 5 / NOT TRANSFERABLE
blue cardboard, 37mm, round, R9

George J. Holliday took over operation of the family business sometime around the turn of the century. At that time it consisted of a general store and turpentine still. During the twenties and thirties, branch stores were opened in Aynor and Jordanville. The business, which still operates today as Pee Dee Farms Corporation, is mainly involved in tobacco-growing and real estate.

A50   A.C.L. CO. / R. L. MONTAGUE (facsimile signature) / TREAS. / GEORGETOWN, S.C.
    GOOD FOR / 50¢ (within wreath) / IN MDSE. ONLY
    bimetallic, 31mm, round, R10

A5   (obverse similar to A50)
    GOOD FOR / 5¢ (within wreath) / IN MDSE. ONLY
    bimetallic, 21mm, round, R8

A1   (obverse similar to A50)
    GOOD FOR / 1¢ (within wreath) / IN MDSE. ONLY
    bimetallic, 19mm, round, R10

B100 ATLANTIC COAST / LUMBER Co. / 1⁰⁰ / GEORGETOWN, S.C.
    GOOD FOR / 1⁰⁰ / IN MERCHANDISE ONLY
    aluminum, 23mm x 45mm, rectangular, R10

B5   (obverse similar to B100 except denomination 5)
    GOOD FOR / 5 / IN / MERCHANDISE ONLY
    aluminum, 17mm x 26mm, rectangular, R10

C25   ATLANTIC COAST LUMBER CO. / 25 / GEORGETOWN, S.C.
    GOOD FOR / 25 / IN MERCHANDISE ONLY
    aluminum, 29mm, octagonal, R10

C5   (obverse similar to C25 except denomination 5)
    GOOD FOR / 5 / IN MERCHANDISE ONLY
    aluminum, 22mm, octagonal, R10

D50   A.C.L. CORPORATION / E. L. LLOYD (facsimile signature) / ASST. TREAS. / GEORGETOWN, S.C.
    GOOD FOR / 50 / PAT / APPLD FOR / IN MERCHANDISE
    bimetallic, 32mm, round, R10

D25   (obverse similar to D50)
    GOOD FOR / 25 / PAT / APPLD FOR / IN MERCHANDISE
    bimetallic, 27mm, round, R10

D10   (obverse similar to D50)
    GOOD FOR / 10 / PAT / APPLD FOR / IN MERCHANDISE
    bimetallic, 25mm, round, R8

D5   (obverse similar to D50)
    GOOD FOR / 5 / PAT. JULY 1899 / IN MERCHANDISE
    bimetallic, 20mm, round, R9

E50   A.C.L. CORP'N / F. S. FARR (facsimile signature) / PRES'T / GEORGETOWN, S.C.
    GOOD FOR / 50¢ / IN MDSE. ONLY
    bimetallic, 31mm, round, R10

FREEMAN S. FARR, President & Gen'l Mgr.   FRANCIS GORDON BROWN, Vice President   H. M. SADLER, JR., Treasurer.   E. L. LLOYD, Secretary.

Atlantic Coast Lumber Co.

GEORGETOWN, S.C.
CAPACITY OF MILLS 600.000 FEET PER DAY
OF ELEVEN HOURS.

OFFICES,

NEW YORK, N.Y.   BOSTON, MASS.

NORFOLK, VA.   GEORGETOWN, S.C.

PLEASE ADDRESS ALL
CORRESPONDENCE TO THE COMPANY.

Georgetown, S.C. Dec. 10, 1902.   *190*

This letterhead provides a panoramic view of the Atlantic Coast Lumber
Company's Georgetown mill.

F50   A.C.L. CORP'N / GEORGETOWN, S.C. / F. S. FARR (facsimile signature)
/ PRES'T / GOOD ONLY IN / LOGGING DEPT
     GOOD FOR / 50¢ / IN MDSE. ONLY
       bimetallic with square aluminum center, 31mm, round, R10

F5   (obverse similar to F50 except period after DEPT)
     GOOD FOR / 5¢ / IN MDSE. ONLY
       bimetallic with square aluminum center, 21mm, round, R10

G5   A.C.L. CORP'N / (facsimile signature illegible) / GOOD ONLY IN /
LOGGING DEPT.
     GOOD FOR / 5 / PAT. / JULY 1899 / IN MERCHANDISE
       bimetallic with square aluminum center, 20mm, round, R10

H   ATLANTIC COAST LUMBER CORPORATION / MONTH OF / 906
(serial #) / FEBRUARY / 1911 / GEORGETOWN, S.C.
     THIS CHECK NOT / NEGOTIABLE OR TRANSFER- / ABLE, ISSUED
FOR PURPOSES / OF IDENTIFICATION AND RECEIPT. /
EMPLOYES' (sic) TIME CHECK / SURRENDER OF THIS CHECK
WILL / CONSTITUTE YOUR RECEIPT FOR / WAGES IN FULL FOR
MONTH / STAMPED ON REVERSE / SIDE.
     green cardboard, 42mm, round, holed as made, R10

I   ATLANTIC COAST LUMBER CO. / 194 (incuse serial #) /
GEORGETOWN, S.C.
     (same except for no serial #)
     brass, 24mm, round, R9

J   ATLANTIC COAST LUMBER CO. / MAY / 574 (serial #) / LOGGING
        DEPT. / GEORGETOWN, S.C. (all incuse)
           (blank)
              brass, 36mm, round, holed as made, R9

K   ATLANTIC COAST LUMBER CO. / 3723 (serial #) / GEORGETOWN, S.C.
        (all incuse)
           (blank)
              brass, 36mm, round, holed as made, R9

L   A.C.L. CORP'N. / 1801 (serial #) / OCT. 1913 / LOG DEPT. (all incuse)
           (blank)
              aluminum, 36mm, round, holed as made, R9

        The Atlantic Coast Lumber Company was formed in 1899 when the
potential value of the vast amounts of standing timber in Georgetown
County was discovered by a group of Northern lumbermen. Options were
taken by the company on this timber and that of surrounding counties. A
large sawmill was built west of town and production began. In 1903 the
company was incorporated with a capital of 1 million dollars.
        The mill was expanded through the years, and included three separate
sawmills, two shipping wharves, several warehouses, and numerous other
buildings, including workers' houses, stores, a hotel, a church, etc. In 1913,
a disastrous fire destroyed two of the sawmills. A new steel and concrete
mill was erected within 10 months. At peak production, the company could
produce 600,000 feet of lumber per day and was properly proclaimed "the
largest lumber manufacturing plant on the Atlantic Coast." Due to the
effects of the Great Depression, the plant was closed in 1932.

M25   EMBA / CAFETERIA / GEORGETOWN, / S.C.
            25 c / IN TRADE (across numerals)
               aluminum, 28mm, round, R10

M10   (obverse similar to M25)
            10 c / IN TRADE (across numerals)
               aluminum, 26mm, round, R9

M5   (obverse similar to M25)
            5 c / IN TRADE (across numeral)
               aluminum, 22mm, round, R9

M1   (obverse similar to M25)
            1 c / IN TRADE (across numeral)
               aluminum, 16mm, round, R10

N   GEORGETOWN COUNTY SCHOOLS
            GOOD FOR / 1 / MEAL / ELEMENTARY
               aluminum, 22mm, round, R10

O   LAFAYETTE BRIDGE: it is believed that the tokens listed in the Atwood -
        Coffee catalog for this company were never issued. A quantity was
        ordered from the token manufacturer, but none have ever been
        discovered in the state.

GEORGETOWN (Continued) 1730

P50 SAMPIT CONTRACTING / COMPANY / (facsimile signature not readable)
GOOD FOR / 50¢ / IN MERCHANDISE
aluminum, 31mm, octagonal, R10

This company had business dealings with the Atlantic Coast Lumber
Company, so it was probably related in some way to the lumber industry.

GILLESPIE SIDING (Chesterfield County) 1740

A10 W. T. HENDRICK JR. / GILLESPIE / SDG. / S.C.
GOOD FOR / 10 / IN MERCHANDISE
brass, 24mm, round, R10

W. T. Hendrick, Jr. operated a general store and cotton gin during the
teens and twenties.

GIVHANS (Dorchester County) 1745

A25 T. J. WRIGHT / 25
(Ingle System - 1909 pat. date)
composition unknown, 24mm, round, R10

Attribution tentative. T. J. Wright operated a general store from 1908
through 1916. Obverse description may not be exact. The token appears
only because of its inclusion in Wagaman's catalog of Ingle System tokens.

GLENDALE (Spartanburg County) 1750

A200 THE D. E. CONVERSE CO. / WILL PAY / $2⁰⁰ / IN / MDSE. ONLY
FOR THE CONVENIENCE OF EMPLOYEES
brass, 27mm, square, R10

A100 (obverse similar to A200 except denomination $1⁰⁰)
(reverse similar to A200)
brass, 28mm, scalloped (8), R9

A50 (obverse similar to A200 except denomination 50¢)
(reverse similar to A200)
brass, 29mm, round, R10

A25 (obverse similar to A200 except denomination 25¢)
(reverse similar to A200)
brass, 26mm, octagonal, R9

A10 (obverse similar to A200 except denomination 10¢)
(reverse similar to A200)
brass, 24mm, square with clipped corners, R9

Dexter Edgar Converse, founder of the D. E. Converse Company.

A5   (obverse similar to A200 except denomination 5¢)
           (reverse similar to A 200)
              brass, 22mm, round, R7

A1   (obverse similar to A200 except denomination 1c)
           (reverse similar to A200)
              brass, 18mm, round, R8

Dexter Edgar Converse began his career in the textile business in 1855, as an employee at the Bivingsville Mill. In 1870, with his brother-in-law A. H. Twichell, he purchased the mill and changed its name to D. E. Converse & Company. At the suggestion of Mrs. Converse, the town's name was changed from Bivingsville to Glendale in 1878. In 1889 D. E. Converse & Co. was dissolved and The D. E. Converse Company was incorporated, with D. E. Converse as president and A. H. Twichell as treasurer. Converse also organized the Clifton Mfg. Co. of Clifton, S.C.; no tokens are known to have been issued by that company.

GOLDVILLE (Laurens County) 1760

A10 G. A. BROWNING, JR. / '10 / GOLDVILLE, S.C.
GOOD FOR / 10 / IN TRADE
aluminum, 24mm, round, R10

A5 (obverse similar to A10)
GOOD FOR / 5 / IN TRADE.
aluminum, 19mm, round, R8

George A. Browning, Jr. operated a general store and cotton gin during the early teens.

B100 GOOD FOR ONE DOLLAR / IN / MERCHANDISE / $1⁰⁰ / JOANNA MERCANTILE / COMPANY / DESIGN PAT. NO. 79195 AUG. 13, 1929
(geometric design with six-pointed star in center)
brass, 32mm, round, R8

B25 (obverse similar to B100 except denomination TWENTY-FIVE CENTS)
(reverse similar to B100)
brass, 29mm, round, R8

B5 (obverse similar to B100 except denomination FIVE CENTS)
(reverse similar to B100)
brass, 25mm, round, R8

C5 JOANNA / MERCANTILE / COMPANY
GOOD FOR / 5¢ / WITH BOTTLE
aluminum, 21mm, octagonal, R10

D5 JOANNA MERCANTILE COMPANY / (picture of eagle's head)
GOOD FOR / 5¢ / IN MERCHANDISE
brass, 20mm, round, R10

The Joanna Mercantile Co. operated as company store for Joanna Cotton Mills from the late 1920s to the late 1950s.

GREAT FALLS (Chester County) 1780

A10 REPUBLIC COTTON MILLS STORES / GREAT FALLS, / S.C.
GOOD FOR / 10¢ / IN MERCHANDISE
aluminum, 26mm, round, R10

This company, which specialized in yarns, combed cloth, and fancy goods, operated from 1912 through the 1940s.

B5 REPUBLIC / PHARMACY / GREAT FALLS / S.C.
GOOD FOR / 5¢ / IN TRADE
brass, 25mm, round, R10

In business during the teens, twenties, and early thirties, this pharmacy was owned and operated by Republic Cotton Mills.

GREENSBORO

Tokens from the Acorn Tavern at the Oaks Motel with a Greensboro, S.C. address are die-cutting errors. The tokens are from Greensboro, N.C.

GREENVILLE   (Greenville County)   1790

A   A & A FOOD STORE / GOOD IN / TRADE / 6 / BOTTLE / CARTON
(blank)
   brass, 22mm, round, R7

B5   BLUDWINE / BOTTLING / AGCY. / GREENVILLE / S.C.
GOOD FOR / 5¢ / AT
   aluminum, 16mm, round, R10

C   BLUE BIRD LINES / B
GOOD FOR / (picture of bus) / ONE FARE
   bronze, 16mm, round, R8 (Atwood 490B)

D   (obverse and reverse similar to C)
   nickel, 23mm, round, R8 (Atwood 490C)

   500 specimens each of 1790 C and 1790 D were struck in 1950.

E5   BROWN & GRUBB / 5
(Ingle System - 1909 pat. date)
   brass, 20mm, round, R10

   In 1913 Brown & Grubb were listed as operators of a grocery store.

F2½   THE BROWN DERBY / 118 / N. MAIN / ST. / GREENVILLE, S.C.
GOOD FOR / 2½ / CENTS / IN TRADE
   aluminum, 20mm, round, R10

   This restaurant and billiard parlor operated during the late 1930s.

G5   BRUCE BROS. / DRUGS / GREENVILLE, / S.C.
GOOD FOR / 5 / CENTS / AT SODA FOUNTAIN
   aluminum, 19mm, round, R10

H25   CAMPERDOWN / MILL / STORE / 1905 / GREENVILLE S.C.
GOOD FOR / 25¢ / IN TRADE
   brass, 26mm, round, R5

   Camperdown Mills, one of the older textile mills in the Greenville area, was in operation as early as 1886. It was located on the Reedy River near the south end of Main Street. A small group of the tokens was discovered when the mill was torn down several years ago.

I100   CAROLINA STORES INC. / STORE / No. 1 / 1⁰⁰ / NON-TRANSFERABLE
(Master Metal Scrip - type I)
   brass, 35mm, round, R9

I50   (obverse similar to I100 except denomination 50)
(Master Metal Scrip - type I)
   brass, 30mm, round, R9

I25   (obverse similar to I100 except denomination 25)
(Master Metal Scrip - type I)
brass, 24mm, round, R9

I10   (obverse similar to I100 except denomination 10)
(Master Metal Scrip - type I)
brass, 21mm, round, R9

I5   (obverse similar to I100 except denomination 5)
(Master Metal Scrip - type I)
brass, 19mm, round, R8

I1   (obverse similar to I100 except denomination 1)
(Master Metal Scrip - type I)
brass, 18mm, round, R8

J100   CAROLINA STORES INC. / STORE / No. 3 / 1⁰⁰ / NON-TRANSFERABLE
(Master Metal Scrip - type I)
nickel-plated brass, 35mm, round, R9

J50   (obverse similar to J100 except denomination 50)
(Master Metal Scrip - type I)
nickel-plated brass, 30mm, round, R9

J25   (obverse similar to J100 except denomination 25)
(Master Metal Scrip - type I)
nickel-plated brass, 24mm, round, R9

J10   (obverse similar to J100 except denomination 10)
(Master Metal Scrip - type I)
nickel-plated brass, 21mm, round, R9

J5   (obverse similar to J100 except denomination 5)
(Master Metal Scrip - type I)
nickel-plated brass, 19mm, round, R9

K100   CAROLINA STORES INC. / STORE / No. 4 / 1⁰⁰ / NON-TRANSFERABLE
(Master Metal Scrip - type I)
brass, 35mm, round, R9

K50   (obverse similar to K100 except denomination 50)
(Master Metal Scrip - type I)
brass, 30mm, round, R9

K25   (obverse similar to K100 except denomination 25)
(Master Metal Scrip - type I)
brass, 24mm, round, R9

K10   (obverse similar to K100 except denomination 10)
(Master Metal Scrip - type I)
brass, 21mm, round, R9

K5   (obverse similar to K100 except denomination 5)
(Master Metal Scrip - type I)
brass, 19mm, round, R8

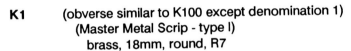

K1   (obverse similar to K100 except denomination 1)
(Master Metal Scrip - type I)
brass, 18mm, round, R7

L100   CAROLINA STORES INC. / STORE / No. 5 / 1⁰⁰ / NON-TRANSFERABLE
(Master Metal Scrip - type I)
brass, 35mm, round, R9

L50   (obverse similar to L100 except denomination 50)
(Master Metal Scrip - type I)
brass, 30mm, round, R9

L25   (obverse similar to L100 except denomination 25)
(Master Metal Scrip - type I)
brass, 24mm, round, R9

L10   (obverse similar to L100 except denomination 10)
(Master Metal Scrip - type I)
brass, 21mm, round, R9

L5   (obverse similar to L100 except denomination 5)
(Master Metal Scrip - type I)
brass, 19mm, round, R9

The Carolina Stores were listed as general stores during the late twenties and early thirties. It is likely that they operated as company stores for one or more of the textile mills in the Greenville area.

M5   CARPENTER / BROS.
GOOD FOR / 5¢ / CIGAR OR SODA
aluminum, 19mm, round, R9

The Carpenter Brothers opened a drug store in 1893. The business was passed down through the family and is still operated by two grandsons of one of the founders.

N1   COCA - COLA / BOTTLING / CO. / GREENVILLE, / S.C.
1¢ / GOOD - FOR / PREMIUMS / ONLY.
brass, 23mm, octagonal, R9

This token was used in place of cash when a patron returned a bottle to the company for a premium. The company has been in business since 1908.

O100   CROSSWELL COMPANY / WOODSIDE / MILL
GOOD FOR / $1⁰⁰ / IN / MERCHANDISE / ONLY
brass, 35mm, round, R5 (varieties exist)

O50   (obverse similar to O100)
GOOD FOR / 50¢ / IN / MERCHANDISE / ONLY
brass, 31mm, round, R6

O25   (obverse similar to O100)
GOOD FOR / 25¢ / IN / MERCHANDISE / ONLY
brass, 28mm, round, R6

O10   (obverse similar to O100)
          GOOD FOR / 10¢ / IN / MERCHANDISE / ONLY
              brass, 25mm, round, R5 (varieties exist)

O5   (obverse similar to O100)
          GOOD FOR / 5¢ / IN / MERCHANDISE / ONLY
              brass, 21mm, round, R4 (varieties exist)

O1   (obverse similar to O100)
          GOOD FOR / 1¢ / IN / MERCHANDISE / ONLY
              aluminum, 25mm, round, R9

          In business from 1917 to the 1940s, the Crosswell Company operated the company store for Woodside Mills.

P   HENRY V. DICK & CO. / CHARLOTTE, N.C. / RALEIGH, N.C. /
          COLUMBIA, S.C. / GREENVILLE, S.C.
              YOU PAY (in script)
              aluminum, 32mm, round, R8

          This wholesale refrigeration, heating, and radio supply dealer operated during the 1940s.

Q5   DOSTER BROS. / DRUGS / GREENVILLE, / S.C.
              GOOD FOR / 5 / CENTS / AT SODA FOUNTAIN
              aluminum, 19mm, round, R10

          This token was issued prior to 1902, when Doster Bros. merged with Joseph Bruce to form the Bruce & Doster Drug Company, a long-lived wholesale and retail drug company. The company is no longer in family hands, but the retail drug store still operates on Main Street. See 1790-G5 for a token issued by Joseph Bruce and his brother before he entered business with Doster Brothers.

R   DUKE POWER CO. / G (stencil cut-out) / GREENVILLE, S.C.
              GOOD FOR / ONE FARE
              zinc, 16mm, round, cut-out, R3 (Atwood 490A)

          100,000 specimens were struck in 1942. Duke Power sold the bus line in 1954.

S100   DUNEAN MILLS STORE / D M / 1̲0̲0̲ / IN TRADE ONLY / GOOD ONLY TO
          / WHOM ISSUED / NON-TRANSFERABLE
              (Master Metal Scrip - type I)
              brass, 39mm, scalloped (12), R9

S50   (obverse similar to S100 except denomination 50)
              (Master Metal Scrip - type I)
              nickel, 35mm, scalloped (11), R9

S10   (obverse similar to S100 except denomination 10)
              (Master Metal Scrip - type I)
              brass, 27mm, scalloped (9), R9

S5   (obverse similar to S100 except denomination 5)
(Master Metal Scrip - type I)
nickel, 24mm, scalloped (8), R9

Dunean Mills, which at one time specialized in fancy weaves, has operated since 1912.

T25   FARMERS AND MERCHANTS BANK, STATE DEPOSITORY / F AND M B (monogram) / GREENVILLE, S.C.
GOOD (swastika) LUCK / WE WILL ACCEPT THIS ON DEPOSIT FOR / 25 CTS. / IF YOU OPEN / A NEW SAVINGS ACCOUNT / OF $5.00 OR MORE, / LEAVING IT IN THE BANK 12 MONTHS / AND WE WILL PAY 4% / INTEREST / ON YOUR SAVINGS / COMPOUNDED QUARTERLY
brass, 31mm, round, R9

U25   FRANKLIN FINANCE / 103 E. WASHINGTON ST. / GREENVILLE, S.C.
25¢
aluminum, 26mm, round, R10

U10   (obverse same as U25)
10¢
aluminum, 26mm, round, R10

U5   (obverse same as U25)
5¢
aluminum, 26mm, round, R10

It is not known exactly how these tokens, which were probably issued in the 1940s or 1950s, were used. See the token listed under town of City View for another issue from this company.

V100   GANTT'S / UNIFORM / OUTLET, / INC. / GREENVILLE, S.C.
GOOD / FOR / $1.00 / OFF NEXT / UNIFORM / PURCHASE / GANTT'S UNIFORM OUTLET, INC.
aluminum, 32mm, round, R9, modern

W100   J. W. GILREATH / 1.00
(Ingle System - 1909 pat. date)
copper, 35mm, round, R10

J. W. Gilreath operated a grocery store from 1908 to 1918.

X50   GREENVILLE / EQUITY / EXCHANGE
GOOD FOR / 50¢ / IN MERCHANDISE
aluminum, 32mm, octagonal, R10

Attribution tentative. The Greenville Exchange was listed as a second-hand furniture dealer in the 1920s and 1930s.

Y500   HADEN MOTOR CO. / USED CARS / AUTO / LOANS / GREENVILLE, S.C.
GOOD FOR / $5.00 / DOWN / PAYMENT / ONE PER SALE
aluminum, 36mm, round, R10

This used-car dealership operated during the 1930s and 1940s.

Z5 J. W. HARRISON / DRUGGIST / OPP. OPERA HOUSE / GREENVILLE, S.C.
  GOOD FOR / 5¢ / CIGAR OR SODA
  aluminum, 25mm, octagonal, clover-shaped c/o, R10
  J. W. Harrison operated a drug store during the early teens.

AA1 IDEAL / ATHLETIC / CLUB / GREENVILLE / S.C. / R.C. GRAY, OWNER
  GOOD FOR / 1¢ / IN EXCHANGE
  aluminum, 20mm, round, R10

AB2½ JIM'S BILLIARD / HALL / GREENVILLE, / SO. CAR.
  GOOD FOR / 2½¢ / IN TRADE
  aluminum, 24mm, round, R10

AC10 JUDSON MILL STORE CO. / GREENVILLE, / S.C.
  GOOD FOR / 10 / IN MERCHANDISE
  aluminum, 24mm, round, R10

AD100 JUDSON MILLS STORE CO. / J M / 1⁰⁰ / IN TRADE ONLY. / GOOD ONLY TO - / WHOM ISSUED / NON-TRANSFERABLE
  (Master Metal Scrip - type I)
  copper, 35mm, round, R9

AD50 (obverse similar to AD100 except denomination 50)
  (Master Metal Scrip - type I)
  copper, 30mm, round, R9

AD25 (obverse similar to AD100 except denomination 25)
  (Master Metal Scrip - type I)
  copper, 24mm, round, R9

AD10 (obverse similar to AD100 except denomination 10)
  (Master Metal Scrip - type I and type II varieties exist)
  copper, 21mm, round, R7

AD5 (obverse similar to AD100 except denomination 5)
  (Master Metal Scrip - type I and type II varieties exist)
  copper, 19mm, round, R7

AD1 (obverse similar to AD100 except denomination 1)
  (Master Metal Scrip - type II)
  brass, 18mm, round, R7

  In the early teens this company was operated by Hobbs-Henderson Co., a retail dry goods and general merchandise firm. Later, Judson Mills operated the store on its own.

AE KASH / & / KARRY / GREENVILLE, S.C.
  DEPOSIT / TOKEN / CARTON / 6 BOTTLES
  aluminum, 26mm, round, R4

  This large discount supermarket was in business from the early 1940s to the early 1980s.

AF   LEWIS & / GREENVILLE / S.C. / HARTZOG.
GOOD FOR / 1 / GLASS / OF / SODA WATER
aluminum, 24mm, round, R10

Lewis & Hartzog operated a drug store circa 1900 to 1916. When Lewis left the business, O. B. Hartzog continued to run it until the early 1930s.

AG1   J. C. LOOPER / 2603 / BUNCOMBE / ROAD
GOOD FOR / 1¢ / IN TRADE
brass, 18mm, scalloped (8), R9

James C. Looper operated a grocery store from the mid-1920s to the 1940s.

AH500   MARTIN - HAWKINS / FURN. / CO. / GREENVILLE / S.C.
GOOD FOR / $5.00 / ON PURCHASE / OF / $50.00 / OR MORE / DURING JUNE 1936
aluminum, 38mm, scalloped (14), R10

AI500   (obverse similar to AH500)
(reverse similar to AH500 except date JUNE 1938)
aluminum, 36mm, round, R10

The Martin-Hawkins Furniture Co. was first listed in 1926. Around 1940 it was purchased by Kimbrells, Inc.

AJ5   MAULDIN / PHARMACY / GREENVILLE, S.C.
GOOD FOR / 5¢ / IN TRADE
aluminum, 19mm, round, R10

The Mauldin Pharmacy was in business during the early teens.

AK10   MILLS MANUFACTURING CO. / 10 / GREENVILLE, / S.C.
GOOD FOR / 10 / IN MERCHANDISE
aluminum, 18mm, round, R10

This company, which specialized in the manufacture of twills and sheetings, began operations circa 1900. Around 1919 its name was changed to Mills Mill, Inc.

AL100   MONAGHAN MILL STORE / V M C / 1$\frac{00}{}$ / NON-TRANSFERABLE
(Master Metal Scrip - type I)
brass, 35mm, round, R9

AL50   (obverse similar to AL100 except denomination 50)
(Master Metal Scrip - type I)
brass, 30mm, round, R9

AL25   (obverse similar to AL100 except denomination 25)
(Master Metal Scrip - type I)
brass, 24mm, round, R9

AL10   (obverse similar to AL100 except denomination 10)
(Master Metal Scrip - type I)
brass, 21mm, round, R9

A postcard view of Monaghan Mills.

AL5   (obverse similar to AL100 except denomination 5)
     (Master Metal Scrip - type I)
     nickel, 19mm, round, R9

AL1   (obverse similar to AL100 except denomination 1)
     (Master Metal Scrip - type I and type II varieties exist)
     brass, 18mm, round, R4

AM1   MONAGHAN MILL STORE / 1 / GREENVILLE, S.C.
     (Master Metal Scrip - type II)
     brass, 21mm, scalloped (8), "M" c/o, R9

AN   MONAGHAN / MILLS
     SPOOLING / 1 / PIECE
     brass, 25mm, octagonal, holed as made, R8

AO   MONAGHAN / MILLS
     SPOOLING / 1 / PIECE (varieties exist)
     brass, 24mm, round, holed as made, R8

    Built circa 1900, Monaghan Mill continues to operate today. The last two tokens (AN and AO) were used as production checks.

AP100 THE HOUSE OF SERVICE / GOOD FOR A / CHARGE ACCOUNT / ON
YOUR TERMS / AT THE / NATIONAL CLOTHING STORES / 120 SOUTH
MAIN ST. / GREENVILLE / S.C. / A SQUARE DEAL TO ALL
      GOOD AS / 1\underline{00}$ CASH / ON YOUR FIRST PURCHASE OF / $10 OR
      MORE / COMPLIMENTS / OF J. NATHAN (facsimile signature) /
      PRESIDENT / GOOD ONLY DURING / 1922
          brass, 32mm, round, R10

AQ5 C. A. PARKINS / GREENVILLE / S.C.
      GOOD FOR / 5¢ / IN TRADE
          aluminum, 19mm, round, R10

AR JAMES E. PAYNE / MFR. OF / SODA WATER / GREENVILLE, S.C.
      GOOD FOR / 1 / BOTTLE / OF BEER
          aluminum, 25mm, octagonal, R10

     James E. Payne moved to Greenville around 1915 and opened a soda
bottling business. He also ran a "near beer" saloon on Laurens Street.
Before coming to Greenville, Payne had operated a distillery in Baltimore
and also some type of bottling works near Augusta, Ga.

AS100 PEOPLES SUPPLY CO. / DUNEAN / MILLS
      GOOD FOR / 1\underline{00}$ / IN / MERCHANDISE / ONLY
          brass, 35mm, round, R6

AS50 (obverse similar to AS100)
      GOOD FOR / 50¢ / IN / MERCHANDISE / ONLY
          brass, 31mm, round, R6

AS25 (obverse similar to AS100)
      GOOD FOR / 25¢ / IN / MERCHANDISE / ONLY
          brass, 28mm, round, R6

AS10 (obverse similar to AS100)
      GOOD FOR / 10¢ / IN / MERCHANDISE / ONLY
          brass, 25mm, round, R6

AS5 (obverse similar to AS100)
      GOOD FOR / 5¢ / IN / MERCHANDISE / ONLY
          brass, 21mm, round, R8

     During the late teens The Peoples Supply Company was company
store for Dunean Mills.

AT10 F. W. POE MFG. C$\underline{o}$ / GOOD FOR / 10 / IN MDSE. /GREENVILLE, S.C.
      (same)
          aluminum, 26mm, octagonal, R10

AT5 (obverse similar to AT10 except denomination 5)
      (same)
          aluminum, 26mm, square with clipped corners, R10

AU100   F. W. POE MFG. Cǫ / GOOD FOR / 100 / CENTS / IN MDSE. / GREENVILLE, S.C.
> (same)
>> brass, 26mm, square, R6 (varieties exist)

AU50   (obverse similar to AU100 except denomination 50 CENTS)
> (same)
>> brass, 29mm, scalloped (4), R6

AU25   (obverse similar to AU100 except denomination 25 CENTS)
> (same)
>> brass, 30mm, scalloped (8), R6

AU10   (obverse similar to AU100 except denomination 10 CENTS)
> (same)
>> brass, 25mm, octagonal, R6

AU5   (obverse similar to AU100 except denomination 5 CENTS)
> (same)
>> brass, 21mm, gear-shaped planchet, R5

AV100   F. W. POE MFG. CO. / GOOD FOR / 100 / CENTS / IN MDSE. / GREENVILLE, S.C.
> (Orco - type I) (varieties exist without cut-out)
>> brass, 32mm, round, arrow-shaped c/o, R6

AW   POE / MILL
> SPOOLING / 1 / PIECE
>> brass, 25mm, round, holed as made, R10

AX   POE / MILL
> WARP DRAWING / 1 / PIECE
>> brass, 24mm, round, holed as made, R10

AY   POE / MILL / 150 (incuse serial #)
> WARP DRAWING / 1 / PIECE (different dies from AX)
>> brass, 24mm, round, R10

    F. W. Poe started in the retail clothing business sometime in the 1880s. By 1904 he had founded the F. W. Poe Mfg. Co., manufacturing cotton goods. The mill was sold to Burlington Mills in the 1940s, and continued in operation until the late 1970s.

AZ5   J. N. POOLE / 5 / GREENVILLE, S.C.
> (picture of head of Liberty within a wreath)
>> brass, 20mm, round, R10

    J. N. Poole operated a saloon during the 1880s.

BA60   QUALITY BOTTLING / WORKS / GREENVILLE, / S.C.
> 20 CHECKS GOOD FOR / 60 / IN SODA WATER
>> brass, 29mm, round, R10

    The Quality Bottling Works was in business in the mid-teens.

BB   SOUTHERN WEAVING CO. / GREENVILLE, / S.C.
GROSS / 5 / YARDS
aluminum, 26mm, round, R10

This company, which specialized in cotton yarns, brake linings, and special tapes, began operating in the mid-1920s.

BC5   STONE DRUG CO. / GREENVILLE, / S.C.
GOOD FOR ONE / 5 / CENT / GLASS OF SODA
aluminum, 24mm, round, R10

The Stone Drug Company was in business from the late teens to the early thirties.

BD1   VERNER / SPRINGS / WATER - CO. / GREENVILLE, / S.C.
1¢ / GOOD - FOR / PREMIUMS / ONLY.
brass, 22mm, round, R8

In business from 1908 to 1940, this company bottled Coca-Cola and other soda water products.

BE10   C. WEST / 10 / 1511 / BUNCOMBE ST.
(Ingle System - 1909 pat. date)
brass, 21mm, round, R10

BE5   (obverse similar to BE10 except denomination 5)
(Ingle System - 1909 pat. date)
brass, 20mm, round, R9

Canton West operated a grocery store from the early 1900s to the 1920s.

BF   WOODSIDE COTTON MILLS
(blank except for numeral "3" counterstamp)
brass, 24mm, round, R9

BG   WOODSIDE COTTON MILLS / (counterstamped "3")
(blank)
aluminum, 24mm, round, R9

BF and BG were probably used as production tokens. For company store tokens, see listings under Crosswell Company.

BH   NATIONAL / WOODSIDE / BANK / GREENVILLE, S.C.
WOODSIDE BUILDING / (picture of building) / 1923
brass, 32mm, round, R5

Woodside Cotton Mills, as depicted on a postcard.

GREENWOOD   (Greenwood County)   1795

A   NEW HOME OF THE OLDEST AND STRONGEST BANK IN
      GREENWOOD COUNTY / (picture of building)
          BANK OF GREENWOOD / CAPITAL $65,000.00 / SURPLUS
      $60,000.00 / STATE DEPOSITORY / & / SAFE DEPOSIT VAULTS /
      YOUR ACCOUNT / SOLICITED / GREENWOOD, S.C.
          brass, 32mm, round, R9

B   BLUE AND WHITE BUS CO., INC. / (picture of bus)
          GOOD FOR / (picture of bus) / ONE SCHOOL FARE
          brass, 23mm, round, c/o, R6 (Atwood 500A)

C   (obverse similar to B)
          GOOD FOR / (picture of bus) / ONE FARE
          nickel, 16mm, round, c/o, R5 (Atwood 500B)

      The Blue and White Bus Co. operated in the 1940s and 1950s. In 1940,
1000 specimens of 1795-B and 2000 of 1795-C were struck.

D   J. C. BURNS & CO. / GOOD / SHOES, / DRY GOODS, / NOTIONS / AND CLOTHING / FOR LESS / MONEY / GREENWOOD, S.C.
J. C. BURNS & CO. / AROUND / THE / CORNER / WALK-A-BLOCK / AND SAVE A / DOLLAR / GREENWOOD'S "BIG BUSY" STORE
aluminum, 39mm, round, R10

J. C. Burns & Co. operated a "racket store," specializing in dry goods, clothing, shoes, and ladies' notions. The business was listed from 1904 to 1930.

E5   J. W. CLEM / GREENWOOD / S.C.
GOOD FOR / 5¢ / IN TRADE
aluminum, 18mm, round, R10

J. W. Clem ran a general store during the teens, twenties, and thirties.

F50   COMMERCIAL BANK / C B (monogram) / GREENWOOD, S.C.
WE WILL ACCEPT THIS ON DEPOSIT FOR / 50 CTS. / IF YOU OPEN A NEW / SAVINGS ACCOUNT OF / 5\frac{00}{}$ / OR MORE, LEAVING IT / IN THE BANK 12 MONTHS / AND PAY 5% INTEREST / ON YOUR SAVINGS / COMPOUNDED QUARTERLY
brass, 31mm, round, R8

G5   THE ENTERPRISE CASH SUPPLY CO. / GREENWOOD / S.C.
GOOD FOR / 5 / CENTS (across numeral) / SODA WATER
aluminum, 24mm, round, R10

This company operated a grocery store circa 1910.

H500   GRENOLA GROCERY CO. / 5$\frac{00}{}$ / GREENWOOD, S.C.
(Orco - type I)
brass, 32mm, scalloped (12), R10

H100   (obverse similar to H500 except denomination 1$\frac{00}{}$)
(Orco - type II)
nickel, 32mm, round, R10

H50   (obverse similar to H500 except denomination 50)
(Orco - type II)
copper, 27mm, round, R9

H25   (obverse similar to H500 except denomination 25)
(Orco - type II)
nickel, 24mm, round, R9

H10   (obverse similar to H500 except denomination 10)
(Orco - type II) (varieties exist)
brass, 21mm, round, R7

H5   (obverse similar to H500 except denomination 5)
(Orco - type II) (varieties exist)
nickel, 19mm, round, R7

During the 1930s this was the company store for Grendel Mills.

I100 GRIFFIN BROS. MERC. CO. / GREENWOOD, / S.C.
   GOOD FOR / 1<u>00</u> / IN TRADE
    brass, 25mm, round, R10

I5 (obverse same as I100)
   GOOD FOR / 5 / IN TRADE
    brass, 25mm, round, R10

    The Griffin Bros. Mercantile Co. was in business from the late 1920s to the early 1940s.

J10 OREGON POOL / PARLOR / GREENWOOD / S.C.
   GOOD FOR / ONE / 10¢ / GAME OF POOL
    aluminum, 23mm, round, R10

    This pool parlor may have been located in the lobby of the Oregon Hotel.

K25 C. M. POLATTY / 25
   (Ingle System - 1914 pat. date)
    brass, 24mm, round, R10

K5 (obverse similar to K25 except denomination 5)
   (Ingle System - 1914 pat. date)
    nickel-plated brass, 20mm, round, R10

    C. M. Polatty operated a general store near Greenwood circa 1910 to 1930.

L PRICE'S BUS LINES / ONE / RIDE / GREENWOOD, S.C.
   (same)
    nickel, 16mm, round, c/o, R6 (Atwood 500C)

    This line operated during the early 1950s. 2000 tokens were struck in 1950.

GREER (Spartanburg County)   1800

A50 BANK OF GREERS / B OF G (monogram) / GREER, S.C.
   WE WILL ACCEPT THIS ON DEPOSIT FOR / 50 CTS. / IF YOU OPEN
   A NEW / SAVINGS ACCOUNT OF / $5<u>00</u> / OR MORE, LEAVING IT / IN
   THE BANK 12 MONTHS / AND PAY 5% INTEREST / ON YOUR
   SAVINGS, / COMPOUNDED
    brass, 31mm, round, R9

B25 T. M. BOBO / GOOD THINGS / TO EAT / GREER, S.C.
   GOOD FOR / 25¢ / IN TRADE
    aluminum, 28mm, round, R10

B5 (obverse similar to B25)
   GOOD FOR / 5¢ / IN TRADE
    aluminum, 20mm, round, R10

    T. M. Bobo ran a grocery store and cafe during the teens.

C   C. A. HERLONG ordered 5000 tokens from the Ingle - Schierloh Company, and they were delivered to him in 1932. No specimens are known in collectors' hands.

D100   VICTOR MILL STORE / 1<u>00</u> / GOOD FOR / MERCHANDISE / ONLY / GREER, S.C.
        (Master Metal Scrip - type I)
          nickel-plated brass, 35mm, round, "V" c/o, R8

D25   (obverse similar to D100 except denomination 25)
        (Master Metal Scrip - type I)
          brass, 24mm, round, "V" c/o, R8

        Varieties of D25 also exist without a cutout.

D10   (obverse similar to D100 except denomination 10)
        (Master Metal Scrip - type I)
          nickel-plated brass, 21mm, round, "V" c/o, R7

D5   (obverse similar to D100 except denomination 5)
        (Master Metal Scrip - type I)
          copper, 19mm, round, "V" c/o, R7

D1   (obverse similar to D100 except denomination 1)
        (Master Metal Scrip - type I)
          copper, 18mm, round, "V" c/o, R7

E100   (obverse similar to D100)
        (Master Metal Scrip - type II)
          nickel, 35mm, round, "V" c/o, R8

E25   (obverse similar to D100 except denomination 25)
        (Master Metal Scrip - type II)
          brass, 24mm, round, "V" c/o, R8

E10   (obverse similar to D100 except denomination 10)
        (Master Metal Scrip - type II) (varieties exist)
          nickel, 21mm, round, "V" c/o, R7

E5   (obverse similar to D100 except denomination 5)
        (Master Metal Scrip - type II)
          copper, 19mm, round, "V" c/o, R7

E1   (obverse similar to D100 except denomination 1)
        (Master Metal Scrip - type II)
          brass, 18mm, round, "V" c/o, R7

       Victor Mill was owned and operated by the Victor - Monaghan Corporation of Greenville. The mill was opened in the early 1900s and continued well into the second half of the century. The token manufacturer's records reveal that 50¢ denominations were struck and delivered to the mill store; no examples are known to exist.

GREERS   (Spartanburg County)   1805

A   GREERS MANUFACTURING CO. / 6 / GREERS, S.C.
         (blank)
              brass, 24mm, round, R9

         Greers Manufacturing Company was an early textile mill in the town of
   Greers (later renamed Greer). This was a production token.

B5   C. M. PONDER / COOL DRINKS / & / FANCY AND HEAVY /
         GROCERIES / GREERS, S.C.
              GOOD FOR / 5 / CENTS (across numeral) / SODA WATER
              aluminum, 25mm, round, R10

         Carl M. Ponder operated a general store and soda water bottling
   company from 1908 to the 1940s.

C   VICTOR - MONAGHAN CO. / 16 / GREERS / PLANT / GREERS, S.C.
         (blank)
              brass, 25mm, round, R9

         This production token was used at the Greers Plant of the Victor -
   Monaghan Company, later called Victor Mill.

HAILE GOLD MINE   (Kershaw County)   1820

A25   THE HAILE GOLD MINING CO. / HAILE GOLD MINE, / S.C.
              GOOD FOR / 25 / IN MERCHANDISE
              aluminum, 28mm, round, R9

A10   (obverse similar to A25)
              GOOD FOR / 10 / IN MERCHANDISE
              aluminum, 24mm, round, R10

         In 1827, Colonel Benjamin Haile, an early settler in the Kershaw area,
   discovered gold in one of the creek beds on his farm. He began to pan the
   creeks on his property on a regular basis, and did so for several years.
   In 1837 the first stamp mill was erected, and actual mining operations were
   begun. The mine continued to operate through the Civil War, as the Hailes
   had some sort of agreement with the Confederacy to supply much needed
   gold and other minerals. Sherman destroyed the whole works during the
   closing days of the war.

         The Haile family sold the mine in 1866 to James Eldridge who, in 1880,
   sold out to a New York syndicate. The new owners resumed operations
   on a large scale. In 1887, Dr. Adolph Thies was hired as foreman, and he
   perfected a process known as "barrel chlorination," which more easily
   extracted the gold from the ore. This process became the technical
   innovation of the day, so much so that Thomas Edison visited Thies to learn
   about it.

         During the two-decade period from 1887 to 1908 the mine did very well.
   Besides several large buildings that housed machinery for the mining
   operations, there was a large office building, company store, post office,
   and boarding house covering an area of 1800 acres. It was during this
   period that tokens were issued.

HAILE GOLD MINE   (Continued)   1820

In 1904 Dr. Thies retired and his son, "Captain" Ernest Thies, took control of the daily operations. On 10 August 1908 the huge boiler that provided power for all of the mining equipment exploded. The force of the blast ruined several buildings, killed "Captain" Thies, and injured several others. The physical and emotional devastation was so great that the mine did not reopen for several years.

Several companies have attempted to work the mine since then. Most have been unsuccessful. The mine was most recently reopened by the Piedmont Mining Company in 1984. The first gold from the reopened mine was poured in April, 1985. Operations have continued on a successful basis since then.

HAMPTON   (Hampton County)   1830

A5   R. H. ANDERSON / HAMPTON / S.C.
        GOOD FOR / 5 / CENTS / IN TRADE
          aluminum, 20mm, round, R10

          R. H. Anderson operated a grocery store circa 1910.

B50   J. C. LIGHTSEY / 50 / NOT / TRANSFERABLE
        GOOD FOR / 50¢ / IN TRADE
          aluminum, 30mm, round, R10

B10   (obverse similar to B50)
        GOOD FOR / 10¢ / IN TRADE
          aluminum, 21mm, round, R10

          J. C. Lightsey ran a sawmill during the teens and twenties.

HARDEEVILLE   (Jasper County)   1838

A100   J. A. COLEMAN, JR. / GENERAL / MERCHANDISE / HARDEEVILLE, S.C.
        GOOD FOR / 1\frac{00}{}$ / IN TRADE
          aluminum, 35mm, round, R7

A50   (obverse similar to A100)
        GOOD FOR / 50¢ / IN TRADE
          aluminum, 31mm, round, R7

A25   (obverse similar to A100)
        GOOD FOR / 25¢ / IN TRADE
          aluminum, 28mm, round, R7

A10   (obverse similar to A100)
        GOOD FOR / 10¢ / IN TRADE
          aluminum, 25mm, round, R7

HARDEEVILLE   (Continued)   1838

A5   (obverse similar to A100)
          GOOD FOR / 5¢ / IN TRADE
          aluminum, 20mm, round, R7

          First listed in 1917, J. A. Coleman, Jr. appears as the owner of
Hardeeville Naval Stores Co., a firm engaged in the manufacture of
turpentine and other similar products. The business continued to operate
until the late 1920s. Although the tokens specifically state "general
merchandise," most likely they were used in conjunction with the naval
stores company. Tokens were also issued by Coleman at a
Swainsboro, Ga. location.

HATTIEVILLE   (Barnwell County)   1850

A10   BRABHAM & CO. / NOT / TRANSFERABLE / HATTIEVILLE / S.C.
          GOOD FOR / 10¢ / IN TRADE
          aluminum, 19mm, round, R10

A5   BRABHAM & CO. / NOT / TRANSFERABLE / HATTIEVILLE, S.C.
          GOOD FOR / 5¢ / IN TRADE
          aluminum, 21mm, round, R10

B5   BRABHAM / & / COMPANY
          GOOD FOR / 5 / IN / MERCHANDISE
          brass, 19mm, round, R9

          This firm operated a general store from the early 1900s to the early
1930s.

HEATH SPRINGS   (Lancaster County)   1855

A5   PEOPLE'S DRUG STORE / HEATH / SPRINGS, / S.C.
          GOOD FOR / 5¢ / IN TRADE
          aluminum, 19mm, round, R10

HEINEMANN   (Williamsburg County)   1858

A10   10 / J P G (all incuse)
          J P G (all incuse)
             brass, 20mm, round, R10

HEINEMANN (Continued) 1858

A5   (obverse similar to A10 except denomination 5)
      (blank)
         brass, 26mm, round, R10

        Issued by Julius Pendergras Gamble in the 1890s or early 1900s, these tokens were used to pay the workers he employed on his large farm in Williamsburg County. In addition to being a large grower of cotton, Gamble also produced some tobacco and timber. His store operated into the 1930s and was the local post office, with Gamble serving as postmaster.

HELENA (Newberry County) 1860

A200   THIS CHECK IS GOOD FOR / IN GOODS / AT THE STORE OF / WM. ZOBEL (facsimile signature) / FAMILY GROCER / HELENA, / NEWBERRY COUNTY / S.C. / TWO DOLLARS
         (outer circle of numeral "2" repeated 15 times) / (inner circle of word "TWO" repeated 7 times) / TWO
         green cardboard, 50mm, square, R10

A10   (obverse similar to A200 except denomination TEN CENTS)
         TEN CENTS / 10 / NOT TRANSFERABLE
         orange cardboard, 38mm, square, R9

        William Zobel operated a general store in 1886.

HEMINGWAY (Williamsburg County) 1865

A25   W. H. GROVER / HEMINGWAY, / S. CAR.
         GOOD FOR / 25¢ / IN TRADE
         brass, 26mm, round, R10

B10   W. C. HEMINGWAY & CO'S / STORE / HEMINGWAY / S.C.
         GOOD FOR / 10 / IN MERCHANDISE
         brass, 24mm, round, R9 (varieties exist)

        W. C. Hemingway & Co. operated several general stores in Williamsburg County. The Hemingway store operated during the teens and twenties. Tokens were also issued at the Lambert, S.C. location.

C10   INGRAM - DARGAN / STORE / HEMINGWAY, / S.C.
         GOOD FOR / 10¢ / IN TRADE
         brass, 25mm, round, R10

        The Ingram - Dargan Lumber Company issued this token circa 1937. The company only operated in Hemingway for three years or so, moving to Conway about 1940.

HICKORY (York County) 1875

A100 J. S. WILKERSON & CO. / HICKORY, / S. CAR.
GOOD FOR / $1⁰⁰ / IN / MERCHANDISE
aluminum, 35mm, round, R9

   This company, which operated a general store and sold wagons and buggies, was listed from 1908 to 1913. Its name was changed to Wilkerson Mercantile Company in 1914. The town is now known as Hickory Grove.

HILTON HEAD (Beaufort County) 1885

A H.H.O.F. CO.
MUST BE CASHED / WEEKLY
brass, 25mm, round, R7

B H.H.O.F. CO. / 461 (serial #) (all incuse)
(blank)
brass, 25mm, round, holed as made, R7

C H.H.P. CO. / 1355 (serial #) (all incuse)
(blank)
brass, 29mm, round, holed as made, R5

   The Hilton Head Oyster Factory Co. (later called the Hilton Head Packing Co.) was in operation during the early 1920s. It was headquartered in Savannah, Ga. The business was later operated by S. V. Toomer.

D50 J. B. HUDSON / HILTON HEAD, / S.C.
GOOD FOR / 50 / IN / MERCHANDISE
brass, 33mm, round, R10

D25 (obverse similar to D50)
GOOD FOR / 25 / IN / MERCHANDISE
brass, 29mm, round, R10

   J. B. Hudson ran a general store in the late 1920s and early 1930s.

HONEA PATH (Anderson County) 1895

A25 T. H. BROCK & CO. / GENERAL / MERCHANDISE / HONEA PATH, S.C.
GOOD FOR / 25 / IN MERCHANDISE
aluminum, 29mm, round, R10

   T. H. Brock & Co. was in business circa 1910.

B5 CHIQUOLA / B.B.
5
aluminum, 20mm, round, R6

B1 (obverse same as B5)
1
aluminum, 20mm, round, R6

C1   CHIQUOLA / B.B.
          1
             brass, 22mm, round, R6

          Presumably these are production tokens from Chiquola Mfg. Co., a textile mill that specialized in the manufacture of sheeting. The "B.B." inscribed on the obverse is thought to stand for "box of bobbins," a unit of work performed by workers in the mill.

HOPKINS   (Richland County)   1900

A5   E. D. HOPKINS, / HOPKINS, S.C.
          GOOD FOR / 5¢ / IN TRADE
             aluminum, 21mm, round, R10

INMAN   (Spartanburg County)   1920

A100   INMAN MILL STORE / 1$\underline{00}$ / I M S / INMAN, S.C.
           (Orco - type IV)
              brass, 32mm, round, c/o, R9

A50   (obverse similar to A100 except denomination 50)
           (Orco - type IV)
              brass, 29mm, round, c/o, R9

A25   (obverse similar to A100 except denomination 25)
           (Orco - type IV)
              brass, 26mm, round, c/o, R8

A10   (obverse similar to A100 except denomination 10)
           (Orco - type IV)
              brass, 23mm, round, c/o, R8

A5   (obverse similar to A100 except denomination 5)
           (Orco - type IV)
              brass, 20mm, round, c/o, R8

A1   (obverse similar to A100 except denomination 1)
           (Orco - type IV)
              brass, 17mm, round, c/o, R7

B1   (obverse similar to A100 except denomination 1)
           (Orco - type IV, dated 1940)
              brass, 17mm, round, c/o, R9

C10   INMAN MILLS STORE / GOOD FOR / 10¢ / IN MERCHANDISE
           (same)
              nickel, 18mm, round, R9 (varieties exist)

A postcard view of Inman Mills, circa 1910.

C1 (obverse similar to C10 except denomination 1¢)
(same)
brass, 19mm, round, R9

D INMAN / MILLS.
SPOOLER / CHECK
aluminum, 25mm, round, R10

Inman Mills began operating circa 1900, producing print cloths and sheeting. The company operated well into the 1960s.

ISLANDTON (Colleton County) 1930

A50 J. S. PADGETT / ISLANDTON, S.C.
GOOD FOR / 50 / IN MERCHANDISE
brass, 31mm, round, R10

A5 (obverse similar to A50)
GOOD FOR / 5 / IN MERCHANDISE
brass, 21mm, round, R10

The J. W. Jenny & Co. store, as it appears on exhibit in the S.C. State Museum.

A50   J. W. JENNY & CO. / JENNYS / S.C.
             GOOD FOR / 50 / IN / MERCHANDISE
             aluminum, 31mm, round, R9

A5   (obverse similar to A50)
             GOOD FOR / 5 / IN / MERCHANDISE
             aluminum, 20mm, round, R10

This firm operated a small country store from the 1890s to the 1930s. The store (and all the merchandise inside) sat undisturbed for many years until the 1980s, when it was all donated to the South Carolina State Museum. On the third floor of the museum, the entire store was reassembled into a fine exhibit highlighting the role of the country store in the local history of the state.

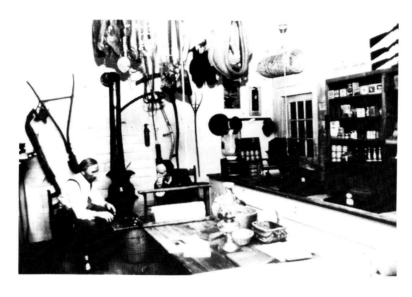

An interior view of the J. W. Jenny & Co. store.

JOHNS ISLAND (Charleston County) 1955

A10 E. M. I. BROWN, / AGENT / GEN. / MDSE. / JOHNS ISLAND / S.C.
GOOD FOR / 10¢ / IN / MERCHANDISE
brass, 23mm, round, R10
During the mid-1920s E. M. I. Brown ran a general store.

JOHNSTON (Edgefield County) 1960

A5 GOOD FOR / 5¢ / J.H. BOUKNIGHT
(blank)
aluminum, 20mm, round, R9
J. H. Bouknight operated a general store near the town of Johnston during the teens.

B5 LA GRONE DRUG CO. / JOHNSTON / S.C.
GOOD FOR ONE / 5¢ / DRINK / OR CIGAR
aluminum, 25mm, octagonal, R10
The LaGrone brothers, Elzie and James, operated a drug store during the mid-teens.

JONESVILLE (Union County)

A100 WALLACE MILL STORE / 1⁰⁰ / GOOD FOR / MDSE. ONLY /
JONESVILLE, S.C.
> (Master Metal Scrip - type I)
> nickel, 35mm, round, "W" c/o, R8

A50 (obverse similar to A100 except denomination 50)
> (Master Metal Scrip - type I)
> brass, 30mm, round, "W" c/o, R8

A25 (obverse similar to A100 except denomination 25)
> (Master Metal Scrip - type I)
> copper, 24mm, round, "W" c/o, R8

A10 (obverse similar to A100 except denomination 10)
> (Master Metal Scrip - type II)
> nickel, 21mm, round, "W" c/o, R7

A5 (obverse similar to A100 except denomination 5)
> (Master Metal Scrip - type I)
> brass, 19mm, round, "W" c/o, R7

> During the teens, twenties, and thirties Wallace Mill was owned and operated by the Victor - Monaghan Corp. of Greenville, a large textile conglomerate. The tokens were probably issued in the thirties.

KEG TOWN (Spartanburg County) 1980

A5 AT L. AND W. SERVICE / STATION / KEG / TOWN, / S.C.
GOOD FOR / 5¢ / IN TRADE / THE OSBORNE REGISTER CO., CIN,O.
(in tiny letters)
> brass, 20mm, round, R10

> Keg Town was actually part of the town of Pacolet.

LADIES ISLAND (Beaufort County) 2000

A L. P. MAGGIONI & CO. / LADIES / ISLAND, / S.C.
WORK ON ONE / POT / PEELED / SHRIMP
> aluminum, 19mm, round, R10

> L. P. Maggioni & Co., headquartered in Savannah, Ga., purchased the Hunt Packing Company around 1920. See listings under Beaufort for tokens of Hunt Packing Co.

LA FRANCE (Anderson County)   2005

A100   PENDLETON MANUFACTURING CO. / STORE / 1$\underline{00}$ / LA FRANCE / S.C.
(Master Metal Scrip - type II)
nickel-plated brass, 35mm, round, "P" c/o, R8

A50   (obverse similar to A100 except denomination 50)
(Master Metal Scrip - type II)
nickel, 30mm, round, "P" c/o, R8

A25   (obverse similar to A100 except denomination 25)
(Master Metal Scrip - type I)
copper, 24mm, round, "P" c/o, R8

A10   (obverse similar to A100 except denomination 10)
(Master Metal Scrip - type II)
nickel-plated brass, 21mm, round, "P" c/o, R7

Varieties are known without a cutout.

A5   (obverse similar to A100 except denomination 5)
(Master Metal Scrip - type II)
brass, 19mm, round, "P" c/o, R7

A1   (obverse similar to A100 except denomination 1)
(Master Metal Scrip - type II) (varieties exist)
copper, 18mm, round, "P" c/o, R5

The Pendleton Manufacturing Company is perhaps the oldest textile plant still operating in South Carolina. It was founded on the present site in 1838. The town, originally called simply Pendleton Factory, was named Autun in 1879 and renamed La France in 1927. (It is rumored that tokens exist showing an Autun address.) In the 1840s and again in the 1860s, paper scrip was issued which is quite scarce today. The listed tokens are from the late 1920s or early 1930s.

LAKE CITY (Florence County)   2010

A5   DEEP RIVER LB'R COR'P. / LAKE CITY, / S.C.
DUE BEARER / 5¢ / IN MERCHANDISE / AT / COMPANY STORE
nickel, 22mm, round, R10

Headquartered in Norfolk, Va. the Deep River Lumber Corp. operated a sawmill near Lake City during the teens and early twenties.

B100   MOORE & WILSON / 1$\underline{00}$
(Ingle System - 1914 pat. date)
composition unknown, 35mm, round, R10

B1   (obverse similar to B100 except denomination 1)
(Ingle System - 1914 pat. date)
composition unknown, 18mm, round, R10

Attribution tentative. Moore & Wilson were listed as meat dealers in 1915. Obverse description may not be exact.

LAKE VIEW   (Dillon County)   2015

A   LAKE VIEW SCHOOL / LUNCH / LAKE VIEW, S.C.
        (blank)
            brass, 23mm, round, R4 (varieties exist)

B   (obverse similar to A)
        (blank)
            aluminum, 23mm, round, R4

LAMBERT   (Williamsburg County)   2020

A25   W. C. HEMINGWAY & CO. / STORE / LAMBERT, S.C.
        GOOD FOR / 25¢ / IN MERCHANDISE
            brass, 28mm, round, R10

        This store was in operation during the teens. For other tokens of the
    company, see Hemingway.

LANCASTER   (Lancaster County)   2025

A5   DABNEY'S LUNCH / 342 / MIDWAY / ST. / LANCASTER, S.C.
        GOOD FOR / 5¢ / IN TRADE
            brass, 20mm, round, R10

        Andrew B. Dabney operated a restaurant and cafe in the 1930s. Other
    denominations are rumored to exist.

B50   LANCASTER / CO-OPERATIVE / STORE / LANCASTER, S.C.
        GOOD FOR / 50 / IN MERCHANDISE
            aluminum, 33mm, round, R9

B10   (obverse similar to B50)
        GOOD FOR / 10 / IN MERCHANDISE
            aluminum, 22mm, round, R10

B5   (obverse similar to B50)
        GOOD FOR / 5 / IN MERCHANDISE
            aluminum, 21mm, round, R9

B1   (obverse similar to B50)
        GOOD FOR / 1 / IN MERCHANDISE
            aluminum, 19mm, round, R9

C1   LANCASTER / CO-OPERATIVE / STORE / LUNCH / STAND /
        LANCASTER, S.C.
        GOOD FOR / 1 / IN / MERCHANDISE
            brass, 18mm, round, R10

        This store operated from the late teens to the early thirties. It probably
    functioned as company store for one of the area's textile mills.

D5   LANCASTER PHARMACY / ON THE SQUARE / HOME / OF NYAL'S /
REMEDIES / LANCASTER, S.C.
> GOOD FOR ONE / 5¢ / SODA OR CIGAR
>> aluminum, 24mm, round, R10

>> The Lancaster Pharmacy was in business during the teens and early
twenties.

E10   J. F. MACKEY & CO. / LANCASTER / S.C.
> WORTH / 10¢ / IN TRADE / AT THE FOUNTAIN
>> aluminum, 23mm, round, R10

E5   (obverse similar to E10)
> WORTH / 5¢ / IN TRADE / AT THE FOUNTAIN
>> aluminum, 20mm, round, R10

>> J. F. Mackey & Co. operated a drug store in downtown Lancaster from
the early 1900s through the 1940s.   The company also operated an
undertaking service and a furniture business.

F5   L. T. THREATT / LANCASTER / S.C.
> GOOD FOR / 5¢ / IN TRADE
>> brass, 24mm, round, R10

>> In 1915 L. T. Threatt was listed as a grocer.

LANDO   (Chester County)   2030

A100   MANETTA MILLS STORE / LANDO / S.C.
> GOOD FOR / 100 / IN MERCHANDISE
>> aluminum, 35mm, round, R7 (varieties exist)

A50   (obverse similar to A100)
> GOOD FOR / 50 / IN MERCHANDISE
>> aluminum, 33mm, round, R7

A25   (obverse similar to A100)
> GOOD FOR / 25 / IN MERCHANDISE
>> aluminum, 29mm, round, R7

A10   (obverse similar to A100)
> GOOD FOR / 10 / IN MERCHANDISE
>> aluminum, 24mm, round, R7 (varieties exist)

A5   (obverse similar to A100)
> GOOD FOR / 5 / IN MERCHANDISE
>> aluminum, 19mm, round, R7 (varieties exist)

A2   (obverse similar to A100)
> GOOD FOR / 2 / IN MERCHANDISE
>> aluminum, 26mm, octagonal, R9

A1   (obverse similar to A100)
            GOOD FOR / 1 / IN MERCHANDISE
            aluminum, 28mm, scalloped (6), R9

B100   (obverse similar to A100)
            GOOD FOR / $1.00 / IN / MERCHANDISE (ornate)
            aluminum, 35mm, round, R9

C25   (obverse similar to A100)
            GOOD FOR / 25 / IN MERCHANDISE (solid numerals)
            aluminum, 28mm, round, R7

C10   (obverse similar to A100)
            GOOD FOR / 10 / IN MERCHANDISE (solid numerals)
            aluminum, 24mm, round, R7

C5   (obverse similar to A100)
            GOOD FOR / 5 / IN / MERCHANDISE (solid numeral)
            aluminum, 19mm, round, R7

D5   (obverse similar to A100)
            GOOD FOR / 5¢ / IN TRADE
            aluminum, 19mm, round, R9

In operation as early as the 1890s, Manetta Mills is still in business. Per Randy Chambers, "The Lando mill store was typical of most textile mill stores in South Carolina. They sold just about everything from ladies' finery to coffins. The Lando complex, however, also offered a barber shop, a beauty salon, and a cafe for the mill employees. It was probably one of the larger mill store complexes in the state."

LANGLEY   (Aiken County)   2035

A500   AIKEN COUNTY STORES INC. / 5⁰⁰ / BATH + LANGLEY + / CLEARWATER, / S.C.
            (Orco - type I)
            brass, 32mm, scalloped (12), "L" c/o, R5

A100   (obverse similar to A500 except denomination 1⁰⁰)
            (Orco - type II)
            nickel, 32mm, round, "L" c/o, R3

A50   (obverse similar to A500 except denomination 50)
            (Orco - type II)
            copper, 27mm, round, "L" c/o, R3

A25   (obverse similar to A500 except denomination 25)
            (Orco - type II)
            nickel, 24mm, round, "L" c/o, R2

A10   (obverse similar to A500 except denomination 10)
       (Orco - type II)
          brass, 21mm, round, "L" c/o, R2

A5   (obverse similar to A500 except denomination 5)
       (Orco - type II)
          nickel, 19mm, round, "L" c/o, R2

A1   (obverse similar to A500 except denomination 1)
       (Orco - type II)
          copper, 18mm, round, "L" c/o, R4

B1   AIKEN COUNTY STORES INC. / 1 / L / BATH + LANGLEY + /
CLEARWATER, / S.C.
       (Orco - type III)
          copper, 17mm, round, no cutout, R4

    Aiken County Stores, Inc. operated the company store for Langley Mills during the 1930s. Prior to that time Langley Mills operated its own store. See listings under Langley Mills Store and Langley Mfg. Co. for other tokens used at this mill.

C10   CHAFEE BROS. (in script) / LANGLEY, / S.C.
       GOOD FOR / 10 / IN / MERCHANDISE
          brass, 25mm, round, R10

C5   (obverse similar to C10, but counterstamped "J")
       GOOD FOR / 5 / IN / MERCHANDISE
          brass, 21mm, round, R9

D5   (obverse similar to C5, but different die and no ctsp.)
       GOOD FOR / 5¢ / IN / MERCHANDISE
          brass, 21mm, round, R8

    The Chafee Bros. operated a general store during the early 1900s. By 1908 only John G. Chafee is listed in business, possibly accounting for the "J" counterstamped on some of the pieces.

E10   LANGLEY MANUFACTURING CO'S. STORE / LANGLEY / S.C.
       GOOD FOR / 10 / IN MERCHANDISE
          aluminum, 24mm, round, R10

F5   THE LANGLEY MILLS STORE / LANGLEY, / S.C.
       GOOD FOR / ONE / 5¢ / DRINK OF COCA - COLA
          brass, 25mm, round, R5

LATHEM (Pickens County)   2040

A100   J. W. LOOPER / MERCHANT / LATHEM, S.C.
       GOOD FOR / 100 / IN MERCHANDISE
          aluminum, 35mm, round, R9

LATHEM (Continued)   2040

A50   (obverse similar to A100)
            GOOD FOR / 50 / IN MERCHANDISE
            aluminum, 33mm, round, R9

A25   (obverse similar to A100)
            GOOD FOR / 25 / IN MERCHANDISE
            aluminum, 29mm, round, R9

            From the early teens to the middle thirties, J. W. Looper ran a general
            store and cotton gin. The town of Lathem was located near Easley.

LATTA (Dillon County)   2045

A5   THE BEATTY CO. / LATTA / ARCADE
            SODA OR CIGARS / 5¢.
            aluminum, 27mm, octagonal, R10

            Attribution tentative.

B25   L.H.S. CAFETERIA
            25 c / IN TRADE (across numerals)
            aluminum, 29mm, round, R5

C25   L.H.S. / CAFETERIA
            25 c / IN TRADE (across numerals)
            aluminum, 29mm, round, R5

D25   (obverse and reverse similar to C25)
            brass, 29mm, round, R5

            These tokens were issued by the Latta High School Cafeteria.

LAURENS (Laurens County)   2050

A5   THE EUREKA DRUG CO. / LAURENS / S.C.
            GOOD FOR / 5¢ / AT FOUNTAIN
            brass, 19mm, round, R10

            The Eureka Drug Company was listed from 1912 to 1933.

B5   LAURENS COTTON MILLS / 5 / LAURENS / S.C.
            GOOD FOR / 5 / CENTS / IN MERCHANDISE
            aluminum, 20mm, round, R10

B1   (obverse similar to B5 except denomination 1)
            GOOD FOR / 1 / CENT / IN MERCHANDISE
            aluminum, 18mm, round, R10

            Laurens Cotton Mills was in operation from the early 1900s to the 1960s.
            The company specialized in print cloths.

C5   PALMETTO DRUG CO. LAURENS, S.C.
           GOOD FOR 5¢ IN TRADE
              aluminum, incomplete description, R10

           This company operated from the turn of the century to the mid-teens.

D5   DR. B. F. POSEY / WHOLESALE / & / RETAIL / DRUGGIST / LAURENS, S.C.
              GOOD FOR / 5¢ / DRINK
              aluminum, 24mm, round, R10

              Dr. B. F. Posey operated a drug store from the late 1880s to the late teens. During the 1890s he also operated a drug store in Union, but no tokens are known from that store.

E10   WASHINGTON FINANCE / N. HARPER ST. / LAURENS, S.C.
              10¢
              aluminum, 26mm, round, R8

E2   (obverse same as E10)
              2¢
              aluminum, 26mm, round, R10

A postcard view of Watts Mills.

F25   WATTS MILLS / LAURENS, / S.C.
              GOOD FOR / 25 / IN MERCHANDISE
              brass, 30mm, octagonal, R10

F1   (obverse similar to F25)
              GOOD FOR / 1 / IN MERCHANDISE
              brass, 18mm, octagonal, R10

              Watts Mills has been in operation since the turn of the century.

LAURINBURG

Tokens issued by the LAURINBURG PLYWOOD CORP. which have a Laurinburg, S.C. address are die-cutting errors. The company was located in Laurinburg, N.C.

LEES (Bamberg County)   2058

A5 THE MAYFIELD CO. / LEES, S.C.
  GOOD FOR / 5¢ / IN / MERCHANDISE
  brass, 20mm, round, R10

  The Mayfield Co. operated a general store in Lees around 1910. See listing under Denmark for another token issued by the company.

LEESVILLE (Lexington County)   2060

A50 MATTHEWS / & / BOUKNIGHT / CO. / LEESVILLE, S.C.
  GOOD FOR / 50 / IN MERCHANDISE
  aluminum, 33mm, round, R10

A25 (obverse similar to A50)
  GOOD FOR / 25 / IN MERCHANDISE
  aluminum, 29mm, round, R10

A10 (obverse similar to A50)
  GOOD FOR / 10 / IN MERCHANDISE
  aluminum, 24mm, round, R9

A5 (obverse similar to A50)
  GOOD FOR / 5 / IN MERCHANDISE
  aluminum, 19mm, round, R9

  This company ran a general store from the early 1890s to the early 1930s.

B10 J. C. SWYGERT & SON, / LEESVILLE, / S.C.
  GOOD FOR / 10 / IN TRADE
  aluminum, 24mm, round, R10

  J. C. Swygert & Son operated a general store during the teens.

LEIGH (Barnwell County)   2065

A50 LEIGH BANANA CASE CO. / COMMISSARY / LEIGH, S.C.
  GOOD FOR / 50¢ / IN TRADE
  nickel, 28mm, round, R9

A25 (obverse similar to A50)
  GOOD FOR / 25¢ / IN TRADE
  nickel, 26mm, round, R9

LEIGH (Continued)

A10   (obverse similar to A50)
        GOOD FOR / 10¢ / IN TRADE
          nickel, 25mm, round, R9

A5   (obverse similar to A50)
        GOOD FOR / 5¢ / IN TRADE
          nickel, 20mm, round, R8

A1   (obverse similar to A50)
        GOOD FOR / 1¢ / IN TRADE
          nickel, 18mm, round, R5 (varieties exist)

    Headquartered in Chicago, Illinois, the Leigh Banana Case Co. made fruit and vegetable crates. In the 1950s the town was closed and all families were forced to move when the Savannah River Nuclear Weapons Plant was built.

LEXINGTON   (Lexington County)

A50   BUDDY PACKING COMPANY NOT INC. / J. E. / HARMAN / MGR. / LEXINGTON / S.C.
        GOOD FOR / 50¢ / IN TRADE
          aluminum, 28mm, round, R5

A25   (obverse similar to A50)
        GOOD FOR / 25¢ / IN TRADE
          aluminum, 26mm, round, R5

A10   (obverse similar to A50)
        GOOD FOR / 10¢ / IN TRADE
          aluminum, 25mm, round, R5

A5   (obverse similar to A50)
        GOOD FOR / 5¢ / IN TRADE
          aluminum, 20mm, round, R5

    J. E. (Ed) Harman packed sandwiches and box lunches for the employees of Lexington Cotton Mill, which was located right across the street. Harman also packaged a patent medicine called KOB Salve ("Knock Out Brand"). His business operated during the 1920s, 1930s, and 1940s.

B5   TAYLOR'S / 5 / LEXINGTON, S.C.
        (Orco - type unknown)
          nickel, 19mm, round, R10

B1   (obverse similar to B5 except denomination 1)
        (Orco - type III)
          copper, 18mm, round, R10

LITTLE ROCK   (Dillon County)   2090

A100   LOYD & CO. / LITTLE ROCK / S.C.
          GOOD FOR / $1<u>00</u> / IN MERCHANDISE
          aluminum, 31mm, round, R10

A1   (obverse similar to A100)
          GOOD FOR / 1 / IN MERCHANDISE
          aluminum, 18mm, round, R10

          This general store was listed in 1926 and 1927.

LOCKHART   (Union County)   2095

A100   LOCKHART MILLS STORE / 1<u>00</u> / LOCKHART, S.C.
          (Orco - type II)
          nickel, 32mm, round, comma-shaped c/o, R9

A50   (obverse similar to A100 except denomination 50)
          (Orco - type II)
          brass, 27mm, round, comma-shaped c/o, R8

A25   (obverse similar to A100 except denomination 25)
          (Orco - type II)
          brass, 24mm, round, comma-shaped c/o, R8

A10   (obverse similar to A100 except denomination 10)
          (Orco - type II)
          brass, 21mm, round, comma-shaped c/o, R8

A5   (obverse similar to A100 except denomination 5)
          (Orco - type II)
          brass, 19mm, round, comma-shaped c/o, R8

A1   (obverse similar to A100 except denomination 1)
          (Orco - type II)
          brass, 18mm, round, comma-shaped c/o, R8

          Lockhart Mills began operations circa 1900. The tokens were issued
          circa 1930, when the company was owned by Monarch Mills of Union.

LODGE   (Colleton County)   2100

A5   F. N. JONES / P.O. / LODGE, S.C. / R.F.D. #1 / ASHTON, S.C.
          GOOD FOR / 5 / IN / MERCHANDISE
          brass, 20mm, round, R10

          During the teens and early twenties F. N. Jones operated a sawmill,
          cotton gin, and general store about 5 miles south of Lodge. The *1920
          Southern Lumberman's Directory* lists a circular sawmill with a 7000 feet
          capacity, a planing mill, a logging railroad with 6 miles of track, and a
          commissary.

LODGE   (Continued)   2100

B10   LODGE MERCANTILE CO. / LODGE, / S.C.
         GOOD FOR / 10 / IN / MERCHANDISE
         aluminum, 24mm, round, R10

B5   (obverse similar to B10)
         GOOD FOR / 5 / IN / MERCHANDISE.
         aluminum, 21mm, round, R10
         This company operated during the teens and twenties.

LONGCREEK   (Oconee County)   2105

A   HORSESHOE LAKE / FARMS / LONGCREEK / S.C.
         GOOD FOR / ONE / BUCKET
         aluminum, 17mm, round, R9, modern

LORIS   (Horry County)   2115

A100   L. D. SUGGS / LORIS, S.C.
         GOOD FOR / 1$\underline{00}$ / IN MERCHANDISE
         brass, 37mm, round, R10

A50   (obverse similar to A100)
         GOOD FOR / 50 / IN MERCHANDISE
         brass, 32mm, round, R10

A25   (obverse similar to A100)
         GOOD FOR / 25 / IN MERCHANDISE
         brass, 27mm, round, R10

A10   (obverse similar to A100)
         GOOD FOR / 10 / IN MERCHANDISE
         brass, 22mm, round, R9

A5   (obverse similar to A100)
         GOOD FOR / 5 / IN MERCHANDISE
         brass, 20mm, round, R9

         During the teens L. D. Suggs operated a sawmill and general store 6
miles west of Loris.

LOWRYVILLE   (Chester County)   2120

A100   E. S. CARTER / 1$\underline{00}$
         (Ingle System - 1914 pat. date)
            composition unknown, 35mm, round, R10

LOWRYVILLE   (Continued)   2120

A25   (obverse similar to A100 except denomination 25)
            (Ingle System - 1914 pat. date)
            brass, 24mm, round, R10

            E. S. Carter ran a general store and cotton gin near Lowryville during
            the late teens and early twenties. In the late 1920s the town's name was
            changed to Lowrys.

LYNCHBURG   (Lee County)   2135

A50   F. A. CRIBBS / GENERAL / MERCHANDISE / LYNCHBURG, S.C.
            GOOD FOR / 50¢ / IN MERCHANDISE
            aluminum, 28mm, round, R7

A25   (obverse similar to A50)
            GOOD FOR / 25¢ / IN MERCHANDISE
            aluminum, 26mm, round, R7

A10   (obverse similar to A50)
            GOOD FOR / 10¢ / IN MERCHANDISE
            aluminum, 25mm, round, R7

A5   (obverse similar to A50)
            GOOD FOR / 5¢ / IN MERCHANDISE
            aluminum, 20mm, round, R7

A1   (obverse similar to A50)
            GOOD FOR / 1¢ / IN MERCHANDISE
            aluminum, 18mm, round, R7

            F. A. Cribbs was in business in the 1930s.

MANNING   (Clarendon County)   2150

A   ARANT'S DRUG STORE / SCHOOL / SUPPLIES / AND / BOOKS
            5 CHECKS / GOOD FOR / ONE / FIVE CENT PENCIL
            aluminum, 25mm, scalloped (12), R10

            J. E. Arant operated his drug store from 1908 to 1945.

B   MANNING TRAINING / ADMISSION / COIN / SCHOOL
            (same)
            aluminum, 28mm, round, R10

C5   JACK G. METROPOL MANNING, S.C.
            GOOD FOR 5¢ IN TRADE
            incomplete description, brass, round, R10

            During the teens Metropol was a fruit dealer and confectioner. During
            the twenties, he was listed as the proprietor of the Boston Candy Kitchen,
            Manning Bottling Works, and Central Cafe.

MANNING   (Continued)   2150

D50   ZEIGLER'S PHARMACY / THE / HOME OF / PURE / DRUGS /
         MANNING, S.C.
         GOOD FOR / 50¢ / IN TRADE
             aluminum, 32mm, round, R10

D25   (obverse similar to D50)
         GOOD FOR / 25¢ / IN TRADE
             aluminum, 28mm, round, R10

         Mrs. H. T. Zeigler operated her pharmacy during the teens and early
twenties.

MAPPUS   (Charleston County)   2155

A100   GOOD FOR / 1⁰⁰ / AT / R. RICHTER
          WULBERN FERTILIZER CO. / W / CHARLESTON, S.C.
              brass, 34mm, round, R10

A10   (obverse similar to A100 except denomination 10¢)
          (reverse similar to A100)
              brass, 20mm, round, R10

          These tokens were issued by Rudolph Richter, who operated a general
store circa 1910. The community of Mappus was located about 7 miles
north of Charleston. The reverse of the tokens features an advertisement
for the Wulbern Fertilizer Co., a manufacturer located in Charleston.

MARION   (Marion County)   2160

A1   AMERICAN WOOD PRODUCTS CORP. / MARION, / S.C.
          GOOD FOR / 1¢ / IN TRADE (varieties exist)
              aluminum, 18mm, round, R6

          This corporation was a subsidiary of the Folding Box Company of
Cleveland, Ohio. The firm, which operated from the late 1920s through the
1940s, made wooden and wire-bound boxes.

B100   BELL LUMBER CO. / MARION / S.C.
          GOOD FOR / $1⁰⁰ / IN / MERCHANDISE
              brass, 35mm, round, R10

B5   (obverse similar to B100)
          GOOD FOR / 5¢ / IN MERCHANDISE
              brass, 21mm, round, R10

B1 (obverse similar to B100)
GOOD FOR / 1¢ / IN MERCHANDISE
brass, 19mm, round, R10

The Bell Lumber Co. operated from the mid-teens to the mid-thirties. Its capacity was 42,000 feet in 1920. The mill featured an electric light plant, commissary, and logging railroad.

C100 CAMP MANUFACTURING CO. / 1⁰⁰ / MARION, S.C.
PAYABLE IN / 1⁰⁰ / MERCHANDISE ONLY
brass, 38mm, scalloped (12), R9

C50 (obverse similar to C100 except denomination 50)
PAYABLE IN / 50 / MERCHANDISE ONLY
brass, 35mm, scalloped (11), R9

C25 (obverse similar to C100 except denomination 25)
PAYABLE IN / 25 / MERCHANDISE ONLY
brass, 32mm, scalloped (9), R8

C10 (obverse similar to C100 except denomination 10)
PAYABLE IN / 10 / MERCHANDISE ONLY
brass, 29mm, scalloped (8), R10

D100 CAMP MFG. CO. / WOODS / STORE / № 5
GOOD FOR / $1⁰⁰ / IN MERCHANDISE
aluminum, 31mm, octagonal, R8

D50 (obverse similar to D100)
GOOD FOR / 50¢ / IN MERCHANDISE
aluminum, 28mm, octagonal, R8

D25 (obverse similar to D100)
GOOD FOR / 25¢ / IN MERCHANDISE
aluminum, 26mm, octagonal, R8

E25 CAMP / MANUFACTURING / CO. / STORE № 5 / NOT TRANSFERABLE
GOOD FOR / 25 / IN MERCHANDISE
brass, 25mm, round, R8

E10 (obverse similar to E25)
GOOD FOR / 10¢ / IN MERCHANDISE
brass, 23mm, round, R10

F10 CAMP MFG. CO. / MILL / STORE / 5
GOOD FOR / 10¢ / IN / MERCHANDISE
brass, 25mm, round, R8

F5 (obverse similar to F10)
GOOD FOR / 5¢ / IN / MERCHANDISE
brass, 20mm, round, R8

Headquartered in Franklin, Va., Camp Manufacturing Company, was incorporated in 1887 by Paul D. Camp and his two brothers, James L. and Robert J.   During the ensuing years the company expanded rapidly, building two more sawmills in Virginia. In the early 1900s it expanded into the Carolinas, building sawmills at one time or another in the following South Carolina towns: Marion, Gourdin, Russsellville, Greeleyville, Andrews, and Saint Stephens.

The company issued quite a few different tokens, most of them identified by either a store number or a city/state address. Store No. 3 was located at one time in Gourdin and later in Russsellville; Store No. 5 was at Marion; and Store No. 6 was at Greeleyville and later in Andrews. The number of the Saint Stephens store is unknown. In his book, *Virginia Tokens*, David Schenkman writes: "The usage of tokens, however, was not restricted to one store; they were accepted at any Camp store... When one store closed, the same number would be assigned to another store, so it isn't always possible to determine which store a token was originally struck for. The use of tokens was discontinued in the mid-1940s. Camp's last company store was closed in 1956."

The author has listed all known Camp tokens that feature a South Carolina address or a store number that was known to have operated in South Carolina. See listings under Russellville for additional tokens of the company.

G5 J. S. DAVIS / DRUGGIST / MARION, S.C.
　　　　GOOD FOR / 5¢ / SODA WATER / OR CIGAR
　　　　　aluminum, 24mm, round, R10

　　　　　J. S. Davis operated a drug store for many years, from as early as 1893 to as late as 1933.

H　　DELMONICO / HOTEL / MARION, S.C.
　　　　GOOD FOR / ONE / ROUND TRIP
　　　　　brass, 25mm, octagonal, R10 (Atwood 650A)

I　　(obverse similar to H)
　　　　GOOD FOR 25¢ IN TRANSPORTATION ON TRUNKS
　　　　　incomplete description, brass, 25mm, round, R10 (Atwood 650B)

　　　　　Per the Atwood-Coffee catalog, "The Delmonico Hotel was built about 1850, constructed of odd-colored brick which had been used as ballast in old sailing ships.   Sometime between 1900 and 1920 the name was changed to the Jenkins Hotel, and the structure was town down in the late 1930s."

J10 D. M. HARPER / GENERAL / MERCHANDISE / MARION
　　　　GOOD FOR / 10¢ / IN / MERCHANDISE
　　　　　zinc, 23mm, round, R10

　　　　　D. M. Harper ran a general store near Marion from the late 1920s to the late 1940s. The composition of the token suggests it was struck during World War II.

K1　R. W. LAWLER STORE / 1¢ / MARION, S.C.
　　　　GOOD FOR / 1¢ / IN TRADE
　　　　　aluminum, 18mm, round, R7

L100   MARION COUNTY LUMBER CO. / $1⁰⁰ / MILL STORE
       MILL STORE / $1⁰⁰ / NOT TRANSFERABLE / SO. S. & S. CO. RICH'D,
       VA. (in tiny letters)
         brass, 35mm, round, R8

L25   (obverse similar to L100 except denomination 25¢)
       MILL STORE / 25¢ / NOT TRANSFERABLE / SO. S. & S. CO. RICH'D,
       VA. (in tiny letters)
         brass, 28mm, round, R8

M100   MARION COUNTY LUMBER CO. / MILL / STORE (ctsp "H")
       GOOD FOR / 1⁰⁰ / IN / MERCHANDISE / NOT TRANSFERABLE
         brass, 35mm, round, R10

M50   (obverse similar to M100)
       GOOD FOR / 50¢ / IN / MERCHANDISE / NOT TRANSFERABLE
         brass, 30mm, round, R10

M10   (obverse similar to M100)
       GOOD FOR / 10¢ / IN / MERCHANDISE / NOT / TRANSFERABLE
         brass, 25mm, round, R10

       This company was in operation from the early 1900s to the late teens.
It was headquartered in Franklin, Virginia and controlled by the Camp
family. See notes following listings of Camp Mfg. Co., Marion, S.C. tokens.

N25   MARION LUMBER MFG. CO. / 25 / MARION, S.C.
       (Orco - type I)
         nickel, 24mm, round, star c/o, R10

N10   (obverse similar to N25 except denomination 10)
       (Orco - type I)
         brass, 21mm, round, no cutout, R9

N5   (obverse similar to N25 except denomination 5)
       (Orco - type II)
         nickel, 19mm, round, no cutout, R9

N1   (obverse similar to N25 except denomination 1)
       (Orco - type I)
         copper, 18mm, round, no cutout, R9

O5   MARION LUMBER MFG. CO. / MARION / S.C.
       GOOD FOR / 5¢ / IN MERCHANDISE
         aluminum, 20mm, round, star cutout, R10

       The Marion Lumber Manufacturing Company was listed from 1921 to
1933.

MARS BLUFF   (Florence County)   2165

A50   H. F. HESTER / MARS / BLUFF, / S.C.
           GOOD FOR / 50 / IN TRADE ONLY
             brass, 33mm, round, R10

B100   G. J. PAIT / MARS BLUFF, / S.C.
           1$\underline{00}$
             aluminum, 38mm, round, R8

B50   (obverse similar to B100)
           50
             aluminum, 31mm, round, R8

B25   (obverse similar to B100)
           25
             aluminum, 27mm, round, R8

B10   (obverse similar to B100)
           10
             aluminum, 24mm, round, R8

B5   (obverse similar to B100)
           5
             aluminum, 21mm, round, R8

C50   J. R. PAIT, / GENERAL / MERCHANDISE / MARS BLUFF, S.C.
           GOOD FOR / 50 / IN / MERCHANDISE
             composition unknown, 33mm, round, R9

             J. R. Pait operated a general store and sawmill in the early teens. Some specimens have been counterstamped "VOID."

D25   W. L. RANKIN LUMBER CO. / MARS / BLUFF, / S.C.
           GOOD FOR / 25 / IN TRADE ONLY
             aluminum, 28mm, round, R10

             The W. L. Rankin Lumber Company operated circa 1910.

MARTINS POINT   (Charleston County)   2170

A10   FRED W. TOWLES / MARTINS POINT, / S.C.
           GOOD FOR / 10¢ / IN TRADE
             brass, 22mm, octagonal, R10

             This truck farmer and general store owner was in business from 1904 to 1923.

Martins Point, P. O., S. C., June 22, 08

F. W. Towles' letterhead provides much information about his business activities.

MAYESVILLE   (Sumter County)   2185

A100   J. F. BLAND / MAYESVILLE / S.C.
GOOD FOR / 1\underline{00}$ / IN TRADE
brass, 35mm, round, R10

A5   (obverse similar to A100)
GOOD FOR / 5¢ / IN TRADE
brass, 21mm, round, R10

James F. Bland ran a general store and sold crossties circa 1905. It is believed that he also operated a large farm and used these tokens to pay his workers. His son, James F., Jr., later operated a vehicle and livestock sales business.

MAYO   (Spartanburg County)   2190

A100   MARY LOUISE MILLS STORE / 1$\underline{00}$ / IN TRADE / ONLY / M L / MAYO, S.C.
(Master Metal Scrip - type II)
nickel, 35mm, round, R9

A50   (obverse similar to A100 except denomination 50)
(Master Metal Scrip - type II)
brass, 30mm, round, R9

A25   (obverse similar to A100 except denomination 25)
(Master Metal Scrip - type I)
copper, 24mm, round, R9

MAYO (Continued) 2190

A10 (obverse similar to A100 except denomination 10)
(Master Metal Scrip - type II)
nickel, 21mm, round, R9

A5 (obverse similar to A100 except denomination 5)
(Master Metal Scrip - type II)
brass, 19mm, round, R9

A1 (obverse similar to A100 except denomination 1)
(Master Metal Scrip - type II)
copper, 18mm, round, R9

B100 (obverse similar to A100)
(Master Metal Scrip - type II)
brass, 35mm, round, R10

Mary Louise Mills was in operation from 1913 to 1938. In 1940, it became Mayo Mills. The company specialized in making cotton yarns.

McBEE (Chesterfield County) 2195

A10 INGRAM & McCOY / McBEE, S.C. / NOT / TRANSFERABLE
GOOD FOR / 10 / IN MERCHANDISE
brass, 24mm, round, R10

During the early 1900s this company operated a shingle mill and general store. After 1910 only J. D. Ingram is mentioned in relation to the business.

B5 J. K. McCOY / McBEE, S.C. / NOT / TRANSFERABLE / SO. S. & S. CO., RICH'D, VA. (in tiny letters)
GOOD FOR / 5¢ / IN MERCHANDISE
brass, 20mm, round, R10

J. K. McCoy was listed as the proprietor of Hotel Hampton from 1913 to 1915. He also operated a "men's furnishings" store at the same time. In the late 1930s he ran a filling station and grocery store.

McCLELLANVILLE (Charleston County) 2200

A10 McCLELLANVILLE CANNING CO. S.C. / 10
SPRAGUE CANNING MACHINERY CO. / CHICAGO
aluminum, 32mm, round, R9

This company canned oysters, etc. from the early 1900s to the early 1920s.

McCOLL   (Marlboro County)   2205

A100   D. J. BOLTON, / McCOLL, / S.C.
GOOD FOR / $1.00 / IN TRADE
aluminum, 38mm, round, R10

Bolton operated a general store from 1913 to 1926.

B10   WILLIAM H. / HUBBARD / McCOLL, S.C.
GOOD FOR / 10¢ / IN / MERCHANDISE / NOT TRANSFERABLE
aluminum, 23mm, square, R10

William H. Hubbard operated a general store and meat counter from the early teens to the early twenties.

C   THE JNO. M. STORE / McCOLL, S.C.: a set of five obverse dies with this inscription are known to exist. No tokens from these dies are known. The business operated as a general store from 1920 to 1927.

D5   IN TRADE / 5 / AT / PEOPLE'S MARKET
(Ingle System - 1909 pat. date)
brass, 20mm, round, R10

E1   PEOPLES MARKET / 1
(Ingle System - 1914 pat. date)
exact inscription and composition unknown, 18mm, round, R10

Attribution tentative. The tokens are listed because of their inclusion in Wagaman's listing of Ingle System tokens. There was a People's Market listed as a meat dealer in McColl in 1913 and 1914.

McNEILS   (Hampton County)   2225

A50   STONE & PATRICK / McNEILS / S.C.
50
aluminum, 33mm, round, R10

A25   (obverse similar to A50)
25
aluminum, 29mm, round, R10

Stone and Patrick were partners in a sawmill from 1904 to 1916.

MEGGETTS   (Charleston County)   2235

A100   THE CARR - CARLTON CO. / MEGGETTS, / S.C.
GOOD FOR / 1.00¢ / IN / MERCHANDISE
aluminum, 35mm, round, R10

A10   (obverse similar to A100)
GOOD FOR / 10 / IN / MERCHANDISE
aluminum, 21mm, round, R10

MEGGETTS (Continued) 2235

A5 (obverse similar to A100)
GOOD FOR / 5 / IN / MERCHANDISE
aluminum, 19mm, round, R10

In business in the teens and early twenties, this company operated one of the larger truck farms in the state. A truck farmer normally planted many acres of the same three or four vegetables, the large harvest usually being destined for shipment and sale to markets in the metropolitan areas of the northern United States. The tokens were issued to the farm hands and were redeemable at a small general store located on the farm. (For more about truck farming, see listings under Yonges Island.)

MILEY (Hampton County) 2250

A100 LIGHTSEY BROTHERS / PINE / CYPRESS / AND / HARDWOOD / MILEY, S.C.
GOOD FOR / 1⁰⁰ / PATD / JULY 1899 / IN MERCHANDISE
bimetallic, 39mm, round, R8

A50 (obverse similar to A100)
GOOD FOR / 50 / PAT. / APPLD. FOR / IN MERCHANDISE
bimetallic, 32mm, round, R8

A25 (obverse similar to A100)
GOOD FOR / 25 / PAT. / APPLD. FOR / IN MERCHANDISE
bimetallic, 28mm, round, R8

A10 (obverse similar to A100)
GOOD FOR / 10 / PAT / APPLD FOR / IN MERCHANDISE
bimetallic, 25mm, round, R8

The Lightsey Brothers' letterhead.

MILEY (Continued)   2250

A5   (obverse similar to A100)
           GOOD FOR / 5 / IN MERCHANDISE
           bimetallic, 20mm, round, R8

B10   LIGHTSEY BROS. INC. / MILEY, S.C. / NOT TRANSFERABLE
           GOOD FOR / 10¢ / IN MERCHANDISE
           aluminum, 25mm, round, R7

B5   LIGHTSEY BROS. INC. / MILEY, S.C. / NOT / TRANSFERABLE
           GOOD FOR / 5¢ / IN MERCHANDISE
           aluminum, 20mm, round, R7

The Lightsey Brothers (Henry and Fred) moved their sawmill operations to Miley from Crocketville around 1910. (See listings under Crocketville for additional tokens.) In 1919 they purchased The Hampton & Branchville Railroad and Lumber Company and the associated properties. In 1926 the railroad was extended toward Cottageville. Henry W. Lightsey died in 1932 and the business continued under the leadership of W. Fred Lightsey. The main sawmill burned down in 1939, but a new mill was quickly constructed.

W. Fred Lightsey died in 1940 and operations were taken over by W. Norris Lightsey and E. Oswald Lightsey. The sawmill was closed in 1956, but the company still holds vast tracts of timber and continues to operate by selling timber off of these tracts.

MILLETTVILLE (Allendale County)   2255

A100   L. J. SMITH / 1$\underline{^{00}}$
           (Ingle System - 1914 pat. date)
           composition unknown, 35mm, round, R10

Attribution tentative, based solely on Wagaman's inclusion in his book on Ingle System tokens.

MONCKS CORNER (Berkeley County)   2270

A25   S. BEHRMANN / AT MY STORE / MONCKS CORNER, / S.C.
           GOOD FOR / 25 / IN / MERCHANDISE
           aluminum, 24mm, round, R10

S. Behrmann operated a general store from 1908 to 1930.

MONT CLARE (Darlington County)   2275

A100   COXE BROS. / STORE / MONT CLARE, S.C.
           GOOD FOR / 1\underline{^{00}}$ / IN TRADE
           aluminum, 31mm, round, R6

MONT CLARE   (Continued)   2275

A50   (obverse similar to A100)
            GOOD FOR / 50¢ / IN TRADE
            aluminum, 28mm, round, R6

A25   (obverse similar to A100)
            GOOD FOR / 25¢ / IN TRADE
            aluminum, 26mm, round, R7

A10   (obverse similar to A100)
            GOOD FOR / 10¢ / IN TRADE
            aluminum, 25mm, round, R6

A5   (obverse similar to A100)
            GOOD FOR / 5¢ / IN TRADE
            aluminum, 20mm, round, R6

    The Coxe Bros. Lumber Company, successors to the Coxe - Ingram Lumber Co., operated a sawmill in Mont Clare during the 1930s and 1940s. Smaller mills were also located at Clio and Society Hill.

MONTMORENCI   (Aiken County)   2280

A   COMPANY / 4470 / C.C.C.
           GOOD FOR / 1 / GAME
           brass, 21mm, round, R10

    On 15 January 1936 Company 4470 of the Civilian Conservation Corps formed the Joseph Wheeler Camp outside Aiken, near the site of the town of Montmorenci. Prior to that time Company 4470 had been stationed at Cassatt, S.C. The token was probably used at both locations and thus is also listed under Cassatt.

MONTROSE   (Chesterfield County)   2285

A10   WELLING & BONNOITT / MONTROSE / S.C.
           10
           aluminum, 24mm, round, R10

    Welling & Bonnoitt were listed as hardware dealers in Darlington. Apparently they also operated a branch store at one time in this small town, located about 20 miles north of Darlington.

MOUNT HOLLY   (Berkeley County)   2300

A100   MT. HOLLY DEVELOPMENT CO. / 100 / IN / MERCHANDISE /
           MT. HOLLY, S.C. / MURDOCK, CIN,O. (in tiny letters)
           GOOD FOR / 100 / IN / MERCHANDISE
           brass, 34mm, round, R10

A25 (obverse similar to A100)
GOOD FOR / 25 / IN / MERCHANDISE
brass, 26mm, round, R9

A10 (obverse similar to A100)
GOOD FOR / 10 / IN / MERCHANDISE
brass, 22mm, round, R10

A5 (obverse similar to A100)
GOOD FOR / 5 / IN / MERCHANDISE
brass, 19mm, round, R10

This company was listed as a general store from 1913 to 1916.

MOUNT PLEASANT (Charleston County) 2305

A10 WM. HODGES / GREEN / GROCER / MT. PLEASANT, S.C.
GOOD FOR / 10¢ / WORTH ICE
brass, 24mm, round, R10

Hodges, a green grocer specializing in the sale of fresh vegetables, was in business from the early teens to the late twenties.

B5 K. BROS. / MT. P. S.C. / 5 (all incuse)
(blank)
brass, 20mm, round, R10

Tentatively attributed to the King Brothers, dealers in general merchandise, naval stores, and lumber during the early teens. In the late twenties they operated a canning company.

C5 WM. MOESSNER, / MT. PLEASANT, / S.C.
GOOD FOR / 5¢ / LOAF OF BREAD
composition unknown, 24mm, round, R10

William Moessner was a baker and grocer from the early 1890s to the early 1930s.

MULLINS (Marion County) 2315

A LEWIS & WILLIAMS / MULLINS, / S.C.
(incuse serial number)
brass, 27mm, round, R10

B20 MULLINS SCHOOL / LUNCH / ROOM
20c
brass, 26mm, round, R9

A   BEN'S / BINGO / MYRTLE BEACH / S.C.
GOOD / FOR ONE / FREE GAME
      aluminum, 38mm, round, R9, modern

B100   N C O / 1.00 / M B A F B
(blank)
      aluminum, 35mm, round, R9 (Curto A649-100)

B25   (obverse similar to B100 except denomination 25)
(blank)
      aluminum, 28mm, round, R9 (Curto A649-25)

C25   (obverse similar to B100 except denomination 25)
(blank)
      red-anodized aluminum, 28mm, round, R9 (Curto A217)

D100   NCOOM / MBAFB
GOOD FOR / 1.00 / IN MERCHANDISE ONLY
      brass, 32mm, round, R7

D25   (obverse similar to D100)
GOOD FOR / .25 / IN MERCHANDISE ONLY
      brass, 27mm, round, R7

D10   (obverse similar to D100)
GOOD FOR / .10 / IN MERCHANDISE ONLY
      brass, 22mm, round, R7

E100   NCOOM / MBAFB
GOOD FOR / 1.00 / IN MERCHANDISE ONLY
      aluminum, 32mm, round, R7

E25   (obverse similar to E100)
GOOD FOR / .25 / IN MERCHANDISE ONLY
      aluminum, 27mm, round, R7

E10   (obverse similar to E100)
GOOD FOR / .10 / IN MERCHANDISE ONLY
      aluminum, 22mm, round, R7

     Myrtle Beach Air Force Base was first activated in 1940 by the Army Air Corps. The 3rd Observation Squadron utilized the runways of the Myrtle Beach Municipal Airport during World War II. After the war the field was deactivated until 1949, when the 9th Air Force took over. The tokens were used in the 1950s and 1960s at the Non-Commissioned Officers' Open Mess.

F100   MYRTLE BEACH / FARMS / COMPANY / 1917 / MYRTLE BEACH, S.C.
PAYABLE ONLY IN MERCHANDISE / 1\frac{00}{}$ / AT THE / COMPANYS / STORE / AND NOT / TRANSFERABLE
      brass, 35mm, round, R8

F50   (obverse similar to F100)
(reverse similar to F100 except denomination 50¢)
      brass, 31mm, round, R8

F25   (obverse similar to F100)
          (reverse similar to F100 except denomination 25¢)
              brass, 28mm, round, R10

F10   (obverse similar to F100)
          (reverse similar to F100 except denomination 10¢)
              brass, 24mm, round, R10

F5   (obverse similar to F100)
          (reverse similar to F100 except denomination 5¢)
              brass, 20mm, round, R8

This firm was a partially owned subsidiary of the Burroughs & Collins Co. of Conway. The tokens were mainly issued to the company's farm workers, although they were also used in the company's lumbering and turpentine operations. The 25¢ and 10¢ denominations were reported by Randy Chambers, but this author (and other S.C. collectors and even the Burroughs heirs) have not been able to verify their existence. For more information on the Burroughs and Collins Company, see listings under The Jerry Cox Co. of Conway.

G   MYRTLE BEACH TROLLEY / (picture of trolley car) / TOKEN
          ONE-WAY / FARE / 50¢
              aluminum, 39mm, round, R6, modern (Atwood 690A)

H   GOOD FOR ONE / FREE GAME / CARPET GOLF / THE PAVILION /
          M.B., S.C.
              GOOD LUCK / (horseshoe and clover leaf)
              aluminum, 34mm, round, R9, modern

I   SLOPPY JOE'S / SOUVENIR / 1 / COUPON / BINGO
              MYRTLE BEACH / SOUTH CAROLINA
              brass, 32mm, round, R7

J   SLOPPY JOE'S / 1 / COUPON / BINGO
              MYRTLE BEACH / SOUTH CAROLINA
              brass, 32mm, round, R7

K   SLOPPY JOE'S / GOOD FOR / 1 / FREE GAME / BINGO
              MYRTLE BEACH / SOUTH CAROLINA
              aluminum, 32mm, round, R7 (varieties exist)

L15   GOOD FOR / 15¢ / G. W. TRASK & SONS / MYRTLE BEACH, S.C.
          (blank)
              tan cardboard, 32mm x 52mm, rectangular, R9

L10   (obverse similar to L15 except denomination 10¢)
          (blank)
              tan cardboard, 32mm x 52mm, rectangular, R9

L7½   (obverse similar to L15 except denomination 7½¢)
          (blank)
              tan cardboard, 32mm x 52mm, rectangular, R9

L5   (obverse similar to L15 except denomination 5¢)
            (blank)
               tan cardboard, 32mm x 52mm, rectangular, R9

               G. W. Trask & Sons ran a large farming operation, planting hundreds of acres in both Carolinas. Metal tokens were issued at the Burton, S.C. location.

NEESES   (Orangeburg County)   2330

A100   R. L. POOLE / 1<u>00</u> / NON-TRANSFERABLE
            (Ingle System - 1914 pat. date)
               nickel-plated brass, 35mm, round, R10

A5   (obverse similar to A100 except denomination 5)
            (Ingle System - 1914 pat. date)
               nickel-plated brass, 20mm, round, R10

               Although attributed by Randy Chambers to Poole Station, this merchant was listed in directories under Neeses from 1914 to 1923, as a general merchandise dealer.

NEWBERRY   (Newberry County)   2335

A25   GOOD FOR / 25 ¢/ IN / TRADE / ILEY W. FANT (all incuse)
            (blank)
               brass, 26mm, round, R10

               The 1890 gazetteer lists Iley W. Fant as a saloon owner.

B5   J. K. JONES / NEWBERRY, / S.C.
            GOOD FOR / 5¢ / GUM / CIGAR & SODA
               aluminum, 19mm, round, R10

               During the teens Jasper Krebs Jones operated a grocery store on the west end of Main Street.

C25   THE / NATIONAL BANK / OF / NEWBERRY / SOUTH CAROLINA
            WE WILL ACCEPT THIS ON DEPOSIT FOR / 25 CTS / IF YOU OPEN A NEW / SAVINGS ACCOUNT / OF $3<u>00</u> OR / MORE, LEAVING IT IN / THE BANK 12 MONTHS AND / PAY 4% COMPOUND / INTEREST / ON YOUR SAVINGS / SEMI-ANNUALLY
               brass, 31mm, round, R9

D   H. O. REECE (incuse) / GOOD FOR / 1 / SHAVE (incuse)
            (blank)
               brass, 24mm, round, R10

               H. O. Reece operated a barber shop and shaving parlor in Newberry during the 1880s and 1890s.

E5   E. SONNENBURG / BAKERY / & / CONFECTIONERY / NEWBERRY, S.C.
GOOD FOR / ONE / 5¢ / LOAF OF BREAD
aluminum, 28mm, scalloped (8), R10

This business operated circa 1905.

The Summer Bros. Company, circa 1910.

F   SUMMER BROS. CO. / NEWBERRY, / S.C.
GOOD FOR / 5 / GALLONS / GASOLINE
aluminum, 24mm, round, R10

George, Charlie, and Hack Summer started a retail grocery and confectionery business in 1886. As the years went by, the business evolved into handling dry goods, hardware, and general merchandise. It was also involved in oil leases in Texas. In 1927 the company was sold to another family member, Clarence T. Summer.

NEW BROOKLAND   (Lexington County)   2340

A50   M. S. GIBSON / GROCERIES / NEW / BROOKLAND, / S.C.
GOOD FOR / 50 / IN / MERCHANDISE
brass, 32mm, round, R10

M. S. Gibson operated a grocery store during the 1920s.   New
Brookland was later absorbed into the city of West Columbia.

NEWRY   (Oconee County)   2350

A   THE COURTNAY MFG. CO.
SPOOLING DEPARTMENT / 7
aluminum, 25mm, round, holed as made, R7

The Courtnay Manufacturing Company operated the cotton mill in
Newry from the early 1900s through the 1940s.   The company store,
operated by Ligon & Ledbetter of Anderson, was called The Newry Store
until the early 1940s, when the Newry Mercantile Company took over.

B100   NEWRY MERCANTILE CO. / 1$\underline{00}$ / NM / CO. / NEWRY, S.C.
(Orco - type IV, dated 1942)
nickel, 32mm, round, "N" c/o, R5

B50   (obverse similar to B100 except denomination 50)
(Orco - type IV, dated 1942)
nickel, 29mm, round, "N" c/o, R5

B25   (obverse similar to B100 except denomination 25)
(Orco - type IV, dated 1942)
nickel, 26mm, round, "N" c/o, R5

B10   (obverse similar to B100 except denomination 10)
(Orco - type IV, dated 1942)
nickel, 23mm, round, "N" c/o, R5

B5   (obverse similar to B100 except denomination 5)
(Orco - type IV, dated 1942)
nickel, 20mm, round, "N" c/o, R5

B1   (obverse similar to B100 except denomination 1)
(Orco - type IV, dated 1942)
nickel, 17mm, round, "N" c/o, R8

C100   THE NEWRY STORE / 1$\underline{00}$ / IN MDSE. / NEWRY, S.C.
(Master Metal Scrip - type II)
brass, 35mm, round, "N" c/o, R7

C50   (obverse similar to C100 except denomination 50)
(Master Metal Scrip - type II)
brass, 30mm, round, "N" c/o, R7

C25   (obverse similar to C100 except denomination 25)
(Master Metal Scrip - type I)
brass, 24mm, round, "N" c/o, R6

C10 (obverse similar to C100 except denomination 10)
(Master Metal Scrip - type II)
brass, 21mm, round, "N" c/o, R6

C5 (obverse similar to C100 except denomination 5)
(Master Metal Scrip - type I)
brass, 19mm, round, "N" c/o, R9

C1 (obverse similar to C100 except denomination 1)
(Master Metal Scrip - type II)
brass, 18mm, round, "N" c/o, R3 (varieties exist)

D5 (obverse similar to C5)
(Master Metal Scrip - type I)
nickel-plated brass, 19mm, round, "N" c/o, R6

E5 (obverse similar to C5)
(Master Metal Scrip - type II)
nickel, 19mm, round, "N" c/o, R6

NEWTONVILLE (Marlboro County) 2355

A100 W. B. ADAMS' SON / NEWTONVILLE, / S.C.
GOOD FOR / 100 / IN MERCHANDISE
brass, 36mm, round, R10

A10 (obverse similar to A100)
GOOD FOR / 10 / IN MERCHANDISE
brass, 24mm, round, R10

W. B. Adams' Son operated a general store in Newtonville during the early 1900s. He also issued tokens bearing an Adamsboro address.

NINETY SIX (Greenwood County) 2360

A100 STAR GROCERY COMPANY / 1 00 / NINETY SIX, S.C.
(Orco - type II) (varieties exist)
nickel, 32mm, round, R7

A50 (obverse similar to A100 except denomination 50)
(Orco - type II)
brass, 27mm, round, R8

A25 (obverse similar to A100 except denomination 25)
(Orco - type II) (varieties exist)
nickel, 24mm, round, R7

A10 (obverse similar to A100 except denomination 10)
(Orco - type II) (varieties exist)
brass, 21mm, round, R6

NINETY SIX   (Continued)

2360

A5   (obverse similar to A100 except denomination 5)
       (Orco - type II)   (varieties exist)
         nickel, 19mm, round, R6

A1   (obverse similar to A100 except denomination 1)
       (Orco - type II and type III varieties exist)
         copper, 18mm, round, R7

      This establishment was the company store for Ninety Six Cotton Mills. J. B. Harris, one of the mill's executives, owned the store and employed his sons-in-law to manage it. It was in business from the early 1920s to the 1960s. The use of tokens was discontinued in the 1940s.

NORTH   (Orangeburg County)

2365

A   THE / NORTH / BAKERY
      GOOD FOR / ONE LOAF / BREAD
        aluminum, 21mm, octagonal, R3

      In 1914 E. G. Holland was listed as owner of this bakery.

NORTH AUGUSTA   (Aiken County)

2370

A   NORTH AUGUSTA BUS CO. / NAB
      GOOD FOR / NAB / ONE FARE
        nickel, 16mm, round, c/o, R5 (Atwood 730A)

B   (obverse and reverse same as A)
        steel, 16mm, round, c/o, R6 (Atwood 730B)

      18,000 specimens of A and 1,000 of B were struck.

NORTH MYRTLE BEACH   (Horry County)

2375

A   ONE FREE GAME / PIRATES' COVE / MINI GOLF / NORTH MYRTLE BEACH, S.C.
      UNITED STATES / (picture of eagle) / 1776 1976 / BICENTENNIAL
        copper, 20mm, round, R6, modern

OLAR   (Bamberg County)

2395

A100   KEARSE / MFG. CO. / OLAR, S.C.
       GOOD FOR / $1⁰⁰ / IN TRADE
         aluminum, 33mm, round, R7

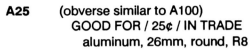

A25   (obverse similar to A100)
GOOD FOR / 25¢ / IN TRADE
aluminum, 26mm, round, R8

A5   (obverse similar to A100)
GOOD FOR / 5¢ / IN TRADE
aluminum, 22mm, round, R8

B100   KEARSE / MFG. CO. / OLAR, S.C.
GOOD FOR / $1⁰⁰ / IN TRADE
brass, 33mm, round, R8

B50   (obverse similar to B100)
GOOD FOR / 50¢ / IN TRADE
brass, 29mm, round, R8

B25   (obverse similar to B100)
GOOD FOR / 25¢ / IN TRADE
brass, 26mm, round, R7

B10   (obverse similar to B100)
GOOD FOR / 10¢ / IN TRADE
brass, 22mm, round, R7

B5   (obverse similar to B100)
GOOD FOR / 5¢ / IN TRADE
brass, 22mm, round, R7

C10   KEARSE / MFG. CO. / OLAR, S.C.
10 c / IN TRADE (across numerals)
aluminum, 26mm, round, R7

C5   (obverse similar to C10)
5 c / IN TRADE (across numeral)
brass, 23mm, round, R7

D1   KEARSE / MANUFACTURING / COMPANY / OLAR, S.C.
GOOD FOR / 1¢ / IN MERCHANDISE
brass, 18mm, round, R9

E100   KEARSE VENEER AND BOX CO. / OLAR, S.C.
GOOD FOR / $1⁰⁰ / IN TRADE
aluminum, 31mm, round, R8

E50   (obverse similar to E100)
GOOD FOR / 50¢ / IN TRADE
aluminum, 28mm, round, R8

E25   (obverse similar to E100)
GOOD FOR / 25¢ / IN TRADE
aluminum, 26mm, round, R8

OLAR (Continued)   2395

E10 (obverse similar to E100)
GOOD FOR / 10¢ / IN TRADE
aluminum, 24mm, round, R8

The Kearse Veneer & Box Company was first listed in 1926. The name was changed to Kearse Manufacturing Company sometime in the mid-1930s. The company manufactured veneers, boxes, and box shooks.

F10 H. O. MORRIS & BRO / 10 / OLAR, S.C.
GOOD FOR / 10 / IN MERCHANDISE
brass, 22mm, round, R10

F5 (obverse similar to F10 except denomination 5)
GOOD FOR / 5 / IN MERCHANDISE
brass, 21mm, round, R9

During the teens H. O. Morris & Brother operated a general store.

ORANGEBURG (Orangeburg County)   2405

A25 J. H. ALBRECHT / LIVERY / STABLES / ORANGEBURG, S.C.
GOOD FOR / 25¢ / ROUND TRIP ON BUS
aluminum, 32mm, round, R10 (Atwood 750A)

J. H. Albrecht operated his livery stables from 1908 to 1923. He later operated a grocery store.

B5 CANNON BROS. / FRUITERS / ORANGEBURG, S.C.
GOOD FOR / 5¢ / SODA WATER OR CIGAR
aluminum, 21mm, round, R10

The Cannon Brothers sold fruit and confections from 1904 to 1923.

C5 GOOD FOR / 5¢ / CLAFLIN CAFETERIA
(blank)
aluminum, 19mm, round, R10

D EDISTO / DAIRY / ORANGEBURG, S.C.
GOOD FOR / 1 / QT. / GOLDEN GUERNSEY MILK
aluminum, 23mm, round, R9

This dairy was listed in the late 1930s and 1940s.

E5 LIGON DRUG CO. / PURE / DRUGS / FINE / CIGARS / ORANGEBURG, S.C.
GOOD FOR / 5¢ / CIGAR / OR / SODA WATER
aluminum, 19mm, round, R10

Listed in 1904 as a retail pharmacy, this business was owned by Reeves, Hazard & Co.

F5 LOWMAN DRUG CO. / THE / REXALL / STORE / ORANGEBURG, S.C.
GOOD FOR ONE / 5¢ / SODA OR CIGAR
aluminum, 24mm, round, R10

This store was in business as early as 1904.

G ORANGEBURG / 194 (serial #) / MFG. CO. (all incuse)
(blank)
   brass, 29mm, square, R10

   This was probably a production token. The Orangeburg Mfg. Co. was listed from 1904 to 1916 as a branch operation of a firm headquartered in Augusta, Georgia. The company, which manufactured cotton goods, was sold in 1917 and became Santee Mills.

H5 ORANGEBURG / STEAM / BAKERY
GOOD FOR ONE / 5¢ / LOAF OF BREAD
   aluminum, 28mm, round, R10

   Henry Von Ohsen operated this bakery during the teens.

I5 ORANGEBURG, S.C. / 5¢ / AND / 10¢ / STORE
GOOD FOR / 5¢ / DRINKS OR CIGARS
   aluminum, 19mm, round, R10

   The Orangeburg 5 & 10 Store operated circa 1910.

J SANTEE MILL / 209 (incuse serial #) / ORANGEBURG, S.C.
(blank)
   brass, 29mm, square, R10

   This cotton mill was listed from 1917 to 1945. A branch operated in Bamberg.

K5 AT / SORENTRUE'S / ARCADE / RUSSELL ST. / ORANGEBURG / S.C.
GOOD FOR / 5¢ / IN TRADE / OR ONE / TUNE / ON ANY INSTRUMENT
   brass, 21mm, round, R9

L5 SPROTT'S / ORANGEBURG, / S.C.
GOOD FOR ONE / 5¢ / DRINK OR CIGAR
   aluminum, 19x26mm, oval, R10

   E. D. Sprott operated Sprott's 5 & 10 Store during the early teens.

PACOLET (Spartanburg County) 2420

A25 PACOLET M'F'G. CO.
GOOD FOR / 25 / IN MERCHANDISE
   aluminum, 24mm, round, R10

   The Pacolet Manufacturing Company, one of the earlier cotton mills in the area, was in business as early as 1893. The company specialized in making cotton sheeting.

The Pacolet Manufacturing Company's general store, as depicted on a postcard.
The company's letterhead is illustrated below.

V. M. MONTGOMERY.   BEN W. MONTGOMERY.
PRES. & TREAS.   ASST. TREAS.

PACOLET MANUFACTURING CO.

TRADE   MARK

BROWN SHEETINGS AND DRILLS.

MILLS NOS 1·2 AND 3. PACOLET. S.C.   CENTRAL OFFICE
MILL NO 4. NEW HOLLAND. GA.   SPARTANBURG. S.C.

PARLER   (Orangeburg County)   2435

A100   THE FARMER'S BANK / 4% / PAID / ON SAVINGS / PARLER, S.C. /
        ELLOREE, S.C.
            GOOD FOR / $ 1.00 / WHEN / ACCOMPANIED BY / $100.00 /
            SAVINGS DEPOSIT
                aluminum, 38mm, round, R10

PARRIS ISLAND   (Beaufort County)   2440

A   REC / PISC / FUND
       (blank)
         nickel, 25mm, round, R5

B   (obverse and reverse same as A)
       brass, 25mm, round, R7 (Curto SC560)

C   (obverse and reverse same as A)
       nickel-plated brass, 25mm, round, R7 (Curto SC561)

       The author has been unable to verify the existence of B and C.

PATRICK   (Chesterfield County)   2445

A10   W. J. NORRIS & BRO. / PATRICK, / S.C.
       GOOD FOR / 10 / IN MERCHANDISE
       aluminum, 24mm, round, R10

PEE DEE   (Marion County)   2455

A10   GREAT SOUTHERN LUMBER & MINING CO. / PEE DEE, / S.C.
       10
       aluminum, 24mm, round, R10

A5   (obverse similar to A10)
       5
       aluminum, 24mm, round, R10

B100   STEVENSON, KREAMER / & / HOCKMAN / NOT / NEGOTIABLE.
       GOOD FOR / $1.00 / IN MDSE. AT / PEE DEE SUPPLY COS' STORE.
       aluminum, 39mm, round, R10

       Stevenson, Kreamer, and Hockman were engaged in the lumber manufacturing business circa 1908. The company was headquartered in Lock Haven, Pennsylvania.

PELZER   (Anderson County)   2460

       It has been reported that over 25 merchants in this small town issued tokens at one time or another. They were utilized primarily as a means of extending credit to customers. Most of the merchants would honor the tokens of their fellow merchants, meeting every Friday to redeem them from each other. With the decline in the use of tokens, the merchants continued their Friday meetings as the town's merchants' association.

A500   ALLISON - CRENSHAW CO. / 5 00 / PELZER, S.C.
       GOOD FOR / 5 00 / IN MERCHANDISE ONLY
       brass, 38mm, scalloped (12), R10

A50   (obverse similar to A500 except denomination 50)
        GOOD FOR / 50 / IN MERCHANDISE ONLY
          brass, 33mm, round, R10

A25   (obverse similar to A500 except denomination 25)
        GOOD FOR / 25 / IN MERCHANDISE ONLY
          brass, 29mm, round, R9

A10   (obverse similar to A500 except denomination 10)
        GOOD FOR / 10 / IN MERCHANDISE ONLY
          brass, 24mm, round, R9

A5   (obverse similar to A500 except denomination 5)
        GOOD FOR / 5 / IN MERCHANDISE ONLY
          brass, 19mm, round, R9

        From 1904 to 1919 this firm was listed as a retail establishment selling general merchandise, clothing, and furniture.

B5   BLUE RIDGE GROCERY CO. / 5 / PELZER, S.C.
        GOOD FOR / 5¢ / IN MERCHANDISE
          brass, 20mm, round, R10

        This establishment was in business from 1908 to the late twenties.

C5   D. B. & M. CO. / PELZER, S.C. (all incuse)
        5 (incuse)
          brass, 24mm, round, R10

        Dexter Broom & Mattress Company was a manufacturing firm circa 1904 to 1912.

D5   EAGLE GROCERY CO. / 5¢ / PELZER, S.C.
        GOOD FOR / 5¢ / IN TRADE
          brass, 19mm, round, R10

        This retail grocery was listed from 1916 to 1933.

E25   HINDMAN & BEAM CO. / 25 / PELZER, S.C.
        PAYABLE IN / 25 / MERCHANDISE ONLY
          brass, 29mm, round, R10

E5   (obverse similar to E25 except denomination 5)
        PAYABLE IN / 5 / MERCHANDISE ONLY
          brass, 19mm, round, R10

        A general store specializing in hardware and farming implements, the Hindman & Beam Co. was in business from the early 1900s to the mid-1920s.

F25   HUDGENS & RAGSDALE / 25 / PELZER, S.C.
        GOOD FOR / 25¢ / IN / MERCHANDISE
          brass, 28mm, round, R10

F10   (obverse similar to F25 except denomination 10)
        GOOD FOR / 10¢ / IN / MERCHANDISE
          brass, 25mm, round, R9

F5 (obverse similar to F25 except denomination 5)
GOOD FOR / 5¢ / IN / MERCHANDISE
brass, 21mm, round, R8

G10 HUDGENS & RAGSDALE / 10¢ / PULZER, S.C. (sic)
GOOD FOR / 10¢ / IN TRADE
brass, 25mm, round, R10

G5 (obverse similar to G10 except denomination 5¢)
GOOD FOR / 5¢ / IN TRADE
brass, 21mm, round, R10

Hudgens & Ragsdale were partners in a retail grocery from the early 1900s to the late teens. On some of their tokens the town name is misspelled. Other tokens list the firm name as Ragsdale, Hudgens & Co. (see below).

H25 J. J. PHILLIPS CO / PELZER S.C. (in script)
GOOD FOR / 25 / IN MERCHANDISE
brass, 24mm, round, R9

H10 (obverse similar to H25)
GOOD FOR / 10 / IN MERCHANDISE
brass, 19mm, round, R10

H5 (obverse similar to H25)
GOOD FOR / 5 / IN MERCHANDISE
brass, 19mm, round, R9

I50 RAGSDALE, HUDGENS & CO. / PELZER, / S.C.
GOOD FOR / 50 / IN MERCHANDISE
brass, 24mm, round, R10

I10 (obverse similar to I50)
GOOD FOR / 10 / IN MERCHANDISE
brass, 19mm, round, R10

J100 WEST PELZER DRUG CO. / MILL NO. 4 / & / FRANKVILLE / PELZER, S.C.
GOOD FOR / 1$\underline{00}$ / IN TRADE
brass, 35mm, octagonal, R10

J25 (obverse similar to J100)
GOOD FOR / 25 / IN TRADE
brass, 29mm, octagonal, R10

J5 (obverse similar to J100)
GOOD FOR / 5 / IN TRADE
brass, 22mm, octagonal, R10

K5 WEST PELZER / DRUG CO. / INC. / PELZER / S.C.
GOOD FOR / 5¢ / CIGAR OR DRINK
aluminum, 19mm, round, R10

This business was listed from 1912 to 1923.

PELZER (Continued)   2460

L   WILLMONT OIL MILLS / 100 LBS. / C.S. HULLS / PELZER, S.C.
         DATE OF REDEMPTION / SUBJECT / TO RULES / POSTED / IN
         OFFICE
           aluminum, 25mm, round, R9

           The Willmont Oil Mills was listed as a manufacturer of cotton seed
         products from 1908 to 1923. Branches were located in Williamston and
         Piedmont.
           In the early 1900s, when "cotton was king," no part of the cotton plant
         was wasted. The seeds were used to make various useful products - cotton
         seed oil, cotton seed meal, and cotton seed hulls, to name a few. This token
         was good for 100 pounds of cotton seed hulls. (See Williamston for a token
         from this company good for 500 pounds of cotton seed meal.)

PENDLETON (Anderson County)   2465

A100   G. A. CANUP / PENDLETON, S.C.
           GOOD FOR / $1<u>00</u> / IN MERCHANDISE
             brass, 35mm, round, R10

A5   (obverse similar to A100)
           GOOD FOR / 5¢ / IN MERCHANDISE
             brass, 20mm, round, R10

           In 1912 G. A. Canup was listed as a general merchandise dealer.

PICKENS (Pickens County)   2475

A20   APPALACHIAN LUMBER CORPORATION / 20¢ / PICKENS, S.C.
           GOOD FOR / MEALS ONLY / 20¢ / AT COMPANY / BOARDING /
           HOUSES
             brass, 32mm, octagonal, R10

B10   ASHMORE / & / NIMMONS / PICKENS, / S.C.
           GOOD FOR / 10 / IN MERCHANDISE
             aluminum, 25mm, scalloped (12), R10

B5   (obverse similar to B10)
           GOOD FOR / 5 / IN MERCHANDISE
             aluminum, 20mm, scalloped (12), R10

           In 1908 Ashmore & Nimmons were partners in a general store.

C10   THE COMPANY STORE / 10 / PICKENS, S.C.
           (Orco - type I)
             nickel, 21mm, round, "B" c/o, R10

C5   (obverse similar to C10 except denomination 5)
           (Orco - type I)
             nickel, 19mm, round, "B" c/o, R10

D100   THE COMPANY STORE No. 2 / 1$\underline{00}$ / PICKENS, S.C.
       (Orco - type I)
         nickel, 32mm, round, "B" c/o, R10

D50   (obverse similar to D100 except denomination 50)
       (Orco - type I)
         nickel, 27mm, round, "B" c/o, R10

D25   (obverse similar to D100 except denomination 25)
       (Orco - type I)
         nickel, 24mm, round, "B" c/o, R10

D10   (obverse similar to D100 except denomination 10)
       (Orco - type I)
         nickel, 21mm, round, "B" c/o, R9

D5   (obverse similar to D100 except denomination 5)
       (Orco - type I)
         nickel, 19mm, round, "B" c/o, R10

    This general store operated during the late 1920s. It probably was affiliated with one of the cotton mills in the area.

E100   FOLGER, THORNLEY & CO. / PICKENS, / S.C.
       GOOD FOR / 100 / IN MERCHANDISE
         aluminum, 36mm, square, counterstamped "HF", R8

E50   (obverse similar to E100)
       GOOD FOR / 50 / IN MERCHANDISE
         aluminum, 33mm, scalloped (12), R8

E25   (obverse similar to E100)
       GOOD FOR / 25 / IN MERCHANDISE
         aluminum, 25mm x 38mm, oval, R8

    Folger, Thornley & Company operated a general store from the late 1890s to the late teens. In 1920 Thornley sold his interest in the business to a man named Hendricks. The remaining tokens were counterstamped with an "H" and an "F" to indicate this change.

F100   HEATH-BRUCE-MORROW CO. / PICKENS, S.C.
       GOOD FOR / 1$\underline{00}$ / IN / MERCHANDISE
         aluminum, 39mm, octagonal, R9

    The Heath-Bruce-Morrow Company operated a general store and hardware business from the early 1900s to the mid-teens.

G100   W. A. PATTERSON / 1$\underline{00}$
       (Ingle System - 1909 pat. date)
         brass, 35mm, round, R10

G1   (obverse similar to G100 except denomination 1)
        (Ingle System - 1909 pat. date)
        brass, 18mm, round, R10

        W. A. Patterson operated a general store from 1912 to 1916. His tokens were previously attributed to Greencastle, Indiana by Lloyd Wagaman. They have since been re-attributed by him to Pickens, by the discovery of more compelling evidence.

H7½   PICKENS MILL / 25 LBS. / PICKENS, S.C.
        ICE CHECK / 7½¢
        aluminum, 25mm, round, R10

I5   PICKENS / MILL / MARKET
        GOOD FOR / 5¢ / IN TRADE
        brass, 21mm, octagonal, R10

        The Pickens Mill was in operation as early as 1908. It specialized in the manufacture of fine sheetings.

PIEDMONT   (Anderson County)   2480

A500 DIXIE MERCANTILE CO. / PIEDMONT, / S.C.
        GOOD FOR / $5<u>00</u> / IN / MERCHANDISE
        brass, 35mm, round, R5

A200 (obverse similar to A500)
        GOOD FOR / $2<u>00</u> / IN / MERCHANDISE
        brass, 35mm, round, R5

A100 (obverse similar to A500)
        GOOD FOR / $1<u>00</u> / IN / MERCHANDISE
        brass, 35mm, round, R5

A50   (obverse similar to A500)
        GOOD FOR / 50¢ / IN MERCHANDISE
        brass, 31mm, round, R5

A25   (obverse similar to A500)
        GOOD FOR / 25¢ / IN MERCHANDISE
        brass, 28mm, round, R5

A10   (obverse similar to A500)
        GOOD FOR / 10¢ / IN MERCHANDISE
        brass, 25mm, round, R5

A5   (obverse similar to A500)
        GOOD FOR / 5¢ / IN MERCHANDISE
        brass, 20mm, round, R5

        The Dixie Mercantile Company was listed from 1908 to 1912 as a general store.

B5   DONNALD & WILSON / CO. / WILLIAMSTON / & / PIEDMONT / S.C.
GOOD FOR ONE / 5¢ / DRINK / OR CIGAR
aluminum, 24mm, round, R10

The Donald & Wilson Company operated drug stores in Piedmont and Williamston during the early teens.

C25   HAMPTON MERCANTILE CO. / 25¢ / PIEDMONT, S.C.
GOOD FOR / 25¢ / IN TRADE
brass, 25mm, octagonal, R10

C5   (obverse similar to C25 except denomination 5¢)
GOOD FOR / 5¢ / IN TRADE
brass, 21mm, octagonal, R10

D5   HAMPTON MERCANTILE CO. / GENERAL / STORE / PIEDMONT, S.C.
GOOD FOR / 5 / IN TRADE
aluminum, 18mm, octagonal, R10

This company operated from the early 1900s to the mid-1930s.

E500 JACKSON CO. / PIEDMONT, / S.C.
GOOD FOR / 500 / IN TRADE
brass, 38mm, round, R4

E100 (obverse similar to E500)
GOOD FOR / 1,00 / IN TRADE
brass, 36mm, round, R3

E50   (obverse similar to E500)
GOOD FOR / 50 / IN TRADE
brass, 33mm, round, R3

E25   (obverse similar to E500)
GOOD FOR / 25 / IN TRADE
brass, 29mm, round, R3

E10   (obverse similar to E500)
GOOD FOR / 10 / IN TRADE
brass, 24mm, round, R3

E5   (obverse similar to E500)
GOOD FOR / 5 / IN TRADE
brass, 19mm, round, R4

F5   (obverse similar to E5 but different style)
GOOD FOR / 5 / IN TRADE (solid numeral, no stars)
brass, 19mm, round, R4

The Jackson Company operated a general store from the early teens to the early thirties. It may have been affiliated with one of the cotton mills in the area.

G25   PIEDMONT / MERCANTILE / CO.
GOOD FOR / 25¢ / IN TRADE
brass, 26mm, round, R10

PIEDMONT (Continued) 2480

G10 (obverse similar to G25)
GOOD FOR / 10¢ / IN TRADE
brass, 23mm, round, R10

G5 (obverse similar to G25)
GOOD FOR / 5¢ / IN TRADE
brass, 20mm, round, R10

This general store was in business during the early teens. It may have served as company store for the Piedmont Mfg. Co., an early textile mill in the area.

PINELAND (Jasper County) 2490

A100 CAROLINA / TURPENTINE / CO. / PINELAND, S.C.
GOOD FOR / 1$\underline{00}$ / IN / MERCHANDISE
brass, 33mm, round, R10

A5 (obverse similar to A100)
GOOD FOR / 5 / IN / MERCHANDISE
brass, 21mm, round, R10

This firm manufactured turpentine and naval stores during the teens.

PINEWOOD (Sumter County) 2495

A25 J. J. BROUGHTON / PINEWOOD, / S.C.
GOOD FOR / 25 / IN TRADE
brass, 24mm, round, R10

PLUM BRANCH (McCormick County) 2505

A5 BRACKNELL & BAKER, / PLUM / BRANCH, / S.C.
GOOD FOR / 5¢ / IN TRADE
aluminum, 19mm, round, R10

Bracknell & Baker were partners in a general store circa 1910 (see notes following listings of J. W. Bracknell & Son tokens).

B500 J. W. BRACKNELL & SON / 5$\underline{00}$ / PLUM BRANCH, S.C.
(Orco - type I)
copper, 32mm, scalloped (12), R10

B100 (obverse similar to B500 except denomination 1$\underline{00}$)
(Orco - type II)
nickel, 32mm, round, R10

PLUM BRANCH   (Continued) 2505

B50 (obverse similar to B500 except denomination 50)
(Orco - type II)
brass, 27mm, round, R10

B25 (obverse similar to B500 except denomination 25)
(Orco - type II)
nickel, 24mm, round, R10

B10 (obverse similar to B500 except denomination 10)
(Orco - type I)
brass, 21mm, round, R10

B5 (obverse similar to B500 except denomination 5)
(Orco - type II)
nickel, 19mm, round, R10

B1 (obverse similar to B500 except denomination 1)
(Orco - type III)
copper, 18mm, round, R8

John Wilson Bracknell started in the general merchandise business in 1902. About 1908 he took in a partner named Baker (see token). By 1912 J. W.'s son had replaced Baker and the business became known as J. W. Bracknell & Son. The tokens were used to facilitate credit with the area's farmers. Instead of making separate entries into the credit ledger for each purchase, only one entry was made at the beginning of the month when tokens were advanced. The farmers then used tokens to make purchases throughout the month. J. W.'s grandson still operates the hardware portion of the business, having sold the grocery portion about 10 years ago.

POMARIA   (Newberry County) 2510

A10 W. D. SUMMER / POOL ROOM
GOOD FOR / 10¢ / IN TRADE
aluminum, 23mm, round, R7

A5 (obverse similar to A10)
GOOD FOR / 5¢ / IN TRADE
aluminum, 21mm, round, R7

W. D. Summer operated a general store from the late teens to the late thirties. Sometime during the twenties he opened a billiard room next to his store.

PORT ROYAL   (Beaufort County) 2515

A25 BAER & CAUSEY / PORT / ROYAL, / S.C.
GOOD FOR / 25 / IN MERCHANDISE
aluminum, 29mm, round, R10

A5   (obverse similar to A25)
  GOOD FOR / 5 / IN MERCHANDISE
  aluminum, 22mm, round, R10

A2½   (obverse similar to A25)
  GOOD FOR / 2½ / IN MERCHANDISE
  aluminum, 19mm, round, R10

A1   (obverse similar to A25)
  GOOD FOR / 1 / IN MERCHANDISE
  aluminum, 17mm, round, R8

This postcard view of the detention barracks was taken circa 1912.

B100   POST EXCHANGE / U.S.N.D.B. / PORT ROYAL, S.C.
  GOOD FOR / 100 / IN MERCHANDISE
  brass, 36mm, round, R7

B50   (obverse similar to B100)
  GOOD FOR / 50 / IN MERCHANDISE
  brass, 33mm, round, R8

B25   (obverse similar to B100)
  GOOD FOR / 25 / IN MERCHANDISE
  brass, 29mm, round, R8

B10   (obverse similar to B100)
  GOOD FOR / 10 / IN MERCHANDISE
  aluminum, 24mm, round, R9

B5   (obverse similar to B100)
         GOOD FOR / 5 / IN MERCHANDISE
         aluminum, 19mm, round, R9

         These tokens were issued by the U.S. Navy Disciplinary Barracks, a military prison located at Port Royal from 1911 to 1915. In October, 1915, the post was transferred to the Marine Corps and was used as a recruit depot. The post's name was soon changed to Parris Island, and many thousands of Marines have received their boot camp training there since then.

POSTON   (Florence County)   2520

A5   BROWN - INGRAM / LUMBER / COMPANY / POSTON, S.C.
         GOOD FOR / 5 / IN MERCHANDISE
         brass, 21mm, round, R10

         From 1923 to 1926 this company was listed as a lumber manufacturer.

PROSPECT HILL PLANTATION   2530
(Georgetown County)

A50   GOOD FOR / 50 / CENTS / IN / MDSE / AT PROSPECT HILL STORE (all incuse)
             50 / CENTS / S.M. WARD (all incuse)
             brass, 29mm, round, holed as made, R8

A25   (obverse similar to A50 except denomination 25 CENTS)
             25 / CENTS / S.M. WARD (all incuse)
             brass, 29mm, round, R7

A10   (obverse similar to A50 except denomination 10 CENTS)
             10 / CENTS / S.M. WARD (all incuse)
             brass, 29mm, round, holed as made, R3

A5   (obverse similar to A 50 except denomination 5 CENTS)
             5 / CENTS / S.M. WARD (all incuse)
             brass, 29mm, round, R3

         Samuel Mortimer Ward (1858-1943) was the grandson of Joshua John Ward, an early Georgetown rice planter. The Prospect Hill Plantation was passed down through the family to S. M. Ward, who also planted rice there. The tokens, used circa 1880 to pay plantation workers, were redeemed at the general store at the plantation.

         The original plantation house (built in 1794) still stands, although it is called "Arcadia" now. In 1819 it was the site of a presidential visit by President James Monroe.

PROSPECT HILL PLANTATION (Continued)   2530

Circa 1900 S. M. Ward entered into partnership with St. Julian M. Lachicotte and A. A. Springs to form S. M. Ward & Company, for the purposes of planting rice on a corporate scale. The business lasted only a few years, as declining rice prices and devastating hurricanes took their toll. S. M. Ward also served as postmaster of Georgetown and as a state senator. (For other tokens issued by Ward, see listings under Richfield Plantation.)

PULZER

Tokens with the inscription HUDGENS & RAGSDALE, PULZER, S.C. are listed under the town of PELZER.

RHEMS (Williamsburg County)   2560

A200   F. RHEM & SONS / RHEMS / S.C.
GOOD FOR / 2$\underline{00}$ / PAT / JULY 1899 / IN MERCHANDISE
bimetallic, 38mm, octagonal, R10

A100   (obverse similar to A200)
GOOD FOR / 1$\underline{00}$ / PAT. / JULY 1899 / IN MERCHANDISE
bimetallic, 36mm, octagonal, R6

A50   (obverse similar to A200)
GOOD FOR / 50 / PAT / JULY 1899 / IN MERCHANDISE
bimetallic, 30mm, octagonal, R6

A25   (obverse similar to A200)
GOOD FOR / 25 / PAT / JULY 1899 / IN MERCHANDISE
bimetallic, 25mm, octagonal, R6

A10   (obverse similar to A200)
GOOD FOR / 10 / PAT / JULY 1899 / IN MERCHANDISE
bimetallic, 23mm, octagonal, R6

F. Rhem & Sons operated a general store and turpentine distillery from the 1870s to the late 1920s. Later the Rhem Real Estate Company was formed to sell the family's land holdings. Virtually all the bimetallic tokens are worn to the point of illegibility.

B100   RHEM REAL ESTATE CO., INC. / RHEMS / S.C.
GOOD FOR / 1\underline{00}$ / IN MERCHANDISE
brass, 31mm, round, R6

B50   (obverse similar to B100)
GOOD FOR / 50¢ / IN MERCHANDISE
brass, 28mm, round, R6

B25   (obverse similar to B100)
GOOD FOR / 25¢ / IN MERCHANDISE
brass, 26mm, round, R6

RHEMS (Continued)   2560

B10   (obverse similar to B100)
          GOOD FOR / 10¢ / IN MERCHANDISE
             brass, 25mm, round, R6

B5   (obverse similar to B100)
          GOOD FOR / 5¢ / IN MERCHANDISE
             brass, 20mm, round, R6

RICHFIELD PLANTATION (Georgetown County) 2565

A200   S. M. WARD & CO. / RICHFIELD
          GOOD FOR / $2⁰⁰ / IN MDSE (last 2 words incuse)
             aluminum, 28mm, scalloped (8), R5

A25   (obverse similar to A200)
          GOOD FOR / 25 / CENTS / IN MDSE (last 2 words incuse)
             aluminum, 26mm, octagonal, R5

This company was a partnership formed by S. M. Ward, St. Julian M. Lachicotte, and A. A. Springs to plant rice on a corporate scale. Several older plantations were bought up, including Richfield. The company did not survive the "killer" hurricanes and declining rice prices of the early 1900s. The tokens were issued at Richfield Plantation, located south of Georgetown near the town of Annandale. (See listings under Prospect Hill Plantation for additional information.)

RIDGELAND (Jasper County)   2570

A100   T. M. BAILEY'S / STORE / RIDGELAND / S.C.
          GOOD FOR / $1⁰⁰ / IN TRADE
             aluminum, 31mm, round, R3 (varieties exist)

A50   (obverse similar to A100)
          GOOD FOR / 50¢ / IN TRADE
             aluminum, 28mm, round, R3

A25   (obverse similar to A100)
          GOOD FOR / 25¢ / IN TRADE
             aluminum, 26mm, round, R3

A10   (obverse similar to A100)
          GOOD FOR / 10¢ / IN TRADE
             aluminum, 25mm, round, R3

A5   (obverse similar to A100)
          GOOD FOR / 5¢ / IN TRADE
             aluminum, 20mm, round, R4

A1   (obverse similar to A100)
  GOOD FOR / 1¢ / IN TRADE
  aluminum, 18mm, round, R5

  T. M. Bailey operated a general store, filling station, and grist mill during the 1930s and 1940s.

B5   LOUIS McCAW / DRUGGIST / RIDGELAND, S.C.
  GOOD FOR / 5¢ / IN TRADE
  aluminum, 20mm, round, R10

  Louis McCaw was in business in the mid-teens.

C100   AT PINCKNEY / OYSTER / CO. / STORE
  GOOD FOR / $1⁰⁰ / IN / MERCHANDISE
  brass, 35mm, round, R3

C50   (obverse similar to C100)
  GOOD FOR / 50¢ / IN MERCHANDISE
  brass, 31mm, round, R3

C25   (obverse similar to C100)
  GOOD FOR / 25¢ / IN MERCHANDISE
  brass, 27mm, round, R3

C10   (obverse similar to C100)
  GOOD FOR / 10¢ / IN MERCHANDISE
  brass, 25mm, round, R3

C5   (obverse similar to C100)
  GOOD FOR 5¢ IN MERCHANDISE / 5
  brass, 21mm, round, R4

C1   (obverse similar to C100)
  GOOD FOR / 1¢ / IN MERCHANDISE
  brass, 19mm, round, R4

D50   RIDGELAND / GROCERY / CO. / RIDGELAND, S.C.
  GOOD FOR / 50¢ / IN MERCHANDISE
  aluminum, 28mm, round, R10

D25   (obverse similar to D50)
  GOOD FOR / 25¢ / IN MERCHANDISE
  aluminum, 26mm, round, R10

  This store operated in the early 1930s.

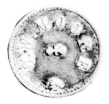

RIDGEWAY   (Fairfield County)   2575

A5   O. W. MOORE
GOOD FOR / 5¢ / IN TRADE
brass, 21mm, round, R10

Attribution tentative. O. W. Moore operated a sawmill and general store near Ridgeway during the teens and twenties.

RITTER   (Colleton County)   2580

A100   COLLETON MERCANTILE & MFG. CO. / RITTER, / S.C.
GOOD FOR / 1$\underline{00}$ / IN MERCHANDISE
aluminum, 38mm, scalloped (12), R8

A50   (obverse similar to A100)
GOOD FOR / 50 / IN MERCHANDISE
aluminum, 33mm, round, R8

A25   (obverse similar to A100)
GOOD FOR / 25 / IN MERCHANDISE
aluminum, 29mm, round, R8

A10   (obverse similar to A100)
GOOD FOR / 10 / IN MERCHANDISE
aluminum, 24mm, square, R8

A5   (obverse similar to A100)
GOOD FOR / 5 / IN MERCHANDISE
aluminum, 21mm, square, R8

B100   AGRICULTURAL LABORER'S CHECK / GOOD FOR 1\underline{00}$ / IN MDSE. / TO ORIGINAL / HOLDER ONLY / COLLETON / MER. & MFG. CO. / RITTER, S.C.
AGRICULTURAL LABORER'S / CHECK / NON / NEGOTIABLE / PAYABLE / IN / MERCHANDISE ONLY
aluminum, 38mm, scalloped (12), R8

B50   (obverse similar to B100 except denomination 50¢)
(reverse similar to B100)
aluminum, 31mm, round, R8

B25   (obverse similar to B100 except denomination 25¢)
(reverse similar to B100)
aluminum, 29mm, octagonal, R8

B5   (obverse similar to B100 except denomination 5¢)
(reverse similar to B100)
aluminum, 21mm, square, R8

B1   (obverse similar to B100 except denomination 1¢)
(reverse similar to B100)
aluminum, 20mm, octagonal, R8

RITTER   (Continued)   2580

C5   SANDERS & LEMACKS / RITTER / S.C.
      LABOR CHECK / 5 / (rest of legend not legible)
        brass, 21mm, round, R10

     Paul Sanders and Ernest Lemacks, brothers-in-law, founded the Sanders & Lemacks Company around the turn of the century. The company was mainly engaged in the lumber business, although some agriculture was undertaken. Around 1908 the Colleton Mercantile & Manufacturing Company was formed when Sanders bought out Lemacks and went into business with his sons (Barion, E. B., and Campbell), and S. P. Sams. The new enterprise was heavily engaged in the lumber business, operating a sawmill and stave factory. It also had agricultural interests (potatoes and cabbage) and a cotton gin. Both sets of Colleton Mercantile & Mfg. tokens were used interchangeably in the lumber and agricultural businesses. The company was dissolved in the 1950s, but the tokens were discontinued in the 1930s. Incidentally, the company redeemed these tokens for cash from any area merchant who had honored them from an employee. The majority of the Sanders & Lemacks tokens were destroyed when the company changed hands.

ROCK HILL   (York County)   2590

A25   B.P.O.E. / 1318
      GOOD FOR / 25¢ / IN TRADE
        aluminum, 23mm, round, R6, modern
        Used in the lodge's "Monte Carlo Night" during the 1960s and 1970s.

B   HAMILTON CARHARTT / COTTON MILL / #1 / ROCK HILL, S.C.
      (blank except for counterstamped "K")
        aluminum, 26mm, round, R10

     This was probably a production token. In business during the teens and twenties, the Hamilton Carhartt mill made men's overalls and work pants.

C5   S. H. McMANUS, / ROCK HILL, / S.C.
      GOOD FOR / 5¢ / IN TRADE
        aluminum, 19mm, round, R10

     McManus operated a grocery store circa 1910.

D5   J. L. PHILLIPS DRUG CO. / (rest of legend not legible)
      GOOD FOR / 5¢ / SODA WATER OR CIGAR
        aluminum, 24mm, round, R10

     This company operated the Rock Hill Drug Company from the early teens through the 1940s.

ROCK HILL   (Continued)   2590

E   WYMOJO YARN / MILLS (all incuse)
       (blank)
          aluminum, 26mm, octagonal, holed as made, R10

          This was probably a production token.   The Wymojo Yarn Mills operated from 1910 to 1933.   In 1926 it was headquartered in Gastonia, N.C.

ROUND   (Colleton County)   2605

A100   A. O. HIOTT / GENL. / MDSE. / ROUND, / S.C.
          GOOD FOR / $1⁰⁰ / IN TRADE / NOT TRANSFERABLE
          aluminum, 31mm, round, R10

          A. O. Hiott was listed from 1910 to 1933 as operator of a general store located one mile northwest of Round. The town is now known as Round O.

RUBY   (Chesterfield County)   2610

A   RUBY CANNING CO. / RUBY, / S.C.
          1 / BUCKET
          brass, 19mm, round, R9

          This cannery was listed in the late 1930s and the 1940s. A branch was also operated in Johns, N.C.

RUSSELLVILLE   (Berkeley County)   2615

A25   CAMP/ MANUFACTURING / CO. / STORE № 3 / RUSSELLVILLE / S.C. / NOT TRANSFERABLE
          GOOD FOR / 25 / IN MERCHANDISE
          brass, 25mm, round, R10

B1   CAMP / MANUFACTURING / CO. / STORE № 3 / NOT TRANSFERABLE
          GOOD FOR / 1¢ / IN MERCHANDISE
          brass, 18mm, round, R9

C100   CAMP MANUFACTURING CO. / 1⁰⁰ / WOODS STORE № 3.
          PAYABLE IN / 1⁰⁰ / MERCHANDISE ONLY
          aluminum, 35mm, octagonal, R8

C50   (obverse similar to C100)
          PAYABLE IN / 50 / MERCHANDISE ONLY
          aluminum, 32mm, octagonal, R8

C25   (obverse similar to C100)
    PAYABLE IN / 25 / MERCHANDISE ONLY
      aluminum, 30mm, octagonal, R8

C10   (obverse similar to C100)
    PAYABLE IN / 10 / MERCHANDISE ONLY
      aluminum, 26mm, octagonal, R8

D5   CAMP MANUFACTURING CO. / 5 / MILL STORE No 3
    GOOD FOR / 5 / IN MERCHANDISE
      aluminum, 26mm, octagonal, R8

    The Camp Manufacturing Company operated a sawmill in Russellville for a period of time. For additional information on the company, see listings under Marion.

SAINT MATTHEWS (Calhoun County)   2620

A5   McLAUGHLIN CO. / ST. MATTHEWS, / S.C.
    GOOD FOR / 5¢ / IN ICE
      brass, 23mm, octagonal, R10

    The McLaughlin Company operated a general store during the late teens and early twenties.

SAINT PAUL (Clarendon County)   2625

A5   CLARENDON COTTON OIL CO. / ST. PAUL, / S.C.
    GOOD FOR / 5 / IN MERCHANDISE
      aluminum, 19mm, round, R10

    This company, which manufactured cottonseed products, was listed from 1904 to 1921.

SALLEY (Aiken County)   2630

A5   R. L. CORBITT & SON
    GOOD FOR / 5¢ / IN TRADE
      brass, 25mm, round, R10

    This general store was listed as R. L. Corbitt & Son only in 1912. From 1913 to 1921 it was listed as R. L. Corbitt & Company.

B100   I. S. HALL, / SALLEY, / S.C.
    GOOD FOR / $1⁰⁰ / IN CASH
      aluminum, 33mm, round, R10

SALLEY (Continued)   2630

C   MADE ONLY BY / SALLEY / COCA - COLA / BOTTLING / CO.
        GOOD FOR / ONE BOTTLE / OF THAT GOOD / GINGER ALE
        aluminum, 24mm, round, R10

        The Salley Coca Cola Bottling Company was in business during the
        late teens.

SALTERS DEPOT (Williamsburg County)   2635

A5   J. M. COOK / 5
        (Ingle System - 1909 pat. date)
        composition unknown, 20mm, round, R10

        Tentative attribution, based on Lloyd Wagaman's inclusion in his
        catalog of Ingle System tokens. J. M. Cook was listed as proprietor of a
        general store from 1893 to 1916.

SALUDA (Saluda County)   2640

A   THE PEOPLES / DRUG CO. / SALUDA, S.C.
        GOOD FOR / ANY / DRINK OR CIGAR / WE SELL / 6 FOR 25¢
        aluminum, 20mm, round, R9

        The Peoples Drug Company was in business from 1917 through the
        late 1940s. The tokens were probably issued in the late teens or early
        twenties.

SANTUCK (Union County)   2652

A5   L. B. JETER JR.
        GOOD FOR 5¢ IN TRADE
        brass, 21mm, round, center hole, R10

        In the 1920s L. B. Jeter, Jr. followed his father into the general
        merchandise business.

SARDINIA (Clarendon County)   2655

A100   McFADDIN - MILLSAPS CO. / SARDINIA, / S.C.
        GOOD FOR / $1⁰⁰ / IN MERCHANDISE
        aluminum, 31mm, round, R10

A50   (obverse similar to A100)
        GOOD FOR / 50¢ / IN / MERCHANDISE
        aluminum, 28mm, round, R10

SARDINIA (Continued)   2655

A10   (obverse similar to A100)
      GOOD FOR / 10¢ / IN MERCHANDISE
        aluminum, 23mm, round, R10

A5   (obverse similar to A100)
      GOOD FOR / 5¢ / IN / MERCHANDISE
        aluminum, 20mm, round, R10
        This general store was in business during the teens.

SEABROOK (Beaufort County)   2665

A   W. H. McLEOD & SON / SEABROOK, S.C. / 29940
      (blank)
        aluminum, 29mm, round, R7, modern
        Probably this was a picker's token, post 1960s.

SENECA (Oconee County)   2675

A5   THE FAIR STORE / J. M. / VICKERY, / PROP. / SENECA, S.C.
      GOOD FOR / 5 / IN MERCHANDISE
        brass, 21mm, round, R10

        J. M. Vickery operated the Fair Store from the early teens to the late twenties. The business sold dry goods, notions, clothing, and shoes.

B5   W. J. LUNNEY / SENECA, / S.C.
      GOOD FOR / ONE / 5¢ / CIGAR OR SODA
        brass, 19mm, round, R9

        Lunney operated a drug store from the 1890s through the 1930s.

C5   SENECA / PHARMACY / SENECA, / S.C.
      SODA OR CIGARS / 5¢.
        aluminum, 31mm, scalloped (8), R8

        This pharmacy was in business from the early 1900s to the early 1930s.

SIMPSONVILLE (Greenville County)   2695

A25   BENSON / GROCERY / CO. / SIMPSONVILLE, S.C.
      GOOD FOR / 25 / IN / MERCHANDISE
        brass, 27mm, round, R9
        The Benson Grocery Company was listed in 1915 and 1916.

SLATER   (Greenville County)   2700

A5   LESTER'S / CAFE / SLATER, / S.C.
       5
           aluminum, 20mm, scalloped (12), R10

A1   (obverse similar to A5)
       1
           brass, 19mm, round, R8

SMOAKS   (Colleton County)   2710

A10   VARN / BROTHERS / CO. / SMOAKS, S.C.
        GOOD FOR / 10¢ / IN / MERCHANDISE
        aluminum, 21mm, round, R10

        The Varn brothers, Aaron Eugene and William Henry, were in business
        during the teens, twenties, and thirties. The company operated a large
        farm, two general stores, and a naval stores business.

SOCIETY HILL   (Darlington County)   2715

A2000   FAT'S TRUCK STOP / $20⁰⁰ / SOCIETY HILL, S.C.
          (same)
              aluminum, 23mm, round, R5

A50   (obverse same as A2000 except denomination 50¢)
        (same)
            aluminum, 23mm, round, R5

A10   (obverse same as A2000 except denomination 10¢)
        (same)
            aluminum, 23mm, round, R5

        These tokens appear to be fairly modern in style. It is not known exactly
        how they were used.

SOUTH CLINTON   (Laurens County)   2720

A100   LYDIA MILLS / SO. CLINTON / S.C.
         GOOD FOR / 1⁰⁰ / IN / MERCHANDISE
         aluminum, 33mm, round, R8

A50   (obverse similar to A100
        GOOD FOR / 50 / IN / MERCHANDISE
        aluminum, 30mm, round, R8

A25   (obverse similar to A100)
        GOOD FOR / 25 / IN / MERCHANDISE
        aluminum, 26mm, round, R8

A10 (obverse similar to A100)
GOOD FOR / 10 / IN / MERCHANDISE
aluminum, 23mm, round, R8

A5 (obverse similar to A100)
GOOD FOR / 5 / IN / MERCHANDISE
aluminum, 20mm, round, R8

A1 (obverse similar to A100)
GOOD FOR / 1 / IN / MERCHANDISE
aluminum, 17mm, round, R8

B100 LYDIA MILLS / SO. CLINTON / S.C. (similar to A100 except different size and style)
GOOD FOR / 1<u>00</u> / IN / MERCHANDISE
aluminum, 35mm, round, R8

B50 (obverse similar to B100)
GOOD FOR / 50 / IN / MERCHANDISE
aluminum, 31mm, round, R9

B25 (obverse similar to B100)
GOOD FOR / 25 / IN / MERCHANDISE
aluminum, 28mm, round, R8

C100 LYDIA MILLS STORE / L (monogram on bust of eagle) / S. CLINTON, S.C.
GOOD FOR / 1<u>00</u> / IN / MERCHANDISE
brass, 33mm, round, R5

C50 (obverse similar to C100)
GOOD FOR / 50 / IN / MERCHANDISE
brass, 30mm, round, R5

C25 (obverse similar to C100)
GOOD FOR / 25 / IN / MERCHANDISE
brass, 26mm, round, R4

C10 (obverse similar to C100)
GOOD FOR / 10 / IN / MERCHANDISE
brass, 23mm, round, R4

C5 (obverse similar to C100)
GOOD FOR / 5 / IN / MERCHANDISE
brass, 20mm, round, R5

C1 (obverse similar to C100)
GOOD FOR / 1 / IN / MERCHANDISE
brass, 18mm, round, R8 (varieties exist)

This company, which specialized in the manufacture of print cloth and sheeting, was in operation as early as 1904.

SOUTH GREENWOOD (Greenwood County)　　　2725

A10　　GRENOLA GROCERY CO. / SOUTH GREENWOOD / S.C.
　　　　GOOD FOR / 10 / IN TRADE
　　　　　　brass, 24mm, round, R10

　　　　The Grenola Grocery Company was company store for Grendel Mills. See listings under Greenwood for additional tokens.

B100　SOUTHSIDE MERCANTILE COMPANY / 1$\underline{00}$ / SOUTH GREENWOOD, S.C.
　　　　　　(Orco - type II)　(varieties exist)
　　　　　　brass, 32mm, round, R1

B50　　(obverse similar to B100 except denomination 50)
　　　　　　(Orco - type II)　(varieties exist)
　　　　　　nickel, 27mm, round, R4

B25　　(obverse similar to B100 except denomination 25)
　　　　　　(Orco - type II)　(varieties exist)
　　　　　　copper, 24mm, round, R2

B10　　(obverse similar to B100 except denomination 10)
　　　　　　(Orco - type II)　(varieties exist)
　　　　　　brass, 21mm, round, R1

B5　　(obverse similar to B100 except denomination 5)
　　　　　　(Orco - type II)　(varieties exist)
　　　　　　nickel, 19mm, round, R1

B1　　(obverse similar to B100 except denomination 1)
　　　　　　(Orco - type III)　(varieties exist)
　　　　　　copper, 18mm, round, R7

　　　　This business, which functioned as company store for Greenwood Cotton Mills, was in operation from the late teens through the late forties.

SOUTH MARION　(Marion County)　　　2730

A100　DAVID O. ANDERSON / SOUTH / MARION, / S.C.
　　　　GOOD FOR / 1\underline{00}$ / IN / MERCHANDISE / NOT / TRANSFERABLE
　　　　　　aluminum, 28mm, square, R10

　　　　David O. Anderson operated a lumber company in the teens and the twenties. The *1920 Southern Lumberman's Directory* lists a 100,000 feet capacity sawmill, a logging railroad, an electric light plant, and a commissary. From 1916 to 1930 the company was listed as the Anderson Lumber Corporation (see listings which follow).

B100　ANDERSON LUMBER CORPORATION / 1$\underline{00}$ / A L C / SOUTH MARION, S.C.
　　　　　　(Orco - type I)
　　　　　　nickel, 32mm, round, double-ended arrow c/o, R10

SOUTH MARION   (Continued)

B50   (obverse similar to B100 except denomination 50)
  (Orco - type I)
    brass, 27mm, round, double-ended arrow c/o, R10

B25   (obverse similar to B100 except denomination 25)
  (Orco - type I)
    copper, 24mm, round, double-ended arrow c/o, R9

B10   (obverse similar to B100 except denomination 10)
  (Orco - type I)
    nickel, 21mm, round, double-ended arrow c/o, R9

B5   (obverse similar to B100 except denomination 5)
  (Orco - type I)
    brass, 19mm, round, double-ended arrow c/o, R9

B1   (obverse similar to B100 except denomination 1)
  (Orco - type I)
    copper, 18mm, round, double-ended arrow c/o, R9

SPARTANBURG   (Spartanburg County)

A500   ARKWRIGHT MILLS STORE / 5<u>00</u> / SPARTANBURG, S.C.
  (Orco - type IV, dated 1948)
    copper, 32mm, scalloped (12), R10

A50   (obverse similar to A500 except denomination 50)
  (Orco - type IV, dated 1948)
    copper, 29mm, round, R9

A10   (obverse similar to A500 except denomination 10)
  (Orco - type IV, dated 1948)
    copper, 23mm, round, R8

A5   (obverse similar to A500 except denomination 5)
  (Orco - type IV, dated 1948)
    copper, 20mm, round, R6

B5   (obverse similar to A500 except denomination 5)
  (Orco - type IV, dated 1951)
    copper, 20mm, round, R6

B1   (obverse similar to A500 except denomination 1)
  (Orco - type IV, dated 1951)
    copper, 17mm, round, R6

   In business as early as 1904, Arkwright Mills is still in operation. The company store only recently closed its doors, being one of the last company-owned general stores in existence in the state. Tokens were last issued in the 1950s, but some early tokens bear an Arkwright, S.C. address. (See listing under Arkwright.)

C100 BEAUMONT MFG. CO'S. STORE / NOT PAYING WAGES / 222 (incuse serial #)
    GOOD FOR MERCHANDISE ONLY / 1$\underline{00}$
      brass, 38mm, round, R4

C50 (obverse similar to C100)
    GOOD FOR MERCHANDISE ONLY / 50
      brass, 30mm, round, R3

C25 (obverse similar to C100)
    GOOD FOR MERCHANDISE ONLY / 25
      brass, 24mm, round, R3

C10 (obverse similar to C100)
    GOOD FOR MERCHANDISE ONLY / 10
      brass, 18mm, round, R4

C5 (obverse similar to C100)
    GOOD FOR MERCHANDISE ONLY / 5
      brass, 21mm, round, R8

D100 BEAUMONT MFG. CO'S. STORE / NOT PAYING WAGES / 376 (incuse serial #)
    GOOD FOR MERCHANDISE ONLY / 1$\underline{00}$
      aluminum, 38mm, round, R6

D50 (obverse similar to D100)
    GOOD FOR MERCHANDISE ONLY / 50
      aluminum, 30mm, round, R3

D25 (obverse similar to D100)
    GOOD FOR MERCHANDISE ONLY / 25
      aluminum, 24mm, round, R3

D10 (obverse similar to D100)
    GOOD FOR MERCHANDISE ONLY / 10
      aluminum, 18mm, round, R10

D5 (obverse similar to D100)
    GOOD FOR MERCHANDISE ONLY / 5
      aluminum, 21mm, round, R10

E1 BEAUMONT MFG. CO'S. STORE / NOT PAYING WAGES
    GOOD FOR MERCHANDISE ONLY / 1
      aluminum, 23mm, round, R3

F100 BEAUMONT MFG. CO'S. STORE / 1$\underline{00}$ / NOT PAYING / WAGES
    (Orco - type II)
      nickel, 32mm, round, R10

F50 (obverse similar to F100 except denomination 50)
    (Orco - type II)
      nickel, 27mm, round, R9

F25   (obverse similar to F100 except denomination 25)
            (Orco - type II)
               nickel, 24mm, round, R9

F10   (obverse similar to F100 except denomination 10)
            (Orco - type II)
               nickel, 21mm, round, R8

F5   (obverse similar to F100 except denomination 5)
            (Orco - type II)
               nickel, 19mm, round, R7

F1   (obverse similar to F100 except denomination 1)
            (Orco - type I and type II varieties exist)
               nickel, 18mm, round, R2

G5   BEAUMONT MFG. CO'S. STORE / 5 / NOT PAYING / WAGES
            (Orco - type unknown)
               red fiber, 19mm, round, R10

H5   BEAUMONT MILL STORE / 5 / NOT PAYING / WAGES
            (Orco - type II)
               green fiber, 20mm, round, R10

    The Beaumont Manufacturing Company, a prolific issuer of tokens, was in business as early as 1893, making twine, rope, and cotton warp. Later it made sheeting, duck, and print cloth. Descriptions of G5 and H5 may not be totally accurate.

I5   BISHOP BROS. / CONFECTIONERS / SPARTANBURG, S.C.
            GOOD FOR / 5 / IN MERCHANDISE
               aluminum, 25mm, round, R10

    The Bishop Brothers were in business circa 1910.

J10   BROWN DERBY / BILLIARD / PARLOR
            GOOD FOR / 10¢ / IN TRADE
               aluminum, 27mm, octagonal, R5

    This establishment was located at 118 Short Wofford Street. Coupon books are also known to exist.

K100   CARLSON'S CLOTHING STORE / LADIES' / READY-TO-WEAR / MILLINERY / MEN'S AND BOYS' / CLOTHING / 137 N. CHURCH ST. / SPARTANBURG, S.C.
            GOOD FOR / $1.00 / ON A PURCHASE OF / $20.00 / OR / 50¢ / ON A $10.00 PURCHASE
               aluminum, 38mm, round, R10

    Carlson's Clothing Store was listed in 1926 and 1927.

L   CHERO NEHI CO. / SPARTANBURG, S.C.
            ONE / WITH / TEN
               aluminum, 26mm, round, R7

    The Chero - Nehi Bottling Co. was in business from the late 1920s to the mid-1940s. It bottled Chero Cola, Nehi Grape, and Nehi Orange sodas.

M5   CITY BAKERY / PHONE 820 / SPARTANBURG, S.C.
     GOOD FOR / 5¢ / LOAF OF BREAD
       aluminum, 25mm, round, R9

       This bakery was listed from 1914 to 1916.

N100 PAUL E CROSBY (facsimile signature) / JEWELER / THE STORE OF
     QUALITY / SPARTANBURG / S.C.
     GOOD FOR / $1.OO / ON ANY / NEW WATCH / ONLY ONE DOLLAR /
     OFF ON / EACH WATCH
       aluminum, 35mm, round, R8

       Paul E. Crosby was first listed in the jewelry business in 1914.

O   D. O. C. / SPARTANBURG, S.C.
     GOOD FOR / 1 / PACK
       brass, 21mm, round, R8

P2½ DELUX / POCKET / BILLIARD / PARLOR / SPARTANBURG
     GOOD FOR / 2½¢ / IN TRADE
       brass, 20mm, round, R10

Q   DUKE POWER CO. / SPARTANBURG, S.C.
     GOOD FOR / ONE FARE
       zinc, 16mm, round, "S" c/o, R3 (Atwood 840A)

R   (obverse and reverse same as Q)
       steel, 16mm, round, "S" c/o, R3 (Atwood 840B)

       Streetcar service ended in Spartanburg in 1935. Duke Power Company later began bus service, and had tokens struck in the early 1940s. 30,000 specimens of Q and 50,000 of R were struck.

S25 THE FIRST NATIONAL BANK / EST. 1871 / (picture of bank building) /
     SPARTANBURG, S.C.
     WE WILL ACCEPT THIS ON DEPOSIT FOR / 25 CTS. / IF YOU OPEN
     A NEW / SAVINGS ACCOUNT OF / $5.00 / OR MORE, LEAVING IT / IN
     THE BANK 12 MONTHS / AND PAY 4% COMPOUND / INTEREST /
     ON YOUR SAVINGS, / JANUARY 1st AND JULY 1st
       brass, 31mm, round, R10

T5   TO DEALERS / WE WILL / REDEEM THIS CHECK / FOR 5¢ CASH /
     WHEN ACCEPTED / IN TRADE FOR / FOREMOST / ICE CREAM /
     PRODUCTS / FOREMOST DAIRIES, INC.
     FOREMOST / 5¢ / NICKEL
       aluminum, 24mm, round, R10

       This non-local maverick token was used in Spartanburg and perhaps other South Carolina cities. Its use has also been attributed to Georgia.

U5 GEILFUSS BAKERY / 66 / E. MAIN STR. / SPARTANBURG, S.C.
     GOOD FOR / A 5¢ / LOAF OF BREAD
       aluminum, 29mm, scalloped (8), R8

       August Geilfuss opened a bakery and confectionery circa 1908 and operated it until 1930 or so.

V10 W. C. HAMMETT / 10
  (Ingle System - 1909 pat. date)
  brass, 21mm, round, R10

V1 (obverse similar to V10 except denomination 1)
  (Ingle System - 1909 pat. date)
  brass, 18mm, round, R10

  From 1913 to 1921 W. C. Hammett was listed as a grocer and meat dealer.

W5 GOOD FOR / ONE 5¢ GLASS / SODA WATER / HEINITSH'S / PHARMACY / SPARTANBURG, S.C.
  BEST / & PUREST / MEDICINES / AT LOWEST / PRICES / HEINITSH'S PHARMACY
  aluminum, 24mm, round, R9

  Harry E. Heinitsh operated a drug store as early as 1893. The business continued into the 1940s as the Heinitsh - Walker Drug Company.

X5 HILLBROOK / FARM / SPARTANBURG / S.C. / ONE PINT MILK
  5
  brass, 21mm, round, R10

  The Hillbrook Dairy Farm was listed in 1914 and 1916.

Y5 HOLMES & JOHNSON / SPARTANBURG / S.C.
  GOOD FOR / 5¢ / CIGAR OR SODA
  aluminum, 19mm, round, R10

  Holmes & Johnson operated a drug store in 1912 & 1913.

Z100 HOME SERVICE FINANCE / 136 DUNBAR ST. / SPARTANBURG, S.C.
  $1
  aluminum, 26mm, round, R9

Z50 (obverse same as Z100)
  50¢
  aluminum, 26mm, round, R9

Z25 (obverse same as Z100)
  25¢
  aluminum, 26mm, round, R9

AA5 HUSEMANN & CO., GOOD FOR 5 CTS. IN TRADE, SPARTANBURG, S.C. (all incuse)
  (blank)
  brass, size unknown, round, R10

  Complete description not available; the listing was obtained from an old auction catalog. F. W. Husemann operated a soda parlor in 1912.

AB100 JONES FURNITURE CO. / 170 - 172 / N. CHURCH ST. / SPARTANBURG, / S.C.
  GOOD FOR / $1.00 / ON ANY / PURCHASE OF / $20.00 / OR OVER
  brass, 38mm, round, R10

  This company operated from the mid 1920s through the late 1940s.

AC10 PASTIME / BILLIARD / PARLOR
GOOD FOR / 10¢ / IN TRADE
aluminum, 27mm, octagonal, R5

The Pastime Billiard Parlor was located at 263 Magnolia Street. Coupon books also exist from this business.

AD QUALITY ICE CREAM CO. / MILK / AND / CREAM / SPARTANBURG, S.C.
GOOD FOR / ONE / PINT / MILK
aluminum, 25mm, round, R10

AE (obverse same as AD)
GOOD FOR / 5¢ / WITH RETURN / OF / EMPTY BOTTLE
aluminum, 25mm, round, R10

This company was in business during the late teens and early twenties.

AF RITZ / BILLIARD / PARLOR
GOOD FOR / 10¢ / IN TRADE
aluminum, 27mm, octagonal, R5

The Ritz Billiard Parlor was located on Library Street. Coupon books are also known from this business.

AG50 SAXON MILLS STORE / SPARTANBURG / S.C.
GOOD FOR / 50 / IN MERCHANDISE
brass, 33mm, round, R10

AG25 (obverse similar to AG50)
GOOD FOR / 25 / IN MERCHANDISE
brass, 29mm, round, R10

AG10 (obverse similar to AG50)
GOOD FOR / 10 / IN MERCHANDISE
brass, 24mm, round, R8 (varieties exist)

AG5 (obverse similar to AG50)
GOOD FOR / 5 / IN MERCHANDISE
brass, 19mm, round, R9

AH10 SAXON MILLS STORE / 10 / MDSE. ONLY / SPARTANBURG, S.C.
(Orco - type II)
brass, 21mm, round, arrow-shaped c/o, R9

AH5 (obverse similar to AH10 except denomination 5)
(Orco - type I) (varieties exist)
nickel, 19mm, round, arrow-shaped c/o, R7

Saxon Mills, a manufacturer of print cloth, was operating by 1904.

AI10 SMOKER BILLIARD PARLOR
GOOD FOR / 10¢ / IN TRADE
aluminum, 28mm, octagonal, R5

AJ10 SPARTAN / MILLS / STORE / SPARTANBURG, S.C.
GOOD FOR / 10¢ (within wreath) / IN MERCHANDISE
aluminum, 24mm, round, R10

AJ5 (obverse similar to AJ10)
GOOD FOR / 5¢ (within wreath) / IN MERCHANDISE
aluminum, 20mm, round, R9

AJ1 (obverse similar to AJ10)
GOOD FOR / 1¢ (within wreath) / IN MERCHANDISE
aluminum, 17mm, round, R5

AK1 (obverse similar to AJ10)
GOOD FOR / 1¢ (within wreath) / IN MERCHANDISE
brass, 17mm, round, R9

AL SPARTAN MILLS / SPARTANBURG, S.C.
(blank)
brass, 24mm, round, R9

This was one of the earlier mills in the Spartanburg area. In operation by 1893, it specialized in making cotton sheeting.

AM TAYLOR - COLQUITT / CO. / 177 (incuse serial #)
(blank)
brass, 36mm, round, holed as made, R10

The Taylor-Colquitt Co., a large manufacturer of treated railroad ties and telephone poles, used this piece as a time or tool check.

AN25 TURNERS / CIGAR / STORE
GOOD FOR / 25¢ / IN / MERCHANDISE
aluminum, 28mm, scalloped (12), R10

This cigar store, which also offered soda water and billiards, was listed from 1912 to 1921.

AO10 WIGWAM / BILLIARD / PARLOR
GOOD FOR / 10¢ / IN TRADE
aluminum, 27mm, octagonal, R8

AP10 WIGWAM / BILLIARD / PARLOR
GOOD FOR / 10¢ / IN TRADE
aluminum, 24mm, round, R9 (varieties exist)

The Wigwam Billiard Parlor was located at 132 Morgan Street. Coupon books are also known from the business.

SPRINGFIELD (Orangeburg County) 2740

A5 CLARK'S PHARMACY / SPRINGFIELD / S.C.
GOOD FOR / 5¢ / IN TRADE
aluminum, 19mm, round, R10

John S. Clark operated a pharmacy from 1910 to 1933.

B100 EDISTO / HARDWOOD / CO. / SPRINGFIELD, / S.C.
GOOD FOR / 1\frac{00}{}$ / IN / MERCHANDISE
brass, 31mm, round, R10

SPRINGFIELD   (Continued) 2740

B25   (obverse similar to B100)
        GOOD FOR / 25¢ / IN / MERCHANDISE
         brass, 26mm, round, R10

        This lumber manufacturer operated from 1927 to 1930.

STONO   (Charleston County) 2755

A50   BULOW STORE / GOOD FOR / 50 / CENTS / WM. L. BRADLEY.
        THIS CHECK / NOT / 1879 / TRANSFERABLE
         copper, 34mm, round, R10

A25   (obverse similar to A50 except denomination 25 CENTS)
        (reverse similar to A50)
         copper, 24mm, round, R8

William L. Bradley.

A10 (obverse similar to A50 except denomination 10 CENTS)
(reverse similar to A50)
copper, 22mm, round, R9

B50 BULOW STORE / GOOD FOR / 50 / CENTS. / WM. L. BRADLEY.
NOT TRANSFERABLE / (geometric design) / 1879
copper, 31mm, round, R9

B25 (obverse similar to B50 except denomination 25 CENTS.)
(reverse similar to B50)
copper, 25mm, round, R9

B10 (obverse similar to B50 except denomination 10 CENTS.)
(reverse similar to B50)
copper, 21mm, round, R9

William L. Bradley's interest in the chemical fertilizer business can be traced back to 1861, when he opened a fertilizer factory in Boston, Massachusetts. Little was known about chemical fertilizers at that time, and Bradley became known as an innovator in the field.

The Bradley Fertilizer Company rapidly expanded, establishing additional manufacturing works in Carteret, NJ, Cleveland, OH, Baltimore, MD, and Charleston, SC. Business offices were also established in Rochester, NY and Augusta, GA.

Bradley's main interest in the Charleston area was connected to the vast amounts of phosphate rock that were discovered in the river beds and surrounding areas. He acted quickly after the initial discoveries, becoming a partner in The Marine and River Phosphate Mining and Manufacturing Company. This corporation, formed in 1870, was granted the "exclusive" right by the state to mine all the phosphate rock from its navigable rivers and streams. Bradley was also heavily involved in the mining of phosphates from land deposits. In the 1870s he bought the old Bulow Plantation and some adjacent land on Rantowle's Creek. By 1884 Bulow Mines had recovered 30,000 tons of phosphate rock and was employing 350 workers. The rock was not processed on site, but was shipped by rail or by barge to Bradley's fertilizer factories.

In December of 1894, at the age of 68, Bradley died in Massachusetts. His two sons, Peter B. and Robert S., continued to oversee the family business interests after his death. (See listings under Ashepoo for tokens issued by the sons.)

SULLIVANS ISLAND (Charleston County) 2765

A10 SO. CA. VOL. H. B. EXCHANGE / 10 / SULLIVAN'S ISLD.
(blank)
aluminum, 29mm, round, R10

This is presumed to be an issue of the South Carolina Volunteer Heavy Battery Exchange. The group was evidently stationed on Sullivan's Island, perhaps at or near Fort Moultrie (which see for additional historical information).

SUMMERTON (Clarendon County) 2770

A5   D. O. RHAME / SUMMERTON / S.C.
        GOOD FOR / 5¢ / IN TRADE
          aluminum, 19mm, round, R10

          Rhame operated a drug store from the early 1900s to the early 1920s.

SUMTER (Sumter County) 2780

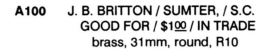

A100   J. B. BRITTON / SUMTER, / S.C.
        GOOD FOR / $1⁰⁰ / IN TRADE
          brass, 31mm, round, R10

A50   (obverse similar to A100)
        GOOD FOR / 50¢ / IN TRADE
          brass, 28mm, round, R10

A10   (obverse similar to A100)
        GOOD FOR / 10¢ / IN TRADE
          brass, 23mm, round, R10

A5   (obverse similar to A100)
        GOOD FOR / 5¢ / IN TRADE
          brass, 20mm, round, R10

A1   (obverse similar to A100)
        GOOD FOR / 1¢ / IN TRADE
          brass, 18mm, round, R9

          J. B. Britton was in business from the mid-teens to the early forties, operating a general store, cotton gin, and sawmill. He was also a contractor and lumber dealer.

B5   BRUNSWICK CIGAR STORE / SUMTER, / S.C.
        GOOD FOR / 5¢ / IN TRADE
          aluminum, 24mm, round, R10

          This business was listed in 1914 and 1915.

C5   WALTER CHEYNE / SUMTER / S.C.
        GOOD FOR / 5 / IN TRADE
          brass, 20mm, round, R10

D100   J. T. COPELAND / 1⁰⁰ / SUMTER, S.C.
        (Orco - type II)
          copper, 32mm, round, R5

D50   (obverse similar to D100 except denomination 50)
        (Orco - type II)
          copper, 27mm, round, R5

D25   (obverse similar to D100 except denomination 25)
        (Orco - type II)
          copper, 24mm, round, R5

D5   (obverse similar to D100 except denomination 5)
            (Orco - type II)
               copper, 19mm, round, R5

D1   (obverse similar to D100 except denomination 1)
            (Orco - type II)
               copper, 18mm, round, R5

            In 1932 J. T. Copeland was listed as a grocer.

E5   DE LORME'S PHARMACY / SUMTER, / S.C.
            GOOD FOR / 5¢ / AT FOUNTAIN
               aluminum, 19mm, round, R10

            This pharmacy was in business as early as 1904. F. G. DeLorme
         continued to operate it through the 1940s.

         H. J. McLaurin, Jr. used this letterhead during the early 1900s.

F100   H. J. McLAURIN JR. / SUMTER, S.C.
            GOOD FOR / 100 / IN MERCHANDISE
               aluminum, 35mm, round, R10

            McLaurin operated a sawmill and lumber yard during the early 1900s.
         The firm, which became known as McLaurin Lumber Company sometime
         prior to 1908, was out of business by 1917.

G25   J. M. / MIMS
            GOOD FOR / 25¢ / IN MERCHANDISE
               aluminum, 26mm, round, R10

            J.M. Mims operated a grocery store during the 1920s and early 1930s.

H100   N C O / SHAW / A.F.B.
            GOOD FOR / 1⁰⁰ / IN TRADE
               brass, 28mm, square, R10

H5   (obverse similar to H100)
GOOD FOR / 5¢ / IN TRADE
brass, 19mm, square, R9

I100   N C O / SHAW A F B
GOOD FOR / 1\frac{00}{}$ / IN TRADE
brass, 35mm, round, R10

I25   (obverse similar to I100)
GOOD FOR / 25¢ / IN TRADE
brass, 29mm, round, R9 (Curto A733-25)

I5   (obverse similar to I100)
GOOD FOR / 5¢ / IN TRADE
brass, 22mm, round, R10 (Curto A733-5)

J100   SHAW AFB / 1974 / NCO CLUB
GOOD FOR / 1\frac{00}{}$ / IN TRADE
blue anodized aluminum, 32mm, round, R8

J25   (obverse similar to J100)
25¢ denomination, description incomplete
blue anodized aluminum, size unknown, round, R10

K100   N C O / SHAW / A.F.B.
GOOD FOR / 1\frac{00}{}$ / IN TRADE
aluminum, 35mm, round, R8

L100   NCO OPEN MESS / SHAW / AFB, / S.C.
GOOD FOR / 1\frac{00}{}$ / IN / MERCHANDISE
brass, 32mm, round, R10

M100   NCO OPEN MESS / SHAW AFB / S.C.
GOOD FOR / 1\frac{00}{}$ / IN / MERCHANDISE
green anodized aluminum, 32mm, round, R5

This Non-Commissioned Officers' Open Mess still uses tokens in its lounge.

N10   STANDARD / CREAMERY / SUMTER, / S.C.
GOOD FOR / 10¢ / WHEN RETURNED / WITH BOTTLE
aluminum, 22mm, octagonal, R9

During the mid-twenties this business was operated by the Sumter Ice & Fuel Company.

O50   THE SUMTER PACKING CO., INC. / SUMTER, / S.C.
GOOD FOR / 50 / IN / MERCHANDISE
brass, 22mm, round, R10

O25   (obverse similar to O50)
GOOD FOR / 25 / IN MERCHANDISE.
brass, 22mm, round, R10

SUMTER (Continued) 2780

O5 (obverse similar to O50)
GOOD FOR / 5 / IN / MERCHANDISE
brass, 22mm, round, R10

    The Sumter Packing Company was in business from the mid-1920s to the early 1940s. It specialized in vegetable and fruit packing.

P1 THE SUMTER PHARMACY / DRUGGISTS / AND / CHEMISTS
GOOD FOR / 1¢ / AT / OUR STORE
aluminum, 21mm, round, R10

Q100 SUMTER TRUCK TERMINAL / (picture of man holding tire) / BUY FISK / DIVISION OF / INDUSTRIAL EQUIPMENT CO. / SUMTER, S.C.
GOOD FOR GOOD FOOD / $1<u>00</u> / IN TRADE / AT SUMTER, S.C. / SUBJECT TO CANCELLATION AT WILL
aluminum, 35mm, round, R9

SWANSEA (Lexington County) 2785

A100 J. C. REYNOLDS / GENERAL / MERCHANDISE
GOOD FOR / 1,00 / IN TRADE
brass, 36mm, round, R10

A5 (obverse similar to A100)
GOOD FOR / 5 / IN TRADE
brass, 19mm, round, R10

    J. C. Reynolds was listed only in 1912. It is believed that he was a partner in Reynolds & Craft, issuers of the following tokens.

B100 REYNOLDS & CRAFT / SWANSEA, / S.C.
GOOD FOR / 100 / IN MERCHANDISE
brass, 36mm, round, R10

B25 (obverse similar to B100)
GOOD FOR / 25 / IN MERCHANDISE
brass, 29mm, round, R9

B10 (obverse similar to B100)
GOOD FOR / 10 / IN MERCHANDISE
brass, 24mm, round, R9

B5 (obverse similar to B100)
GOOD FOR / 5 / IN MERCHANDISE
brass, 19mm, round, R10

    Reynolds & Craft operated a general store circa 1908 to 1910.

TATUM   (Marlboro County)   2795

A25   THE I. BLUM COMPANY / TATUM, / S.C,
GOOD FOR / 25¢ / IN MERCHANDISE
aluminum, 28mm, round, R10

This general store operated during the early 1920s.

TAYLORS   (Greenville County)   2800

A25   BARNEY'S / CAFE / TAYLORS, S.C.
GOOD FOR / 25¢ / IN TRADE
aluminum, 26mm, round, R10

A5   (obverse similar to A25)
GOOD FOR / 5¢ / IN TRADE
aluminum, 20mm, round, R10

B25   J. W. HUDGENS / LUNCH / TAYLORS, S.C.
GOOD FOR / 25 / IN TRADE
aluminum, 26mm, octagonal, R10

B5   (obverse similar to B25)
GOOD FOR / 5 / IN TRADE
aluminum, 20mm, octagonal, R10

B1   (obverse similar to B25)
GOOD FOR / 1 / IN TRADE
aluminum, 18mm, round, R9

C1   J. W. HUDGENS / LUNCH / TAYLORS, / S.C.
GOOD FOR / 1¢ / IN TRADE
aluminum, 20mm, octagonal, R10

D5   SOUTHERN / BLEACHERY / STORE
5 / CENTS (partially illegible, description incomplete)
aluminum, 24mm, round, R10

Southern Bleachery, a large textile mill, was located near Taylors.

THICKETY   (Cherokee County)   2805

A5   J. H. GRAHAM / 5
(Ingle System - 1914 pat. date)
composition unknown, 20mm, round, R10

Obverse description may not be exact. Attribution tentative, based solely on its presence in Wagaman's catalog. A general store owner named J. H. Graham was listed in 1914 and 1915.

TILLMAN   (Jasper County)   2813

A100   W. M. RITTER LUMBER CO. / 1$\underline{00}$
        (Orco - type II)
        nickel, 32mm, round, "R" c/o, R8

A50   (obverse similar to A100 except denomination 50)
        (Orco - type II)
        brass, 27mm, round, "R" c/o, R8

A25   (obverse similar to A100 except denomination 25)
        (Orco - type II)
        nickel, 24mm, round, "R" c/o, R8

A10   (obverse similar to A100 except denomination 10)
        (Orco - type II)
        brass, 21mm, round, "R" c/o, R8

A5   (obverse similar to A100 except denomination 5)
        (Orco - type II)
        nickel, 19mm, round, "R" c/o, R8

In 1890 the W. M. Ritter Lumber Company was organized in West Virginia by William McClellan Ritter, a Pennsylvania lumberman who parlayed his company into one of the largest lumber companies in the eastern United States. Later moving his headquarters to Columbus, Ohio, Ritter amassed holdings that included millions of acres of timberland in six states. Sawmills were first built in West Virginia, and later in Virginia, Kentucky, Tennessee, North Carolina, and South Carolina.

The tokens were probably used at commissaries in all of the above-named states. The sawmill at Tillman was built in the early 1930s and continued to the 1950s. A subsidiary, The Colleton Cypress Company, operated in Colleton, S.C., but it is not known whether the tokens were used there.

TIMMONSVILLE   (Florence County)   2815

A   LANGSTON'S / BAKERY / TIMMONSVILLE, S.C.
        GOOD FOR / ONE LOAF / OF / BREAD
        aluminum, 25mm, square, R10

        During the early teens L. M. Langston operated a bakery and grocery.

TRENTON   (Edgefield County)   2830

A5   B. B. BOUKNIGHT / A / TRENTON, / S.C.
        GOOD FOR / 5 / IN TRADE
        aluminum, 19mm, round, R9

TRENTON (Continued)   2830

B5   S. H. MANGET / TRENTON, S.C.
          GOOD FOR / 5¢ / CIGAR / OR / SODA
          brass, 24mm, round, R10

          Manget operated a grocery store from the early 1900s to the early
          1930s.

TUCAPAU (Spartanburg County)   2835

A25   STARTEX MILL STORE / 25 / TUCAPAU, S.C.
          (Orco - type II)
          brass, 24mm, round, star-shaped c/o, R9

A10   (obverse similar to A25 except denomination 10)
          (Orco - type II) (varieties exist)
          brass, 21mm, round, star-shaped c/o, R7

A5   (obverse similar to A25 except denomination 5)
          (Orco - type II and type III varieties exist)
          brass, 19mm, round, star-shaped c/o, R6

          Startex Mills bought out Tucapau Mills around 1937. The company,
          still in business, makes print cloth.

B25   TUCAPAU MILLS STORE / 25 / TUCAPAU, S.C.
          (Orco - type I)
          nickel, 24mm, round, umbrella-shaped c/o, R8

B10   (obverse similar to B25 except denomination 10)
          (Orco - type I)
          nickel, 21mm, round, umbrella-shaped c/o, R8

455

J.F. CLEVELAND. PRESIDENT.
SPARTANBURG, S.C.

T. E. MOORE, TREAS. & GEN'L MANG'R.
WELLFORD, S.C.

TUCAPAU MILLS
COTTON GOODS.

Tucapau, S.C. Jany 1st 1908

SHIPPING. POINT,
WELLFORD, S. C.

Tucapau Mills' letterhead, circa 1908.

TUCAPAU   (Continued)

B5   (obverse similar to B25 except denomination 5)
        (Orco - type I)
          nickel, 19mm, round, umbrella-shaped c/o, R8

B1   (obverse similar to B25 except denomination 1)
        (Orco - type I)
          brass, 18mm, round, umbrella-shaped c/o, R8

C100   TUCAPAU MILLS STORE / 19 1$\underline{00}$ 33 / TUCAPAU, S.C.
        (Orco - type II)
          brass, 32mm, round, T-shaped c/o, R8

C50   (obverse similar to C100 except denomination 50)
        (Orco - type II)
          brass, 27mm, round, T-shaped c/o, R7

C25   (obverse similar to C100 except denomination 25)
        (Orco - type I)
          brass, 24mm, round, T-shaped c/o, R7

C10   (obverse similar to C100 except denomination 10)
        (Orco - type I)
          brass, 21mm, round, T-shaped c/o, R8

C5   (obverse similar to C100 except denomination 5)
        (Orco - type II)
          brass, 19mm, round, T-shaped c/o, R8

        Tucapau Mills, makers of print cloth, was in operation by 1904. It was
purchased by Startex Mills circa 1937. The name "Tucapau" comes from
an old Indian word meaning "strong cloth". The town now goes by the
name of Startex.

TURBEVILLE   (Clarendon County)

A1   D. E. & J. F. TURBEVILLE / TURBEVILLE / S.C.
        GOOD FOR / 1¢ / IN / MERCHANDISE
          aluminum, 18mm, round, R10

        D. E. & J. F. Turbeville operated a general store from 1916 to 1926. In
1927 they were listed as general store and sawmill.

TYLERS   (Laurens County)

A5   H. C. TYLER / CORPORATION / COMMISSARY / TYLERS, S.C.
        GOOD FOR / 5¢ / IN MERCHANDISE
          aluminum, 20mm, round, R10

ULMERS (Allendale County)

A100 G. A. BEST
GOOD FOR / $1̲0̲0̲ / IN TRADE
brass, 21mm, round, R10

A5 (obverse same as A100)
GOOD FOR / 5¢ / IN TRADE
brass, 21mm, round, R10

G. A. Best operated a general store from the early 1900s to the early 1930s.

B10 BREON LUMBER CO. INC. / DRY GOODS / GROCERIES / & / PROVISIONS / ULMERS, S.C.
GOOD FOR / 10¢ / IN MERCHANDISE
aluminum, 23mm, octagonal, R10

Headquartered at Williamsport, Pa., this company operated in Ulmers circa 1905.

UNION (Union County)

A CORN ROCKER BEARINGS, STONE SHUTTLE CHECKS, SNOW STOP MOTION / BAHAN / TEXTILE MACHINERY / COMPANY / COTTON MILL / SPECIALTIES / UNION, S.C. & / LAWRENCE, / MASS.
MEMBERSHIP EMBLEM OF THE DON'T WORRY CLUB / (picture of swastika with other good luck symbols) / GOOD LUCK
brass, 32mm, round, R8

B50 GOOD FOR / 50¢ / WITH EMPTY CRATE / COCA COLA / BOTTLES / COCA COLA BOTTLING CO. / UNION, S.C
(same)
aluminum, 38mm, round, R8

The Union Coca Cola Bottling Company was in operation by 1908.

C100 S. C. CROSBY / 1̲0̲0̲
(Ingle System - 1909 pat. date)
brass, 35mm, round, R9

C50 (obverse similar to C100 except denomination 50)
(Ingle System - 1909 pat. date)
brass, 31mm, round, R9

C25 (obverse similar to C100 except denomination 25)
(Ingle System - 1909 pat. date)
brass, 24mm, round, R9

C10 (obverse similar to C100 except denomination 10)
(Ingle System - 1909 pat. date)
brass, 21mm, round, R9

C5   (obverse similar to C100 except denomination 5)
 (Ingle System - 1909 pat. date)
  brass, 20mm, round, R9

C1   (obverse similar to C100 except denomination 1)
 (Ingle System - 1909 pat. date)
  brass, 18mm, round, R9

  S. C. Crosby operated a grocery store and cafe circa 1910 to 1916.

D25   EXCELSIOR CANTEEN / UNION, / S.C.
  GOOD FOR / 25¢ / IN TRADE / THE OSBORNE REGISTER CO. CIN,O.
  (in tiny letters)
  aluminum, 26mm, round, R10

D5   (obverse similar to D25)
  GOOD FOR / 5¢ / IN TRADE / (Orco signature)
  aluminum, 20mm, round, R9

D1   (obverse similar to D25)
  GOOD FOR / 1¢ / IN TRADE / (Orco signature)
  aluminum, 18mm, round, R9

  Excelsior Knitting Mills operated a canteen for its employees for many years. The mill, which has been in operation since 1904, manufactured hosiery and sheeting.

E25   B. L. FOWLER / 25
 (Ingle System - 1909 pat. date)
  brass, 24mm, round, R10

E10   (obverse similar to E25 except denomination 10)
 (Ingle System - 1909 pat. date)
  brass, 21mm, round, R10

E1   (obverse similar to E25 except denomination 1)
 (Ingle System - 1909 pat. date)
  brass, 18mm, round, R10

  B. L. Fowler was listed as a grocer from 1908 to 1922.

F5   GOODMAN'S / VARIETY / BAKERY / UNION, / S.C.
  GOOD FOR / A 5¢ / LOAF OF BREAD
  aluminum, 25mm, round, R10

G   C. H. HAMPTON / UNION, / S.C.
  GOOD FOR / ONE / TUNE
  brass, 21mm, round, R9

H5   (obverse same as G)
  GOOD FOR / 5¢ / IN TRADE
  brass, 21mm, round, R9

I5   J. F. JOHNSON / UNION, S.C.
  GOOD FOR / 5¢ / IN TRADE
  aluminum, 19mm, round, R10

J5   KELLER'S DRUG STORE / UNDER / HOTEL / UNION / UNION, S.C.
GOOD FOR ONE / 5 / CENT / GLASS OF SODA
   aluminum, 24mm, round, R10

   George T. Keller was listed as a druggist for the years 1913 and 1914.

K5   A. KERHULAS
GOOD FOR / 5¢ / IN TRADE
   brass, 21mm, round, center hole, R8

   From the early teens through the early thirties Antones Kerhulas operated a fruit stand and confectionery.

L100   MRS. M. J. MABRY / 1$\underline{00}$
(Ingle System - 1909 pat. date)
   brass, 35mm, round, R9

L10   (obverse similar to L100 except denomination 10)
(Ingle System - 1909 pat. date)
   brass, 21mm, round, R10

L1   (obverse similar to L100 except denomination 1)
(Ingle System - 1909 pat. date)
   brass, 18mm, round, R10

   Mrs. Mabry operated a grocery store from 1910 to 1927.

M25   MONARCH AND OTTARAY MILL STORES / 25 / M & O / UNION, / S.C.
(Orco - type II)
   brass, 24mm, round, flower-shaped c/o, R10

M10   (obverse similar to M25 except denomination 10)
(Orco - type II)
   brass, 21mm, round, flower-shaped c/o, R9

M5   (obverse similar to M25 except denomination 5)
(Orco - type II)
   brass, 19mm, round, flower-shaped c/o, R9

M1   (obverse similar to M25 except denomination 1)
(Orco - type II)
   brass, 18mm, round, flower-shaped c/o, R8

   During the 1930s Monarch Mills and Ottaray Mills were operated by the same owner. The mills have been in operation since the early 1900s.

N   COMPLIMENTS / OF / PEPSI-COLA / BOTTLING CO. / UNION, S.C.
GOOD FOR / A BOTTLE OF / PEPSI-COLA (in script)
   aluminum, 18mm, round, R10

   The Union Pepsi Cola Bottling Company was listed only during 1913.

O5   J. J. PURCELL / UNION / S.C.
GOOD FOR / 5 / IN TRADE
   brass, 24mm, round, R10

   This grocer, confectioner, and billiard parlor owner was in business during the early teens.

P500   UNION - BUFFALO MILLS STORE / 5⁰⁰ / UNION, S.C.
　　　　(Orco - type I)
　　　　nickel, 32mm, scalloped (12), "U" c/o, R7

P100   (obverse similar to P500 except denomination 1⁰⁰)
　　　　(Orco - type I)
　　　　nickel, 32mm, round, "U" c/o, R7

P50   (obverse similar to P500 except denomination 50)
　　　　(Orco - type I)
　　　　nickel, 27mm, round, "U" c/o, R7

P25   (obverse similar to P500 except denomination 25)
　　　　(Orco - type I)
　　　　nickel, 24mm, round, "U" c/o, R7

P10   (obverse similar to P500 except denomination 10)
　　　　(Orco - type I)
　　　　nickel, 21mm, round, "U" c/o, R7

P5   (obverse similar to P500 except denomination 5)
　　　　(Orco - type I)
　　　　nickel, 19mm, round, "U" c/o, R7

P1   (obverse similar to P500 except denomination 1)
　　　　(Orco - types I, II, and III varieties exist)
　　　　nickel, 18mm, round, "U" c/o, R4

Q5   UNION - BUFFALO MILL STORE / UNION, S.C.
　　　　GOOD FOR / 5 / IN MERCHANDISE ONLY
　　　　brass, 19mm, round, banana-shaped c/o, R10

　　　Union Cotton Mills was organized in 1895 by the Duncan and Eaves families. By 1908 the company had expanded with the construction of a mill in nearby Buffalo, and had become known as Union-Buffalo Mills Company. In 1949 the company was sold to United Merchants. The mill is still in operation.

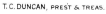

CAPITAL STOCK $1,100,000.

Union, S. C.   NOV 26 1904

This letterhead depicts the Union Cotton Mills during its early years.

UNION (Continued) 2855

R5 UNION DRUG CO. / DISTRIBUTORS / UNION / S.C.
GOOD FOR / 5¢ / CIGAR OR SODA
aluminum, 19mm, round, R10

This company was in business during the 1890s and early 1900s.

S10 VAUGHN BUS LINE / UNION, / S.C. (varieties exist)
GOOD FOR / 10¢ / IN TRADE
brass, 23mm, round, R6 (Atwood 880A)

T10 VAUGHAN BUS LINE
GOOD FOR / 10¢ / IN TRADE
brass, 23mm, round, R6 (Atwood 880B)

The Vaughan Bus Line started operating in 1949 and was out of business by June 1951 (due to the death of the owner, G. Frank Vaughan). "Vaughn" is misspelled on 2855-S10.

VARNVILLE (Hampton County) 2862

A5 VARNVILLE DRUG CO. / VARNVILLE, / S.C.
GOOD FOR / 5¢ / IN MERCHANDISE
aluminum, 20mm, round, R10

This company operated during the late teens and twenties.

WALHALLA (Oconee County) 2875

A100 KENNETH COTTON MILLS STORE / 1⁰⁰ / IN TRADE ONLY
(Master Metal Scrip - type II)
nickel, 35mm, round, "K" c/o, R7

A50 (obverse similar to A100 except denomination 50)
(Master Metal Scrip - type II)
brass, 30mm, round, "K" c/o, R7

A25 (obverse similar to A100 except denomination 25)
(Master Metal Scrip - type II)
copper, 24mm, round, "K" c/o, R7

A10 (obverse similar to A100 except denomination 10)
(Master Metal Scrip - type II)
nickel, 21mm, round, "K" c/o, R7

A5 (obverse similar to A100 except denomination 5)
(Master Metal Scrip - type II)
brass, 19mm, round, "K" c/o, R7

The Kenneth Cotton Mills was listed from 1926 through the 1940s, as a manufacturer of bedspreads.

B100 WALHALLA MILL STORE / 1$\underline{00}$ / WALHALLA, S.C. /
NON-TRANSFERABLE
    (Master Metal Scrip - type II)
    nickel-plated brass, 35mm, round, "W" c/o, R8

B50 (obverse similar to B100 except denomination 50)
    (Master Metal Scrip - type II)
    brass, 30mm, round, "W" c/o, R8

B25 (obverse similar to B100 except denomination 25)
    (Master Metal Scrip - type II)
    copper, 24mm, round, "W" c/o, R8

B10 (obverse similar to B100 except denomination 10)
    (Master Metal Scrip - type II)
    nickel-plated brass, 21mm, round, "W" c/o, R8

B5 (obverse similar to B100 except denomination 5)
    (Master Metal Scrip - type II)
    brass, 19mm, round, "W" c/o, R8

B1 (obverse similar to B100 except denomination 1)
    (Master Metal Scrip - type II)
    copper, 18mm, round, "W" c/o, R8

    Walhalla Mills was a branch of the Victor - Monaghan Corporation of Greenville. The company store was listed from 1921 to 1938.

WALTERBORO (Colleton County) 2880

A5 E. HUBSTER'S / BAKERY / WALTERBORO / S.C.
    GOOD FOR / ONE / 5¢ / LOAF OF BREAD
    aluminum, 25mm, scalloped (12), R8

    Ernest Hubster operated a bakery at 418 Washington Street from the late 1800s to 1930. His son, Edward, then took over until 1937. Tokens were sold at a discount of twenty-five for $1.00.

B25 TERRY & SHAFFER / EGG / CHECK / WALTERBORO, S.C.
    GOOD FOR / 25 / IN / MERCHANDISE
    brass, 29mm, round, R10

    Terry & Shaffer ran a general store as early as 1893. The business closed in the early 1920s.

C25 WALTERBORO / LUMBER CO. / WALTERBORO, S.C.
    GOOD FOR / 25 / IN TRADE
    brass, 25mm, round, R10

    Headquartered in Ridgeway, Pa., this company operated from the early teens to the early twenties.

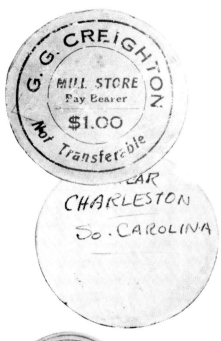

WANDO (Berkeley County)   2885

A100   G. G. CREIGHTON / MILL STORE / PAY BEARER / $1.00 / NOT TRANSFERABLE
      (blank)
        orange cardboard, 45mm, round, R10

A5   (obverse similar to A100 except denomination 5¢)
      (blank)
        green cardboard, 45mm, round, R10

        G. G. Creighton ran a sawmill during the early 1900s.

WARE SHOALS (Greenwood County)   2890

A   WARE SHOALS / DAIRY / Q 1 T. / MILK
      GOOD FOR / ONE / QT. / MILK
        brass, 29mm, round, R10

B   WARE SHOALS / DAIRY / P 1 T. / MILK
      GOOD FOR / ONE / PINT / OF / MILK   (varieties exist)
        brass, 25mm, round, R8

        This dairy was operated by the Ware Shoals Manufacturing Company during the early 1930s.

C5   GOOD AT WARE SHOALS / DEPT. STORE / ONLY / FOR 5¢
      GOOD FOR / 5¢ / IF RETURNED / WITH BOTTLE
        aluminum, 25mm, octagonal, R10

        The Ware Shoals Department Store functioned as company store for the Ware Shoals Manufacturing Company during the teens, twenties, and thirties.

D   WARE SHOALS MFG. CO. / #18
      (blank)
        aluminum, 26mm, round, R10

E   WARE SHOALS MFG. CO. / #20
      (blank)
        aluminum, 26mm, round, R10

F   WARE SHOALS MFG. CO. / #20
      (blank)
        aluminum, 22mm, octagonal, R10

        This company was in operation as early as 1904. Headquartered in New York City, it made sheetings, shirtings, and print cloths. The tokens were probably production checks.

WARRENVILLE (Aiken County) 2895

A100 C. D. KENNEY & SONS / 1⁰⁰ / WARRENVILLE, S.C.
(Orco - type II)
brass, 32mm, round, c/o, R10

A50 (obverse similar to A100 except denomination 50)
(Orco - type II)
copper, 27mm, round, c/o, R9

A25 (obverse similar to A100 except denomination 25)
(Orco - type II)
nickel, 24mm, round, c/o, R10

A10 (obverse similar to A100 except denomination 10)
(Orco - type II)
brass, 21mm, round, c/o, R10

A5 (obverse similar to A100 except denomination 5)
(Orco - type II)
nickel, 19mm, round, c/o, R9

A1 (obverse similar to A100 except denomination 1)
(Orco - type III)
copper, 18mm, round, c/o, R8

C. D. Kenney & Sons operated general stores in Warrenville and Graniteville during the 1920s, 1930s, and 1940s.

B100 A. G. T. SPRADLEY / 1⁰⁰
(Ingle System - 1909 pat. date)
brass, 35mm, round, R10

B25 (obverse similar to B100 except denomination 25)
(Ingle System - 1909 pat. date)
brass, 24mm, round, R10

A. G. T. Spradley operated a grocery near Warrenville from 1913 to 1916.

WATEREE (Richland County) 2900

A10 ALEX. G. CLARKSON / WATEREE / S.C.
GOOD FOR / 10 / IN / MERCHANDISE
aluminum, 25mm, round, R10

Clarkson operated a general store as early as 1893. He also operated the Farmers Supply Company in Eastover circa 1905.

A product label of Breslauer, Lachicotte & Co.

A10   BRESLAUER, LACHICOTTE & CO. / WAVERLY / MILLS, / S.C.
          GOOD FOR / 10 / IN MERCHANDISE
          aluminum, 24mm, round, R9

A5   (obverse similar to A10)
          GOOD FOR / 5 / IN MERCHANDISE
          aluminum, 19mm, round, R9

   This firm operated a cannery and sauce-making company from 1890 to 1919. The cannery was originally built near Litchfield in 1890, but in 1900 was moved to Oaks Plantation, on Pawleys Island.

B5   WAVERLY SUPPLY CO. / WAVERLY MILLS, / S.C.
          GOOD FOR / 5 / CENTS (within curl of 5) / IN TRADE
          aluminum, 25mm x 38mm, rectangular, R10

C50   WAVERLY SUPPLY CO. / F / WAVERLY / MILLS, / S.C.
          GOOD FOR / 50 / CENTS / IN TRADE
          aluminum, 35mm, scalloped (4), R10

C40   (obverse similar to C50)
          GOOD FOR / 40 / CENTS / IN TRADE.
          aluminum, 31mm, scalloped (16), R9

C20   (obverse similar to C50)
          GOOD FOR / 20 / CENTS / IN TRADE
          aluminum, 26mm, hexagonal, R10

   This general store operated from 1904 to 1921.

WELLFORD   (Spartanburg County) 2910

A1   BERRY - FORTUNE CONSTRUCTION CO. / WELLFORD, / S.C.
GOOD FOR / 1 / IN / MERCHANDISE
    aluminum, 19mm, round, R10

      The Berry - Fortune Construction Company was listed only during 1913 and 1914.

WESTMINSTER   (Oconee County) 2920

A100   J. & J. S. CARTER / 1<u>00</u>
    (Ingle System - 1909 pat. date)
    copper, 35mm, round, R9

A50   (obverse similar to A100 except denomination 50)
    (Ingle System - 1909 pat. date)
    copper, 31mm, round, R10

A1   (obverse similar to A100 except denomination 1)
    (Ingle System - 1909 pat. date)
    copper, 18mm, round, R10

      J. & J. S. Carter, a father and son partnership, opened a general store circa 1904. The father (John) did not participate in the business after 1914 but his son, Jesse Sevier, operated it into the 1920s. The following tokens were used by the same firm; the additional "J" in the name is a die-cutting error.

B100   J. J. & J. S. CARTER / 1<u>00</u>
    (Ingle System - 1909 pat. date)
    copper, 35mm, round, R10

B50   (obverse similar to B100 except denomination 50)
    (Ingle System - 1909 pat. date)
    copper, 31mm, round, R10

B1   (obverse similar to B100 except denomination 1)
    (Ingle System - 1909 pat. date)
    copper, 18mm, round, R10)

C100   S. W. DICKSON & CO. / 1<u>00</u>
    (Ingle System - 1914 pat. date)
    composition unknown, 35mm, round, R10

C50   (obverse similar to C100 except denomination 50)
    (Ingle System - 1914 pat. date)
    composition unknown, 30mm, round, R10

C25   (obverse similar to C100 except denomination 25)
        (Ingle System - 1914 pat. date)
           composition unknown, 24mm, round, R10

      S. W. Dickson & Company operated a grocery and general store from 1913 to 1915. In 1916, and prior to 1912, the business was listed only as S. W. Dickson.

D50   SHELDON FURNITURE CO. / AT
        GOOD FOR / 50¢ / WITH EACH / 10⁰⁰ / CASH PURCHASE
           nickel-plated brass, 31mm, round, R10

      This company was in business from 1908 to 1923.

F5   STONECYPHER DRUG CO. / WESTMINSTER, / S.C.
        DRINK / 5¢ / CIGAR
           aluminum, 19mm, round, R10

      The Stonecypher Drug Company operated from the early 1900s to the early 1920s.

WHITE HALL   (Colleton County)   2930

A50   D. C. HEYWARD / WHITE HALL, / S.C.
        GOOD FOR / 50 / IN / MERCHANDISE
           brass, 31mm, round, R10

      Born in 1864, Duncan Clinch Heyward was the son of a prominent South Carolina rice planter. At the age of six he was orphaned and went to live with his maternal grandmother. As he was growing up, he became enamored of being a rice planter. Upon reaching adulthood he began planting rice on the Whitehall Plantation in Colleton County.

      It was unfortunate that Heyward started his business at a time when the profitability of rice-planting in South Carolina was declining. By 1905 the industry in the state was all but dead, having been dealt successive blows by competition from other states and vicious hurricanes. Realizing that his rice-planting days were drawing to a close, he turned his attention to other horizons.

      In 1902, at the age of 37, Heyward was elected governor of South Carolina as the result of his first campaign for public office. He was elected to a second term without opposition in 1904. He later (1937) penned an excellent book called *Seed From Madagascar* on South Carolina rice culture.

      The tokens were utilized to pay workers employed by Heyward on the plantation. They could be redeemed at the general store which he operated.

WHITE STONE SPRINGS   (Spartanburg County)   2935

A   HEALTHFUL - MADE RIGHT - TASTE RIGHT / TRY IT / FROM / WHITE
STONE / LITHIA SPRINGS / CO. / WHITE STONE SPRINGS / S.C.
GOOD FOR ONE GLASS / OR / SPLIT BOTTLE / OF / WHITE STONE /
LITHIA WATER, / GINGER ALE, / OR / SODA WATER
aluminum, 30mm, round, R10

The White Stone Lithia Springs Company operated a health resort and
bottling company circa 1900.

A. STANLEY STANFORD
Proprietor and Manager

DR. WM. F. HALE
Resident Physician

JOHN H. MCCOACH
Assistant Manager

Wbite Stone Lithia Springs Ibotel

Wbite Stone Springs, S. C., *Aug 21 - 04*

The White Stone Lithia Springs Hotel is depicted on the establishment's
letterhead.

WHITMERE

Tokens from the GLENN - LOWRY MFG. CO. of WHITMERE, S.C. are
die-cutting errors. The town's name is actually Whitmire, and the tokens
are listed there.

WHITMIRE   (Newberry County) 2940

A100   GLENN - LOWRY MFG. CO. / GENERAL / MERCHANDISE / WHITMERE, S.C.
>   GOOD FOR / $1⁰⁰ / IN MERCHANDISE
>   brass, 35mm, octagonal, R9

A50   (obverse similar to A100)
>   GOOD FOR / 50¢ / IN MERCHANDISE
>   brass, 32mm, octagonal, R9

A25   (obverse similar to A100)
>   GOOD FOR / 25¢ / IN MERCHANDISE
>   brass, 29mm, octagonal, R9

A10   (obverse similar to A100)
>   GOOD FOR / 10¢ / IN MERCHANDISE
>   brass, 25mm, octagonal, R9

A5   (obverse similar to A100)
>   GOOD FOR / 5¢ / IN MERCHANDISE
>   brass, 20mm, octagonal, R9

A1   (obverse similar to A100)
>   GOOD FOR / 1¢ / IN / MERCHANDISE
>   brass, 18mm, octagonal, R9

B10   (obverse similar to A100)
>   GOOD FOR / 10¢ / IN MERCHANDISE
>   brass, 25mm, round, R9

The Glenn-Lowry Manufacturing Company operated a cotton mill from the early 1900s to the mid-1920s. Sometime around 1925, the mill was sold to Aragon-Baldwin Cotton Mills, headquartered in Rock Hill. The town's name is misspelled as "Whitmere" on the tokens.

C5   L.C.L. COOPERATIVE / STORES / GENERAL / MERCHANDISE / WHITMIRE, S.C.
>   GOOD FOR / 5¢ / IN MERCHANDISE
>   aluminum, 21mm, octagonal, R10

This store was listed only in 1922 and 1923.

WHITNEY   (Spartanburg County) 2945

A5   WHITNEY MFG. CO. / WHITNEY / S.C.
>   GOOD FOR / 5 / IN GOODS / AT OUR STORE
>   aluminum, 21mm, round, R10

B100   WHITNEY / MILL STORE / WHITNEY, / S.C.
>   GOOD FOR / $1⁰⁰ / IN / MERCHANDISE
>   brass, 35mm, round, R10

WHITNEY (Continued) 2945

B50 (obverse similar to B100)
GOOD FOR / 50¢ / IN / MERCHANDISE
brass, 31mm, round, R9

B25 (obverse similar to B100)
GOOD FOR / 25¢ / IN / MERCHANDISE
brass, 28mm, round, R9

B10 (obverse similar to B100)
GOOD FOR / 10¢ / IN / MERCHANDISE
brass, 26mm, round, R8

C10 WHITNEY / MILL STORE / WHITNEY / S.C.
GOOD FOR / 10¢ / IN / MERCHANDISE
brass, 25mm, round, R8

C5 (obverse similar to C10)
GOOD FOR / 5¢ / IN / MERCHANDISE
brass, 20mm, round, R8

C1 (obverse similar to C10)
GOOD FOR / 1¢ / IN / MERCHANDISE
brass, 18mm, round, R7 (varieties exist)

D5 WHITNEY MILL STORE / WHITNEY, / S.C.
GOOD FOR / 5¢ / IN TRADE
brass, 20mm, round, R8

   The Whitney Manufacturing Company was in operation as early as the turn of the century. In the 1940s it was purchased by Springdale Finishing of Canton, Mass. The mill store was in operation from the early teens to the forties.

WILLIAMSTON (Anderson County) 2950

A500 AIKEN STORES INC. / 5̲0̲0̲ / A S / WILLIAMSTON, S.C.
(Orco - type IV, dated 1939)
brass, 32mm, scalloped (12), "W" c/o, R7

A100 (obverse similar to A500 except denomination 1̲0̲0̲)
(Orco - type IV, dated 1939)
nickel, 32mm, round, "W" c/o, R3

A50 (obverse similar to A500 except denomination 50)
(Orco - type IV, dated 1939)
copper, 29mm, round, "W" c/o, R3

A25 (obverse similar to A500 except denomination 25)
(Orco - type IV, dated 1939)
nickel, 26mm, round, "W" c/o, R3

A10   (obverse similar to A500 except denomination 10)
            (Orco - type IV, dated 1939)
            brass, 23mm, round, "W" c/o, R3

A5   (obverse similar to A500 except denomination 5)
            (Orco - type IV, dated 1939)
            nickel, 20mm, round, "W" c/o, R3

            Aiken Stores Inc. operated the company store for one of the Williamston area cotton mills during the late thirties and early forties.

B5   DONNALD & WILSON / CO. / WILLIAMSTON / & / PIEDMONT / S.C.
            GOOD FOR ONE / 5¢ / DRINK / OR CIGAR
            aluminum, 24mm, round, R10

            This company operated drug stores in Williamston and Piedmont in the early teens. The token is also listed under Piedmont.

C200   EMPIRE / MERCANTILE / CO. / WILLIAMSTON, / S.C.
            GOOD FOR / 2.00 / IN MERCHANDISE
            brass, 36mm, round, R9

C100   (obverse similar to C200)
            GOOD FOR / 100 / IN MERCHANDISE
            brass, 36mm, round, R9

C50   (obverse similar to C200)
            GOOD FOR / 50 / IN MERCHANDISE
            brass, 33mm, round, R9

C25   (obverse similar to C200)
            GOOD FOR / 25 / IN MERCHANDISE
            brass, 29mm, round, R9

C10   (obverse similar to C200)
            GOOD FOR / 10 / IN MERCHANDISE
            brass, 24mm, round, R8

C5   (obverse similar to C200)
            GOOD FOR / 5 / IN MERCHANDISE
            brass, 19mm, round, R7

            The Empire Mercantile Company sold general merchandise and fertilizer during the mid-teens.

D5   GOSSETT MILLS STORE / 5 / PRODUCE / ONLY / WILLIAMSTON, S.C.
            (Orco - type II)
            brass, 19mm, round, R10

            Headquartered in nearby Anderson, Gossett Mills operated a cotton mill in Williamston during the late 1920s.

E50   HUDGENS MERCANTILE CO. / WILLIAMSTON, / S.C.
            GOOD FOR / 50 / IN MERCHANDISE
            brass, 33mm, round, R9

E5 (obverse similar to E50 except no comma after WILLIAMSTON)
GOOD FOR / 5 / IN MERCHANDISE
brass, 19mm, round, R9

The Hudgens Mercantile Company was listed only in 1908. The firm sold meats, groceries, and ice.

F500 VICTOR / MERCANTILE / CO. / WILLIAMSTON, / S.C.
GOOD FOR / 5.00 / IN MERCHANDISE
brass, 36mm, round, R9

F100 (obverse similar to F500)
GOOD FOR / 100 / IN MERCHANDISE
brass, 36mm, round, R9

F50 (obverse similar to F500)
GOOD FOR / 50 / IN MERCHANDISE
brass, 33mm, round, R9

F25 (obverse similar to F500)
GOOD FOR / 25 / IN MERCHANDISE
brass, 29mm, round, R9

F10 (obverse similar to F500)
GOOD FOR / 10 / IN MERCHANDISE
brass, 24mm, round, R9

F5 (obverse similar to F500)
GOOD FOR / 5 / IN MERCHANDISE
brass, 19mm, round, R8

The Victor Mercantile Company was listed from 1910 to 1917.

G200 WILLIAMSTON / MERCANTILE / CO. / 2⁰⁰ / WILLIAMSTON / S.C.
GOOD FOR / $2⁰⁰ / IN / MERCHANDISE
brass, 31mm, round, R9

G100 (obverse similar to G200 except denomination 1⁰⁰)
GOOD FOR / $1⁰⁰ / IN / MERCHANDISE
brass, 31mm, round, R9

G50 (obverse similar to G200 except denomination 50)
GOOD FOR / 50¢ / IN / MERCHANDISE
brass, 28mm, round, R9

G25 (obverse similar to G 200 except denomination 25)
GOOD FOR / 25¢ / IN / MERCHANDISE
brass, 26mm, round, R9

G10 (obverse similar to G200 except denomination 10)
GOOD FOR / 10¢ / IN / MERCHANDISE
brass, 23mm, round, R9

G5　　(obverse similar to G200 except denomination 5)
　　　　　GOOD FOR / 5¢ / IN MERCHANDISE
　　　　　　　brass, 20mm, round, R7

　　　　　This company operated from the mid-twenties to the late forties.

H50　WILLIAMSTON MILL STORE / 50¢
　　　　　PRODUCE / CHECK
　　　　　　　brass, 29mm, round, R10

　　　　　The Williamston Mill Store was in business as early as 1912. The Williamston Cotton Mills, first listed in 1904, manufactured cotton and woolen goods; it operated into the late 1920s.

I　　　WILLMONT OIL MILLS / 500 LBS. / C.S. MEAL / WILLIAMSTON, S.C.
　　　　　DATE OF REDEMPTION / SUBJECT / TO RULES / POSTED / IN OFFICE
　　　　　　　brass, 28mm, round, R10

　　　　　This company, which manufactured cotton seed products, operated branches in Pelzer, Piedmont, and Williamston. The token was "good for" 500 pounds of cotton seed meal.

WINNSBORO (Fairfield County)　　　　　　2960

A5　　C. A. ROBINSON / FANCY / GROCERY / WINNSBORO / S.C.
　　　　　GOOD FOR / 5¢ / IN TRADE
　　　　　　　aluminum, 19mm, round, R10

　　　　　Charles A. Robinson was in business as early as 1908 and as late as 1938.

B500　WINNSBORO MILLS / 5$\underline{00}$ / WINNSBORO, S.C.
　　　　　(Orco - type I)
　　　　　　　nickel, 32mm, scalloped (12), "W" c/o, R10

B100　(obverse similar to B500 except denomination 1$\underline{00}$)
　　　　　(Orco - type I)
　　　　　　　copper, 32mm, round, "W" c/o, R9

B50　　(obverse similar to B500 except denomination 50)
　　　　　(Orco - type I)
　　　　　　　brass, 27mm, round, "W" c/o, R9

B25　　(obverse similar to B500 except denomination 25)
　　　　　(Orco - type I)
　　　　　　　copper, 24mm, round, "W" c/o, R9

B10　　(obverse similar to B500 except denomination 10)
　　　　　(Orco - type I)
　　　　　　　brass, 21mm, round, "W" c/o, R7 (variety with a "CW" c/o known)

WINNSBORO (Continued)

B5 (obverse similar to B500 except denomination 5)
(Orco - type I)
copper, 19mm, round, "W" c/o, R7

B1 (obverse similar to B500 except denomination 1)
(Orco - type I) (varieties exist)
brass, 18mm, round, "W" c/o, R6

C WINNSBORO / MILLS / ONE BOX
(blank)
aluminum, 31mm, round, holed as made, R9

D100 WINNSBORO MILLS / STORE / W / WINNSBORO, S.C.
GOOD FOR / $1⁰⁰ / IN MERCHANDISE
aluminum, 35mm, round, R10

Winnsboro Mills, owned and operated by the U.S. Rubber Company of New York City, manufactured tire cord for use in automobile tires. 2960C was probably some type of production token.

WITHERBEE (Berkeley County)

A100 AT CHERRY & COMPANY'S STORE / WITHERBEE, / S.C.
GOOD FOR / 1⁰⁰ / IN MERCHANDISE
brass, 38mm, round, R7

A50 (obverse similar to A100)
GOOD FOR / 50 / IN MERCHANDISE
brass, 31mm, round, R7

A25 (obverse similar to A100)
GOOD FOR / 25 / IN MERCHANDISE
brass, 27mm, round, R7

A10 (obverse similar to A100)
GOOD FOR / 10 / IN MERCHANDISE
brass, 24mm, round, R7

Cherry & Company operated a general store in Witherbee during the twenties and thirties. The firm also had a store in Charleston.

WOODRUFF (Spartanburg County)

A100 G. E. BLACK / 1⁰⁰ / B / WOODRUFF, S.C.
(Master Metal Scrip - type II)
nickel-plated brass, 35mm, round, R9

A50 (obverse similar to A100 except denomination 50)
(Master Metal Scrip - type II)
nickel-plated brass, 30mm, round, R9

A25 (obverse similar to A100 except denomination 25)
(Master Metal Scrip - type II)
nickel-plated brass, 24mm, round, R9

A10 (obverse similar to A100 except denomination 10)
(Master Metal Scrip - type II)
nickel-plated brass, 21mm, round, R8

A5 (obverse similar to A100 except denomination 5)
(Master Metal Scrip - type II)
nickel-plated brass, 19mm, round, R8

A1 (obverse similar to A100 except denomination 1)
(Master Metal Scrip - type II)
nickel-plated brass, 18mm, round, R8

Black ran a general store during the twenties and early thirties. He may
have been associated with one of the cotton mills in the area.

B100 G. E. / GRUBBS / 1 $\underline{00}$ / MDSE. ONLY
(Master Metal Scrip - type II)
brass, 35mm, round, R9

B50 (obverse similar to B100 except denomination 50)
(Master Metal Scrip - type II)
brass, 30mm, round, R8

B25 (obverse similar to B100 except denomination 25)
(Master Metal Scrip - type II)
brass, 24mm, round, R8

B10 (obverse similar to B100 except denomination 10)
(Master Metal Scrip - type II)
brass, 21mm, round, R8

B5 (obverse similar to B100 except denomination 5)
(Master Metal Scrip - type II)
brass, 19mm, round, R8

B1 (obverse similar to B100 except denomination 1)
(Master Metal Scrip - type II)
brass, 18mm, round, R7

G. E. Grubbs was listed only in the late 1930s, as operator of a general
store and filling station. The tokens were ordered in 1929 according to the
manufacturer's records, so he must have been in business during that
period.

C10 J. L. SWINK, JR. / WOODRUFF, S.C.
GOOD FOR / 10¢ / IN MERCHANDISE
aluminum, 24mm, round, R10

WOODRUFF (Continued) 2970

C5 (obverse similar to C10)
GOOD FOR / 5¢ / IN MERCHANDISE
aluminum, 19mm, round, R10

During the late 1920s Jessie L. Swink, Jr. operated a restaurant and grocery store.

D50 THE VILLAGE STORE / WOODRUFF, / S.C.
GOOD FOR / 50¢ / IN MERCHANDISE
aluminum, 31mm, round, R10

D5 (obverse similar to D50)
GOOD FOR / 5¢ / IN MERCHANDISE
aluminum, 20mm, round, R10

E5 AT THE / VILLAGE / STORE
GOOD FOR / 5 / IN TRADE
brass, 19mm, round, R9

This general store was listed from 1922 to 1930.

YEMASSEE (Beaufort County) 2980

A5 J. B. BISSELL / 5 (all incuse)
GOOD / FOR 5 CENTS / FOR LABOR UNDER / SPECIAL CONTRACT
/ PAYABLE JAN. 1 / 1885 (all incuse)
brass, 31mm, round, R10

John Bennett Bissell, a prominent rice planter during the 1860s, 1870s, and 1880s, planted Bonny Hall Plantation and Bonny Dune Plantation (both located on the Combahee River near Yemassee). He also kept a home in Charleston, on Rutledge Avenue.

YONGES ISLAND (Charleston County) 2985

A50 WM. C. GERATY, / YOUNGS / ISLAND, / B.F. / S.C.
GOOD FOR / 50 / IN / MERCHANDISE
brass, 31mm, round, R9

A25 (obverse similar to A50)
GOOD FOR / 25 / IN / MERCHANDISE
brass, 30mm, round, R9

A10 (obverse similar to A50)
GOOD FOR / 10 / IN / MERCHANDISE
brass, 26mm, round, R9

A5 (obverse similar to A50)
GOOD FOR / 5 / IN / MERCHANDISE
brass, 22mm, round, R9

William C. Geraty's letterhead and the sign on his railroad car provide much
information about his business.

The growing of produce for market (termed "truck") in South Carolina began in 1868, when William C. Geraty and his partner, Frank W. Towles, began a small scale operation on Yonges Island. At that time Towles was just a silent partner, still residing in New York. The business grew over the years, and in the early 1900s Geraty claimed that he was the largest shipper of cabbage plants in the world. By this time he had specialized in raising cabbage plants from seed, then shipping the young plants to other farms where they were replanted and raised to maturity.

Geraty also raised other vegetables - cantaloupes, asparagus, beans, and potatoes in particular - and was a dealer in Sea Island cotton seed. He also operated a general store and paid off his field workers in tokens. Note the spelling of Yonges Island on the tokens, letterhead, and picture of the railroad car. Obviously the name was frequently misspelled. Geraty died in the winter of 1908 but the company continued in his name for some years, being operated by his heirs.

B8   VARN, BYRD & CO. / 8 (all incuse)
      (blank)
         brass, 25mm, round, R6

Varn, Byrd & Company's multi-colored letterhead.

C8   VARN, BYRD & CO. / 8 (all incuse) (different dies)
      (blank)
         brass, 24mm, round, R7

D8   V. B. & CO. / 8 (all incuse)
      (blank)
         brass, 26mm, octagonal, R8

E8   V B & CO. / 8 (all incuse, beaded border)
      (blank)
         brass, 26mm, octagonal, R10

F8   V. B. & CO. / 8 (all incuse)
           (blank)
               aluminum, 24mm, round, R10

     Varn, Byrd & Company operated an oyster and vegetable cannery on Yonges Island circa 1910. Headquartered in Savannah, Georgia, the company also manufactured oyster shell lime. In 1913 it became known as the Varn & Platt Company and operated into the 1920s.

G100 YONGES ISLAND MERCANTILE CO.
               1$\underline{^{00}}$
               brass, 35mm, round, R10

G5   (obverse similar to G100)
               5
               brass, 22mm, round, R10

     This firm was listed from 1912 to 1914, and later from 1926 to 1933. In 1912 it was affiliated with the William C. Geraty Company (see listings).

YORKVILLE (York County)   **2990**

A10   PAYABLE TO BEARER AT OFFICE / ON / 4TH MONDAY. / CAROLINA / BUGGY / CO.
               10 (surrounded by rays)
               nickel, 18mm, round, R9

     Attribution tentative. A company by this name was listed in Yorkville (later shortened to York) in an 1893 mercantile directory. The company was incorporated with a capital of $46,200 (a good deal of money at the time), which hints at a fairly large operation.

YOUNGS ISLAND

     Tokens from WM. C. GERATY of YOUNGS ISLAND, S.C. are die-cutting errors. The tokens were used on Yonges Island, which see.

BIBLIOGRAPHY

Chambers, Randy, "South Carolina Tokens." *TAMS Journal*, 1977.

Coffee, John M. Jr. and Harold V. Ford, *The Atwood - Coffee Catalogue of United States and Canadian Transportation Tokens* (4th Edition) 1983. American Vecturist Association.

Curto, James J., *Military Tokens of the United States, 1866- 1969, Book I.*

Curto, James J., *Military Tokens of the United States, 1866-1978, Book II.*

Mitchell, Ralph A. and Russel Rulau, "Embossed or Shell Store Cards." *TAMS Journal*, 1961.

Rulau, Russell, *Hard Times Tokens* (2nd Edition), 1981. Krause Publications, Inc.

Rulau, Russell, *U.S. Merchant Tokens, 1845-1860* (2nd Edition), 1985. Krause Publications, Inc.

Rulau, Russell, *United States Trade Tokens, 1866-1889*, 1983. Krause Publications, Inc.

Schenkman, David E., *Virginia Tokens*, 1980. The Virginia Numismatic Association.

Wagaman, Lloyd E., *A Checklist and Aid to Attributing Ingle System Scrip*, 1987. The Indiana-Kentucky-Ohio Token and Medal Society.

STREET NAMES ON SOUTH CAROLINA TOKENS

Archdale Street	Charleston	King Street	Charleston
Assembly Street	Columbia	Lady Street	Columbia
Broad Street	Charleston	Line Street	Charleston
Buncombe Road	Greenville	Main Street	(various towns)
Buncombe Street	Greenville	Meeting Street	Charleston
Calhoun Street	Charleston	Midway Street	Lancaster
N. Church Street	Spartanburg	N. Market Street	Charleston
Columbus Street	Charleston	Queen Street	Charleston
Devine Street	Columbia	Railroad Avenue	Batesburg
E. Bay Street	Charleston	Russell Street	Orangeburg
E. Washington Street	Greenville	Second Street	Cheraw
Elizabeth Street	Charleston	Shepard Street	Charleston
Forest Drive	Columbia	Saint Philip Street	Charleston
Gates Street	Columbia	30 Avenue	Conway
Gervais Street	Columbia	Washington Street	Columbia

INDEX

This index includes issuers of maverick and also self-identified tokens. Issuers of maverick tokens are identified with an asterisk (*). In determining placement, the word "The" has been disregarded.

A

A. & A. Food Store *	Greenville	Anderson Chemical & Mercantile Co.	Anderson
A.B.C. Cigar Store	Charleston	Anderson Cotton Mill Store *	Anderson
A.C.L. Co.	Georgetown	David O. Anderson	South Marion
A.C.L. Corp'n, Logging Dept. *	Georgetown	Anderson Lumber Corporation	South Marion
A.C.L. Corporation	Georgetown	Anderson Mills Store *	Anderson
Abbeville Cotton Mills *	Abbeville	R. H. Anderson	Hampton
W. W. Abbott	Columbia	Anderson Steam Bakery *	Anderson
Ackerman Drug Co.	Bishopville	Apalache Mills *	Arlington
Adams Pharmacy Inc.	Conway	Apalache Plant *	Arlington
W. B. Adams' Son	Adamsboro	Appalachian Lumber Corp.	Pickens
W. B. Adams' Son	Newtonville	Appin Dairy	Bennettsville
Addison Mills *	Edgefield	Appleton Mill Store	Anderson
Aiken County Stores Inc.	Bath	Arant's Drug Store *	Manning
Aiken County Stores Inc.	Clearwater	Arcade Place	Columbia
Aiken County Stores Inc.	Langley	Arcadia Mills *	Arcadia
Aiken Manufacturing Co's Stores	Bath	Arcadia Mills Store	Arcadia
Aiken Stores, Inc.	Anderson	Arkwright Mills	Arkwright
Aiken Stores, Inc.	Calhoun Falls	Arkwright Mills Store	Spartanburg
Aiken Stores, Inc.	Williamston	Ashley Co.	Ellenton
J. H. Albrecht	Orangeburg	Ashmore & Nimmons	Pickens
D. W. Alderman & Sons Company	Alcolu	Atkinson's Drug Store	Anderson
Allison - Crenshaw Co.	Pelzer	Atlantic Coast Lumber Co.	Georgetown
American Wood Products Corp.	Marion	Awensdaw Mercantile Co. *	Awensdaw

B

B. P. K. / P.O. Fruit Store	Columbia	Leon Banov	Charleston
B.P.O.E. 1318 *	Rock Hill	Barney's Cafe	Taylors
Badham Lumber Co. *	Cosby	Bernard S. Baruc	Charleston
Baer & Causey	Port Royal	Base Hospital, Post Exchange	Camp Jackson
Bahan Textile Machinery Co.	Union	Batesburg Drug Co.	Batesburg
T. M. Bailey's Store	Ridgeland	H. Baum *	Camden
R. L. Baker	Charleston	Beatty Co., The *	Latta
J. Q. Ballentine *	Columbia	Beaufort/Jasper R.T.A.	Burton
Bank of Greenwood *	Greenwood	Beaumont Mfg. Co's. Store *	Spartanburg
Bank of Greers	Greer	Beaumont Mill Store *	Spartanburg

S. Behrmann	Moncks Corner	Bradley Lumber & Mfg. Co.	Ashepoo
Bell Lumber Co.	Marion	Wm. L. Bradley, Bulow Store *	Stono
J. R. Bellamy & Sons	Beaufort	W.J.H. Brandt *	Charleston
Belton Grocery Co.	Belton	Breon Lumber Co., Inc.	Ulmers
Belton Mercantile Co.	Belton	Breslauer, Lachicotte & Co.	Waverly Mills
Belton Service Company *	Belton	J. B. Britton	Sumter
Ben's Bingo	Myrtle Beach	W. H. Britton & Co. *	Bennettsville
Benson Grocery Co.	Simpsonville	T. H. Brock & Co.	Honea Path
Berry & Keller, Druggists	Buffalo	Brogan Mill Store *	Anderson
Berry - Fortune Construction Co.	Wellford	Brogan Mills *	Anderson
G. A. Best *	Ulmers	J. J. Broughton	Pinewood
Birlant's, "The Smile Store"	Charleston	Brown Derby, The	Greenville
Bishop Bros.	Spartanburg	Brown Derby Billiard Parlor *	Spartanburg
E. E. Bishop *	Charleston	E. M. I. Brown	Johns Island
J. B. Bissell *	Charleston	Brown - Ingram Lumber Company	Poston
G. E. Black	Woodruff		
J. F. Bland	Mayesville	J. S. Brown	Elliott
Blue and White Bus Co., Inc.	Greenwood	G. A. Browning, Jr.	Goldville
Blue Bird Lines *	Greenville	Bruce Bros.	Greenville
Blue Ridge Grocery Co.	Pelzer	F. A. Bruce, Jr. & Co.	Branchville
Bluestein Brothers, J.S. Bluestein, Prop.	Charleston	Brunswick Cigar Store	Sumter
		Buddy Packing Company, Not Inc.	Lexington
I. Blum Company, The	Tatum		
T. M. Bobo	Greer	Buffalo Cotton Mills *	Buffalo
D. J. Bolton	McColl	Bulow Store, Wm. L. Bradley *	Stono
S. W. Boozer	Chapin	V. Z. Burke *	Columbia
B. B. Bouknight	Trenton	J. C. Burns & Co.	Greenwood
J. H. Bouknight *	Johnston	E. P. Burton Lumber Co.	Charleston
Brabham & Company *	Hattieville	M. F. Bush *	Ellenton
J. W. Bracknell & Son	Plum Branch	Busy Bee *	Aiken
Bracknell & Baker	Plum Branch	G. W. Byars & Co. *	Chester

C

C A F B (Charleston Air Force Base) *	Charleston	Camp Manufacturing Co., Store No. 5 *	Marion
C.C.C., Company 4470 *	Cassatt	Camp Mfg. Co., Mill Store 5 *	Marion
C.C.C., Company 4470 *	Montmorenci	Camp Mfg. Co., Woods Store No. 3 *	Russellville
C.C.C., Company 4471 *	Bishopville		
Calhoun Mills Store *	Calhoun Falls	Camp Mfg. Co., Woods Store No. 5 *	Marion
O. G. Calhoun	Bordeaux		
Camden Drug Co.	Camden	Camperdown Mill Store	Greenville
Camp Manufacturing Co.	Marion	Cannon Bros.	Orangeburg
Camp Manufacturing Co., Store No. 3 *	Russellville	G. A. Canup	Pendleton

Capital Cabana Motor Inn	Columbia
Carlson's Clothing Store	Spartanburg
Carolina Buggy Co. *	Yorkville
Carolina Shoe Shop	Anderson
Carolina Stores Inc., Store No. 1 *	Greenville
Carolina Stores Inc., Store No. 3 *	Greenville
Carolina Stores Inc., Store No. 4 *	Greenville
Carolina Stores Inc., Store No. 5 *	Greenville
Carolina Transit Co.	Columbia
Carolina Turpentine Co.	Pineland
Carpenter Bros. *	Greenville
Carr - Carlton Co., The	Meggetts
E. S. Carter *	Lowryville
Carter - Evans Lumber Co.	Cartersville
J. & J. S. Carter *	Westminster
J. J. & J. S. Carter *	Westminster
H. M. Cassels	Ellenton
C. H. Castens, Jr. *	Charleston
Chafee Bros.	Langley
Charleston C. Ry. & Lt. Co. *	Charleston
Charleston Canning Co. *	Charleston
Charleston Hunting & Fishing Club *	Charleston
Charleston News Agency *	Charleston
Chas. A.F.B. (Charleston Air Force Base)	Charleston
Cheraw Amusement Co. *	Cheraw
Chero Nehi Co.	Spartanburg
Cherokee Drug Co.	Gaffney
Cherry & Company's Store	Witherbee
Chesnee Mills Store	Chesnee
Chester Drug Co., The	Chester
Chesterfield Brick Co.	Chesterfield
W. B. Chestnut & Co.	Conway
Walter Cheyne	Sumter
Chick Springs Co. *	Chick Springs
Chiquola, B.B. *	Honea Path
Chiquola Club	Cheraw
Choppee School *	Choppee
Christal Store	Gable
Citizens & Southern Bank of South Carolina *	Charleston
City Bakery	Spartanburg
City Transit, Camden *	Camden
Claflin Cafeteria *	Orangeburg
Clarendon Cotton Oil Co.	Saint Paul
Clark Furniture Co.	Chester
Clark's Pharmacy	Springfield
Alex. G. Clarkson	Wateree
Clemson Agricultural College, The	Clemson College
Cleremont Cafe *	Charleston
Clinton Cotton Mill Store *	Clinton
Clio Drug Co.	Clio
J. F. Cloud	Chester
Clover Cotton Manfg. Co. *	Clover
Co. F, 51st Infantry *	Camp Wadsworth
Co. G, 51st Infantry *	Camp Wadsworth
Coburg Dairy	Charleston
Coca - Cola Bottling Co.	Greenville
Coca - Cola Bottling Co.	Union
W. D. Coggeshall, Floyd Farm	Darlington
Cohannet Mills *	Fingerville
J. A. Coleman, Jr.	Hardeeville
Colleton Mercantile & Mfg. Co.	Ritter
Columbia Bowling Center	Columbia
Columbia Candy Kitchen *	Abbeville
Columbia Dairies *	Columbia
Columbia Electric Street Railway	Columbia
Columbia Office Supply	Columbia
Commercial Bank	Greenwood
Community Store, The	Central
Company C, 52nd Inf. *	Camp Wadsworth
Company Store, The	Pickens
Company Store No. 2, The	Pickens
Conestee Mills Store *	Conestee
D. E. Converse Co., The *	Glendale
Conway Drug Co.	Conway
Conway Lumber Co.	Conway
Conway Trading Company	Conway
J. M. Cook *	Salters Depot
J. T. Copeland	Sumter
R. L. Corbitt & Son *	Salley
W. L. Corley & Co.	Columbia
J. R. Cornwell *	Columbia
Cosmopolitan Club *	Charleston

C (Continued)

Courtnay Mfg. Co., The * — Newry
Covington Company, Inc. — Clio
Coward Store,
   Coxe Lumber Company * — Coward
Cowpens Drug Store — Cowpens
Cowpens Mfg. Co., The * — Cowpens
Cowpens Mill Store * — Cowpens
Jerry Cox Co., The — Conway
Cox Mfg. Co. Store * — Anderson
Coxe Bros. Store — Mont Clare

Coxe Lumber Company,
   Coward Store * — Coward
F. G. Craddock * — Fairfax
G. G. Creighton Mill Store * — Wando
Crescent Drug Co. — Beaufort
F. A. Cribbs — Lynchburg
G. W. Crosby — Camden
Paul E. Crosby — Spartanburg
S. C. Crosby * — Union
Crosswell Company,
   Woodside Mill * — Greenville

D

D. B. & M. Co. (Dexter Broom
   & Mattress Co.) — Pelzer
D. O. C. — Spartanburg
Dabney's Lunch — Lancaster
Dargan Lumber Co. * — Effingham
Darlington Mfg. Co. * — Darlington
Darlington Veneer
   Company Inc. * — Darlington
Davis Cafe — Charleston
J. S. Davis — Marion
Deep River Lumber Co. — Lake City
Delmonico Hotel — Marion
DeLorme Drug Co. Inc. — Charleston
DeLorme's Pharmacy — Sumter
Delux Pocket Billiard Parlor * — Spartanburg
R. R. Derrick — Anderson
Dewey * — Charleston
Henry V. Dick & Co. — Columbia
Henry V. Dick & Co. — Greenville

S. W. Dickson & Co. * — Westminster
Dillon High School Cafeteria * — Dillon
Dixie Mercantile Co. — Piedmont
Dodson & Agnew * — Donalds
Donnald & Wilson Co. — Piedmont
Donnald & Wilson Co. — Williamston
Dorchester Lumber Co. * — Badham
Doster Bros. — Greenville
W. B. Drake — Drake
Draughon's College * — Columbia
Drayton Mills Store * — Drayton
Duke Power Co. — Greenville
Duke Power Co. — Spartanburg
Dunean Mills, Peoples
   Supply Co. * — Greenville
Dunean Mills Store * — Greenville
P. M. Durham * — Central
Duval Brokerage Co. — Charleston

E

E. P. B. Lbr. Co.
   (E. P. Burton Lumber Co.) * — Charleston
Eagle Confectionery * — Columbia
Eagle Grocery Co. — Pelzer
Easley Mill No. 1,
   J.C. Mundy & Co. * — Easley
Eddy Lake Cypress Co. * — Eddy Lake
Edisto Dairy — Orangeburg
Edisto Farms Dairy — Columbia
Edisto Hardwood Co. — Springfield

Edisto River Lumber Co. — Embree
Edward's Cafe & Pool Room — Anderson
Edwards Lumber Co. — Dovesville
Ellerbe's * — Florence
Emba Cafeteria — Georgetown
Empire Mercantile Co. — Williamston
Enoree Mfg. Company — Enoree
Enoree Mill Store — Enoree
Enterprise Cash Supply Co.,
   The — Greenwood

E (Continued)

Equinox Mill Store	Anderson	Eureka Store, The Veneer Mfg. Co.	Conway
Erwin & Co. Inc.	Gaffney		
Erwin - Hermitage Co. Inc.	Camden	Excelsior Canteen	Union
Eureka Drug Co., The	Laurens		

F

The Fair Store, J.M. Vickery, Prop.	Seneca	Floyd Farm, W.D. Coggeshall	Darlington
		Folger, Thornley & Co.	Pickens
Fairfax Cool Spot	Fairfax	Follin Bros. Company *	Charleston
Fairwold Farms Dairy	Columbia	Foremost Dairies, Inc. *	Spartanburg
lley W. Fant *	Newberry	Fort Jackson	Fort Jackson
Farmers and Merchants Bank	Greenville	Fort Moultrie, Post Exchange *	Fort Moultrie
Farmer's Bank, The	Elloree	Fountain Inn Mfg. Co. *	Fountain Inn
Farmer's Bank, The	Parler	B. L. Fowler *	Union
Fat's Truck Stop	Society Hill	Franklin Finance	City View
Federal Clothing Stores	Charleston	Franklin Finance	Greenville
Federal Clothing Stores	Columbia	Franklin Process Spinning Mills Inc. *	Fingerville
Field Signal Service Exchange 105 *	Camp Sevier	F. W. Free Co.	Bamberg
Frank Fields	Charleston	W. G. Fricks	Easley
First National Bank, The	Spartanburg	Frogmore Factory, Geo. W. Lowden *	Frogmore
Florence Coach Co. *	Florence		
Florence Daily Times, The	Florence	B. A. Fulmer *	Columbia
Florence V.F.W. Post #3181	Florence	R. P. Funderburk *	Columbia

G

Gantt's Uniform Outlet	Greenville	Gray Line	Charleston
Geer Drug Co., The *	Charleston	R. C. Gray, Owner, Ideal Athletic Club	Greenville
Geilfuss Bakery	Spartanburg		
Gem Restaurant, The	Columbia	Great Southern Lumber & Mining Co.	Pee Dee
Georgetown County Schools *	Georgetown		
Wm. C. Geraty	Yonges Island	Greenville Equity Exchange *	Greenville
M. S. Gibson	New Brookland	Greers Manufacturing Co.	Greers
J. W. Gilreath *	Greenville	Greers Plant, Victor - Monaghan Co.	Greers
Glenn - Lowry Mfg. Co.	Whitmire		
Glenwood Cotton Mills	Easley	Grenola Grocery Co.	Greenwood
Gluck Mill Store	Anderson	Grenola Grocery Co.	South Greenwood
Goodman's Variety Bakery	Union	Griffin Bros. Merc. Co.	Greenwood
Gossett Mills Store	Williamston	W. H. Grover	Hemingway
J. H. Graham *	Thickety	G. E. Grubbs *	Woodruff
Granby Mercantile Co.	Columbia	Gunter's Drug Store	Batesburg
Graves - Denton Lumber Co.	Ashepoo	J. L. Guy, Jr.	Blaney

H

H.H.O.F. Co. (Hilton Head Oyster Factory)*	Hilton Head	Hermitage Cotton Mills Store	Camden
H.H.P. Co. (Hilton Head Packing Co.) *	Hilton Head	Herring Brothers *	Florence
Haden Motor Co.	Greenville	H. F. Hester	Mars Bluff
Hagen Bros.	Abbeville	D. C. Heyward	White Hall
Haile Gold Mining Co., The	Haile Gold Mine	Heyward's Pharmacy	Columbia
I. S. Hall	Salley	High School of Charleston	Charleston
Hamilton Carhartt Cotton Mill	Rock Hill	H. C. Hill	Allendale
W. C. Hammett *	Spartanburg	Hillbrook Farm	Spartanburg
C. H. Hampton	Union	Hindman & Beam Co.	Pelzer
Hampton Mercantile Co.	Piedmont	A. O. Hiott	Round
Hampton Mills Cooperative Store, The *	Columbia	Wm. Hodges	Mt. Pleasant
		J. F. Hoffman *	Anderson
W. C. Hane *	Fort Motte	Hoffman Lumber Co.	Columbia
Hardin & Fox *	Batesburg	W. P. Hogarth & Sons	Brunson
J. E. Harman, Mgr., Buddy Packing Co.	Lexington	Geo. J. Holliday *	Galivants Ferry
		Holmes & Johnson	Spartanburg
D. M. Harper *	Marion	Holmes School	Florence
Harris Music Co.	Darlington	Home Service Finance	Spartanburg
J. W. Harrison	Greenville	E. D. Hopkins	Hopkins
H. R. Harter *	Fairfax	Horry Transit Co. *	Conway
W. C. Hatchell *	Bingham	Horseshoe Lake Farms	Longcreek
Haverty Furniture Co. *	Columbia	M. C. Howie	Alcolu
Haviland Stevenson & Co.	Charleston	William H. Hubbard	McColl
A. H. Hayden, Jr.	Columbia	E. Hubster's Bakery	Walterboro
Heath - Bruce - Morrow Co.	Pickens	Hudgens & Ragsdale	Pelzer
Heinitsh's Pharmacy	Spartanburg	J. W. Hudgens	Taylors
W. C. Hemingway & Co. Store	Lambert	Hudgens Mercantile Co.	Williamston
W. C. Hemingway & Co's. Store	Hemingway	C. C. Humphries *	Gaffney
Henderson Packing Co. *	Burton	T. E. Hunnicutt	Easley
W. T. Hendrick, Jr.	Gillespie Siding	Hunt Pkg. Co. *	Beaufort
C. A. Herlong	Greer	S. D. Hurst	Camden
		Husemann & Co.	Spartanburg

I

Ideal Athletic Club, R.C. Gray, Owner	Greenville	Charles Ingram Store, Inc.	Florence
		Ingram - Dargan Store	Hemingway
Ideal Steam Bakery	Darlington	Inman Mills *	Inman
Ingram & McCoy	McBee	Inman Mills Store *	Inman

J

Jackson Co.	Piedmont	Jones Billiard Parlor & Cafe	Anderson
At Jeans	Clinton	F. N. Jones	Ashton
J. W. Jenny & Co.	Jennys	F. N. Jones	Lodge
L. B. Jeter, Jr.	Santuck	Jones Furniture Co.	Spartanburg
Jim's Billiard Hall	Greenville	J. K. Jones	Newberry
Jno. M. Store, The	McColl	X. C. Jones	Branchville
Joanna Mercantile Co. *	Goldville	Judson Mills Store Co. *	Greenville
J. F. Johnson	Union		

K

K. Bros. *	Mt. Pleasant	E. L. Kelly	Dorlen
Kafer's Bakery *	Florence	Kenneth Cotton Mills Store *	Walhalla
Kash & Karry	Greenville	C. D. Kenney & Sons	Warrenville
Kearse Mfg. Co.	Olar	A. Kerhulas *	Union
Kearse Veneer & Box Co.	Olar	Kimbrells Inc.	Columbia
Keller's Drug Store	Union	J. M. Kirkland & Co.	Ehrhardt

L

L. & W. Service Station	Kegtown	Lightsey Brothers	Miley
L.C.L. Cooperative Store	Whitmire	Henry W. Lightsey	Crocketville
L.H.S. Cafeteria (Latta High School) *	Latta	J. C. Lightsey	Hampton
La Grone Drug Co.	Johnston	W. Fred Lightsey	Crocketville
Lafayette Bridge	Georgetown	Ligon Drug Co.	Orangeburg
Lake View School	Lake View	Limestone Mills Store	Gaffney
Lancaster Co-operative Store	Lancaster	Lipscomb & Richardson	Gaffney
Lancaster Co-operative Store Lunch Stand	Lancaster	Lockhart Mills Store	Lockhart
Lancaster Pharmacy	Lancaster	Lodge Mercantile Co.	Lodge
Jno. J. Landers *	Charleston	J. C. Looper *	Greenville
Langley Manufacturing Co's. Store	Langley	J. W. Looper	Lathem
Langley Mills Store, The	Langley	M. A. Lorenzi *	Charleston
Langston's Bakery	Timmonsville	Los Gringos *	Charleston
Laurens Cotton Mills	Laurens	Mary Louise Mills Store	Mayo
R. W. Lawler Store	Marion	Geo. W. Lowden, Frogmore Factory *	Frogmore
Leigh Banana Case Co. Commissary	Leigh	Lowman Drug Co.	Orangeburg
Lester's Cafe	Slater	Loyd & Co.	Little Rock
J. B. Letton	Columbia	Lucky 13 Lounge	Columbia
Lewis & Hartzog	Greenville	W. J. Lunney	Seneca
Lewis & Williams	Mullins	Chas. G. Luther, Ph.G.	Beaufort
C. M. Lide	Columbia	Lydia Mills	South Clinton
Lightsey Bros. Inc.	Miley	Lydia Mills Store	South Clinton
		Lyric Soda Parlor	Columbia

MBAFB, NCO (Myrtle Beach Air Force Base) *	Myrtle Beach	J. K. McCoy	McBee
		McCullough & Fergerson	Chester
Mrs. M. J. Mabry *	Union	McFaddin - Millsaps Co.	Sardinia
J. F. Mackey & Co.	Lancaster	McLaughlin Co.	Saint Matthews
L. P. Maggioni & Co.	Ladies Island	H. J. McLaurin, Jr.	Sumter
Manetta Mills Store	Lando	W. H. McLeod & Son	Seabrook
S. H. Manget	Trenton	S. H. McManus	Rock Hill
Manning Training School *	Manning	McMillans Drug Store *	Columbia
J. Mannos	Charleston	Jack G. Metropol	Manning
T. W. Mappus	Charleston	Metropolitan Cigar Co. *	Charleston
D. Marchetti *	Charleston	Mills Manufacturing Co.	Greenville
Marine Corps Air Station Theatre *	Beaufort	J. M. Mims *	Sumter
		MOD Store, J.G. Richards *	Columbia
Marion County Lumber Co. Mill Store *	Marion	Wm. Moessner	Mt. Pleasant
		Monaghan Mill *	Greenville
Marion Lumber Mfg. Co.	Marion	Monaghan Mill Store *	Greenville
Marlboro Drug Co.	Bennettsville	Monarch and Ottaray Mill Stores	Union
Marshall Bath House *	Charleston		
Martin Bros.	Anderson	Montgomery Lumber Co.	Causey
Martin - Hawkins Furniture Co.	Greenville	Moore & Wilson *	Lake City
J. V. Martin Jr. High School *	Dillon	O. W. Moore *	Ridgeway
Mary Louise Mills Store	Mayo	J. L. Morehead	Gaffney
J. O. Massenburg *	Big Oak Island	H. O. Morris & Bro.	Olar
Massie Lumber Co.	Dovesville	W. M. Motte	Denmark
Matthews & Bouknight Co.	Leesville	Mt. Holly Development Co.	Mt. Holly
Matthews Drug Store	Denmark	Mullins School Lunch Room *	Mullins
Mauldin Pharmacy	Greenville	J. C. Mundy & Co., Easley Mill No. 1 *	Easley
Mayfair Mills Store	Arcadia		
Mayfield Co., The	Denmark	Mutual Dry Goods	Buffalo
Mayfield Co., The	Lees	Mutual Mercantile Co.	Arlington
Maynard Lumber Corp. *	Cheraw	Myrtle Beach Farms Company	Myrtle Beach
Louis McCaw	Ridgeland	Myrtle Beach Trolley *	Myrtle Beach
McClellanville Canning Co. *	McClellanville		

N.L.H.L. Co., The (N.L. Hoover Lumber Co.) *	Cashs Depot	A. J. H. Nolte *	Charleston
		H. Nolte	Charleston
Nabors & Adair *	Clinton	Norris Cotton Mills Store	Cateechee
National Bank of Newberry, The	Newberry	W. J. Norris & Bro.	Patrick
National Clothing Stores	Greenville	North Augusta Bus Co. *	North Augusta
New Cabana Club	Columbia	North Bakery, The *	North
Newry Mercantile Co.	Newry	Norton Drug Co.	Conway
Newry Store, The	Newry		

O

Olympia Candy Co.	Anderson	Oregon Pool Parlor	Greenwood
Orangeburg 5 and 10 Store	Orangeburg	Orr Cotton Mills Store	Anderson
Orangeburg Mfg. Co. *	Orangeburg	Orr Gray & Co.	Anderson
Orangeburg Steam Bakery *	Orangeburg	Owen & Paul *	Columbia

P

P. B. G. (Peter B. Gretes)	Columbia	J. L. Phillips Drug Co. *	Rock Hill
PISC, REC FUND *	Parris Island	Pickens Mill	Pickens
P.O. Fruit Store / B. P. K.	Columbia	Pickens Mill Market *	Pickens
Pacolet Mfg. Co. *	Pacolet	Piedmont Mercantile Co. *	Piedmont
J. S. Padgett	Islandton	J. F. Pieper	Charleston
G. J. Pait	Mars Bluff	Pinckney Oyster Co. Store *	Ridgeland
J. R. Pait	Mars Bluff	J. S. Pinkussohn Cigar Co.	Columbia
Palace Confectionery	Columbia	J. S. Pinkusson Co. *	Charleston
Palmetto Commissary Co. Store	Columbia	Pirates Cove Mini Golf	North Myrtle Beach
Palmetto Cotton Mills *	Columbia	Planters Hotel	Charleston
Palmetto Drug Co.	Laurens	Plaza News Stand *	Columbia
Palmetto Pharmacy	Columbia	Henry Plenge	Charleston
C. A. Parkins	Greenville	F. W. Poe Mfg. Co.	Greenville
Pastime Billiard Parlor *	Spartanburg	Poe Mill *	Greenville
W. A. Patterson *	Pickens	C. M. Polatty *	Greenwood
The Pavilion	Myrtle Beach	C. M. Ponder	Greers
Peace's Super Market	Calhoun Falls	J. N. Poole	Greenville
Pee Dee Supply Cos' Store *	Pee Dee	R. L. Poole *	Neeses
Peeler & Lemmond	Gaffney	J. A. Porter	Barnwell
Pendleton Manufacturing Co. Store	La France	Dr. B. F. Posey	Laurens
Peoples Drug Co.	Bamberg	Post Exchange	Charleston
Peoples Drug Co., The	Saluda	Post Exchange, Fort Moultrie *	Fort Moultrie
Peoples Drug Store, The	Batesburg	Post Exchange, U.S.N.D.B.	Port Royal
Peoples Market *	McColl	H. F. Prator *	Bishopville
Peoples Supply Co., Dunean Mills *	Greenville	Price's Bus Lines	Greenwood
Pepsi Cola Bottling Co.	Union	W. R. Pritchard	Charleston
Petty & Co.	Chester	Prospect Hill Store, S.M. Ward *	Prospect Hill Plantation
J. J. Phillips Co.	Pelzer	J. J. Purcell	Union

Q

Quality Bottling Works	Greenville	Quality Ice Cream Co.	Spartanburg

REC, PISC, FUND *	Parris Island	F. Rhem & Sons	Rhems
C. J. F. Rabens *	Charleston	Rhem Real Estate Co., Inc.	Rhems
H. R. Rabins *	Charleston	J. G. Richards, MOD Store *	Columbia
Ragsdale, Hudgens & Co.	Pelzer	R. Richter,	Mappus
W. L. Rankin Lumber Co.	Mars Bluff	Wulbern Fertilizer Co. *	
Rapid Transit Company,	Gaffney	Ridgeland Grocery Co.	Ridgeland
Zone 1 *		Ridgell Drug Co.	Batesburg
Rapid Transit Company,	Gaffney	J. B. Riedlinger	Columbia
Zone 2 *		Rikard & Son	Batesburg
Rapid Transit Company,	Gaffney	W. F. P. Riser	Bowman
Zone 3 *		W. M. Ritter Lumber Co. *	Tillman
Rawl's Pool Room	Batesburg	Ritz Billiard Parlor *	Spartanburg
Redick's Pharmacy	Fountain Inn	J. T. Rivers	Brunson
H. O. Reece *	Newberry	C. A. Roach *	Bingham
P. R. Reese *	Columbia	Roberts Canning Co. *	Beaufort
Rephan's Sanitary Dairy	Charleston	C. A. Robinson	Winnsboro
Republic Cotton Mills Stores	Great Falls	J. E. Rodgers	Fountain Inn
Republic Pharmacy	Great Falls	L. C. Rodgers *	Gaffney
Reynolds & Craft	Swansea	Rosemary Amusement Co.	Anderson
J. C. Reynolds *	Swansea	Ruby Canning Co.	Ruby
D. O. Rhame	Summerton		

S.C. Electric & Gas Co. *	Columbia	Geo. W. Seignious	Charleston
S.C. Penitentiary Canteen *	Columbia	Selected Dairies Inc.	Florence
S.C. Power Co. *	Charleston	Seminole Manufacturing	Clearwater
S. E. F. (S.E. Follin) *	Charleston	Company Store	
Geo. Sabbagha *	Columbia	Seneca Pharmacy	Seneca
S. A. Sabbagha *	Columbia	Shaw A.F.B.	Sumter
Salley Coca - Cola Bottling	Salley	(Shaw Air Force Base) *	
Co. *		Sheldon Furniture Co. *	Westminster
Sampit Contracting Company *	Georgetown	Shelmore *	Awensdaw
Sanders & Lemacks	Ritter	Shelmore O.P. Co. *	Awensdaw
Santee Mercantile Co.	Ferguson	Shelmore Oyster Products	Awensdaw
Santee Mill	Orangeburg	Co. *	
Santee River Cypress Lumber	Ferguson	Shipyard River Mercantile Co.	Charleston
Co. *		Simpson - Moore Drug Co. *	Cowpens
The Savoy,	Columbia	Winslow Sloan *	Clemson College
S.T. Wesberry, Prop. *		Sloppy Joe's	Myrtle Beach
Saxon Mills Store	Spartanburg	Small's Grocery	Columbia
J. H. Schmonsees	Charleston	L. J. Smith *	Millettville
C. H. Schultz *	Charleston	Smithdeal Music Co., The	Columbia
Scofield Auto-Music Co.	Columbia	Smithdeal's *	Columbia
Seaside Cannery	Charleston	Smoker Billiard Parlor *	Spartanburg
J. C. Seegers & Co.	Columbia	So. Ca. Vol. H.B. Exchange *	Sullivans Island

S (Continued)

E. Sonnenburg	Newberry	Stevenson, Kreamer & Hockman *	Pee Dee
Sorentrue's Arcade	Orangeburg		
South Atlantic Lumber Co.	Cordesville	H. D. Still & Sons' Store	Blackville
South Carolina Baptist Hospital	Columbia	Stone & Patrick	McNeils
South Carolina State Prison *	Columbia	Stone Drug Co.	Greenville
Southern Bleachery Store *	Taylors	Stonecypher Drug Co.	Westminster
Southern States Lumber Co.	Dunbarton	H. A. Stramm	Charleston
Southern Weaving Co.	Greenville	Suburban Transit Co. *	Columbia
Southside Mercantile Co.	South Greenwood	Suburban Transit Lines, Inc. *	Anderson
Southside Pool Room	Anderson	L. D. Suggs	Loris
Spartan Mills	Spartanburg	F. C. W. Suhrstedt *	Charleston
Spartan Mills Store	Spartanburg	Summer Bros. Co.	Newberry
T. T. Speaks *	Fairfax	W. D. Summer Pool Room *	Pomaria
A. G. T. Spradley *	Warrenville	Sumter Packing Co., The	Sumter
Sprott's	Orangeburg	Sumter Pharmacy, The *	Sumter
Standard Creamery	Sumter	Sumter Truck Terminal	Sumter
Star Grocery Co.	Ninety Six	Sunshine Laundry & Cleaners	Columbia
Startex Mill Store	Tucapau	J. L. Swink, Jr.	Woodruff
Stenhouse & Co.	Charleston	J. C. Swygert & Son	Leesville

T

T. C.	Columbia	Neil W. Trask	Burton
Taylor's	Lexington	G. W. Treadway	Cheraw
Terry & Shaffer	Walterboro	Tucapau Mills Store	Tucapau
Thomas Dairy	Fairfax	D. E. & J. F. Turbeville	Turbeville
Thomas Drug Store	Columbia	Turner's Cigar Store *	Spartanburg
L. T. Threatt	Lancaster	A. C. Tuxbury Lbr. Co., Camp 1	Bethera
Time Finance Co., Inc.	Columbia		
B. Timmons	Edgefield	A. C. Tuxbury Lumber Co. *	Charleston
W. C. Tolar	Dillon	A. C. Tuxbury Lumber Co., Camp 2 *	Charleston
Fred W. Towles	Martins Point		
Toxaway Mill Store	Anderson	Twin Lakes *	Columbia
G. W. Trask & Sons	Burton	H. C. Tyler Corporation Commissary	Tylers
G. W. Trask & Sons	Myrtle Beach		

U

U.B.M. Co. (Union - Buffalo Mills Co.) *	Buffalo	Union - Buffalo Mills Store	Fairmont
		Union - Buffalo Mills Store	Union
U.S.N.D.B., Post Exchange	Port Royal	Union Drug Co.	Union
U.S.S. Denebola *	Charleston	Union Station Drug Co.	Columbia
Union - Buffalo Mills Store	Buffalo		

V

V. B. & Co. (Varn, Byrd & Co.) *	Yonges Island	Verner Springs Water Co.	Greenville
Van Metre's	Columbia	J. M. Vickery, Prop., The Fair Store	Seneca
Varn Brothers Co.	Smoaks		
Varn, Byrd & Co. *	Yonges Island	Victor Mercantile Co.	Williamston
Varnville Drug Co.	Varnville	Victor Mill Store	Greer
Vaughan Bus Line *	Union	Victor - Monaghan Co., Greers Plant	Greers
Vaughn Bus Line	Union		
The Veneer Mfg. Co., Eureka Store	Conway	Village Store, The *	Woodruff
		Vosburg Co., The	Cashs Depot

W

W A I M (Radio Station)	Anderson	Whitney Mfg. Co.	Whitney
Walhalla Mill Store	Walhalla	Whitney Mill Store	Whitney
Wallace Mill Store	Jonesville	A. W. Wieters	Charleston
John Wallach	Charleston	O. H. Wieters	Charleston
Wall's Drug Store	Batesburg	Wigwam Billiard Parlor *	Spartanburg
Walterboro Lumber Co.	Walterboro	W. W. Wilbur	Charleston
S. M. Ward, Prospect Hill Store *	Prospect Hill Plantation	J. S. Wilkerson & Co.	Hickory
S. M. Ward & Co., Richfield *	Richfield Plantation	Williamston Mercantile Co.	Williamston
Ware Shoals Dairy *	Ware Shoals	Williamston Mill Store *	Williamston
Ware Shoals Dept. Store *	Ware Shoals	Willmont Oil Mills	Pelzer
Ware Shoals Mfg. Co. *	Ware Shoals	Willmont Oil Mills	Williamston
Washington Finance	Laurens	Winnsboro Mills *	Winnsboro
Watts Mills	Laurens	Winnsboro Mills Store	Winnsboro
Waverly Supply Co.	Waverly Mills	Wonderland	Charleston
Welling & Bonnoitt	Montrose	Woodside Cotton Mills *	Greenville
S. T. Wesberry, Prop., The Savoy *	Columbia	Woodside Mill, Crosswell Company *	Greenville
C. West *	Greenville	Woodside National Bank	Greenville
West End Dairy	Charleston	T. J. Wright *	Givhans
West Pelzer Drug Co.	Pelzer	Wulbern Fertilizer Co., R. Richter *	Mappus
J. W. White	Chester		
White Stone Lithia Springs Co.	White Stone Springs	Wymojo Yarn Mills *	Rock Hill

X, Y, Z and

G. K. Xepapas	Columbia	Zeigler's Pharmacy	Manning
Y.M.C.A.	Columbia	Wm. Zobel	Helena
Yonges Island Mercantile Co. *	Yonges Island	51st Inf., K *	Camp Wadsworth
Youngs Pharmacy	Clinton		